# Christian History
# Made Easy

D0840068

Timothy Paul Jones, Ph.D.

ROSE
PUBLISHING

Torrance, California

© 2009 Timothy Paul Jones
Rose Publishing, Inc.
4733 Torrance Blvd., #259
Torrance, California 90503 U.S.A.
Email: info@rose-publishing.com
www.rose-publishing.com

All Scripture quotations, unless otherwise noted, are taken from the *Holy Bible, New International Version®. NIV®.* Copyright © 1973, 1978, 1984 by International Bible Society. Used by permission of Zondervan. All rights reserved.

Layout design by Nancy Bishop, cover design by Sergio Urquiza

Character illustrations on pages 10, 25, 37, 53, 68, 85, 97, 99, 106, 111, 129, 143, 158, 177, and 180 were created by Stephen Hesselman.

Rose Publishing is in no way liable for any context, change of content, or activity for the websites listed. Inclusion of a work does not necessarily mean endorsement of all its contents or of other works by the same author(s).

Library of Congress Cataloging-in-Publication Data

Jones, Timothy P. (Timothy Paul)
   Christian history made easy / Timothy Paul Jones. – [Rev. ed.].
        p. cm. – (Rose Bible basics)
   Includes index.
   Summary: "An overview of the development and history of Christianity from AD 1 to the 21st century"–Provided by publisher.
   ISBN 978-1-59636-328-1 (pbk.)
   1.  Church history.  I. Title.
   BR145.3.J66 2009
   270–dc22

                                    2008056128

## About the Author

Timothy Paul Jones has authored, co-authored, or edited more than a dozen books, including *Conspiracies and the Cross* and the CBA bestseller *The Da Vinci Codebreaker.* After fourteen years in vocational ministry, he now serves as professor of leadership and church ministry at Southern Baptist Theological Seminary in Louisville, Kentucky. In addition to receiving the Bachelor of Arts in biblical studies and the Master of Divinity with a focus on historical theology, Timothy has earned the Doctor of Philosophy degree from Southern Seminary. His academic research has earned the Scholastic Recognition Award from the North American Professors of Christian Education, as well as the Baker Book House Award for theological studies. Timothy, his wife Rayann, and their daughter Hannah reside in the city of St. Matthews in Louisville, Kentucky.

Printed by Regent Publishing Services Ltd.
Printed in China
August 2015,12th printing

CHRISTIAN
HISTORY MADE Easy

# Contents

introduction
Why Does
Church
History
Matter?
06

chapter 1
The
Gospels, the
Apostles,
Then...
What?
09

chapter 2
Balancing
the Past
with the
Present
21

chapter 3
The Church
Wins...and
Loses
33

chapter 4
Servant-
Leaders or
Leaders of
Servants?
47

chapter 5
From
Multiplication
to Division
63

chapter 6
God Never
Stops
Working
79

Continued
on next page

CHRISTIAN
HISTORY MADE Easy

# Contents

chapter 7

Everything
Falls Apart
91

chapter 8

Wild Pigs
in a Dirty
Vineyard
105

chapter 9

Change
Doesn't
Always Do
You Good
121

chapter 10

You Say
You Want a
Revolution?
135

chapter 11

Optimism
Has Its
Limits
149

chapter 12

Modern,
Postmodern
...and
Beyond
165

Study Guide
189

Index
222

# Foreword

Church history is being stolen from us, and I don't think we should stand for it anymore.

Church history is being stolen by professional historians who have discarded reporting tales of tragedy, valor, and pathos for writing textbooks crammed with dates, social analysis, and political posturing. It's being shoplifted by television, which lulls us into an entertainment stupor, so that our minds can no longer grasp anything more complicated than Wheel of Fortune. And we're pickpocketed by our own foolishness, this panting after the latest, the new, the "now."

How do we bring church history back? We can write it in a way that shows its relevance. We can follow Augustine's dictum that communication should entertain while it informs. We can be honest about Christian failures—which have been manifold—and yet refuse to wallow in cynicism. We can make sure we don't produce textbooks but books filled with people and stories we will never forget.

Okay, I admit it. I'm biased when it comes to church history.

What I'm saying is that good history should read like *Christian History* magazine, because that's precisely the sort of history that I worked for several years to produce there. And that is precisely what drew me to *Christian History Made Easy*. I know good history when I see it, and I see it here.

The study of church history can do many things for us, to name a few: it gives perspective; it frees us from faddishness; it shows God's working in the world; it gives wisdom; it implants hope deep within us. If you're looking for such things—or perhaps just wondering how you and your fellow believers ended up at this time and place in the larger scheme—reading Christian history, and this book in particular, is one place to begin.

Mark Galli
Managing Editor, *Christianity Today*

# Introduction

## Why does church history matter?

In a classic *Peanuts* comic strip, Sally carefully labels her paper, "Church History." As Charlie Brown glances over her shoulder, Sally considers her subject.

"When writing about church history," Sally scrawls, "we have to go back to the very beginning. Our pastor was born in 1930."

Charles Schulz's comic strip may be amusing, but it isn't too far from the truth. In sermons and devotional books, Christians encounter names like Augustine and Calvin, Spurgeon and Moody. Their stories are interesting. Truth be told, though, most church members have a tough time fitting these stories together. The typical individual's knowledge of church history ends with the apostles and doesn't find its footings again until sometime in the twentieth century.

Still, the story of Christianity deeply affects every believer in Jesus Christ. The history of the Christian faith affects how we read the Bible. It affects how we view our government. It affects how we worship. Simply put, the church's history is our family history. Past Christians are our mothers and fathers in the faith, our aunts and uncles, our in-laws and—in a few cases—our outlaws!

When a child in Sunday School asks, "How could Jesus be God and still be like me?" she's not asking a new question. She is grappling with an issue that, in AD 325, three hundred church leaders discussed in a little village named Nicaea [ni-SEE-ah], now the city of Iznik in the nation of Turkey. Even if you've never heard of Iznik or Nicaea, what those leaders decided will influence the way that you frame your response to the child's question.

If you've ever wondered, "Why are there so many different churches?" the answer is woven somewhere within two millennia of political struggles and personal skirmishes. When you read words like "predestined" or "justified" in the apostle Paul's letter to the Romans, it isn't only Paul and your pastor who affect how you respond. Even if you don't realize it, Christian thinkers such as Augustine and John Calvin and Jonathan Edwards also influence how you understand these words.

So, if the history of Christianity affects so much of what we do, what's the problem? Why isn't everyone excited about this story? Simply this: A few pages into many history books, and the story of Christianity can suddenly seem like a vast and dreary landscape, littered with a few interesting anecdotes and a lot of dull dates.

Despite history's profound effect on our daily lives, most church members will never read Justo González's thousand-page *The Story of Christianity*. Only the most committed students will wade through all 1,552 pages of Ken Latourette's *A History of Christianity*. Fewer still will learn to apply church history to their lives. And so, when trendy novels and over-hyped television documentaries attempt to reconstruct the history of Christianity, thousands of believers find themselves unable to offer intelligent answers to friends and family members.

What we don't seem to recognize is that church history is a *story*. It's an exciting story about ordinary people that God has used in extraordinary ways. What's more, it's a story that every Christian ought to know.

That's why I wrote this book.

*Christian History Made Easy* is a summary of the church's story, written in words that anyone can understand. I haven't cluttered the text with abstract facts and figures and footnotes. *Christian History Made Easy* is a collection of stories. Together, these stories are intended to sketch one small portion of what God has been up to for the past 2,000 years.

When I wrote the first edition of this book, I was not a professional scholar. I was a young pastor in a small town in rural Missouri. A decade later, I have pastored a much larger congregation, and I do now bear the titles of "professor" and "Ph.D." Yet this book still bears the marks of that original context.

In the months that formed the first edition of this book, I spent my days among small-town farmers and school-teachers, in hayfields and hospitals, with lonely widows and life-loving youth. As I wrote, I thought not only about Augustine and Luther and Calvin and Jonathan Edwards, but also about a tiny congregation that graciously referred to me as their pastor, though they probably knew more about pastoral ministry than I did. I loved those people—Thelma's pure and simple heart that could express Christ's love through the larded crust of a gooseberry cobbler, Harold and Kathrine's gentle reprimands that prodded me toward pastoral maturity, the transformation that I witnessed in the home of John and Laura. Today, I cherish those people even more than I did then, because I see more clearly what God was doing in my life through them. It was for those ordinary people that I wrote *Christian History Made Easy,* because I longed for them to grasp what it means to be surrounded by "so great a cloud of witnesses," the saints not only of the present but also of the past (Hebrews 12:1).

I remain indebted to Carol Witte and Gretchen Goldsmith for taking a chance on a then-unknown author and publishing this manuscript; to Jeff Cochran for providing many of the books that undergirded the original research; to Robin Sandbothe, Connie Edwards, Daniel Schwartz, Barbara Harrell Brown, Lianna Johns, and Larry Sullivan for proofreading the first draft of the manuscript; Kenny McCune, Brent McCune, and Amy Ezell for their help on the learning activities; to W. T. Stancil for proof-reading above and beyond the call of duty; Stephanie, Heather, Diane, and Christy at the McDonald's on Highway 50 in Sedalia, Missouri, who fueled the original project with copious amounts of cholesterol and Diet Coke; to the Starbucks baristas at Frankfort Avenue in Louisville, Kentucky, who fueled this updated edition; to my wife and to our daughter Hannah—ten years ago, who could have dreamed what God would do in our lives?

This book is dedicated to my parents, Darrell and Patricia. By chance, you gave me life. By choice, you gave me love. By wisdom, you let me forge my own path. By grace, you gave me wings to fly. This first book will always be for you.

—Timothy Paul Jones

**5 EVENTS you should know**

1. **Jerusalem Council (AD 49 or 50):** Church recognized that Gentiles did not need to become Jews to follow Jesus Christ (Acts 15).

2. **Fire in Rome (AD 64):** Flames destroyed nearly three-fourths of capital city. Emperor Nero blamed and persecuted the Christians.

3. **Destruction of Jerusalem Temple (AD 70):** After a Jewish revolt, Emperor Vespasian ordered his son, Titus, to regain Jerusalem. Titus torched the city and leveled the temple.

4. **Pliny's Letter to Emperor Trajan (around AD 112):** Pliny, governor of Pontus, asked Trajan how to handle Christians. Trajan ordered Pliny not to pursue Christians. Only when people were accused of being Christians were they to be hunted down.

5. **Martyrdom of Polycarp (AD 155):** Polycarp of Smyrna—modern Izmir, Turkey—was burned alive because he would not offer incense to the emperor.

**10 NAMES you should know**

1. **Peter (martyred between AD 65 and 68):** Leading apostle of the early church.

2. **Paul (martyred between AD 65 and 68):** Early Christian missionary and apostle.

3. **Nero (AD 37-68):** Roman emperor, persecuted Christians after fire in Rome.

4. **Clement of Rome (died, AD 96):** Leading pastor of Rome in the late first century. The fourth pope, according to Roman Catholics. Perhaps mentioned in Philippians 4:3.

5. **Josephus (AD 37-100):** Jewish writer. His historical works tell about early Christianity and the destruction of the Jewish temple.

6. **Ignatius (AD 35-117):** Apostolic church father and leading pastor in Syrian Antioch. Wrote seven important letters while traveling to Rome to face martyrdom.

7. **Papias (AD 60-130):** Apostolic church father. Wrote about the origins of the Gospels.

8. **Polycarp (AD 69-155):** Apostolic church father. Preserved Ignatius' writings.

9. **Justin Martyr (AD 100-165):** Christian philosopher and apologist. Martyred in Rome.

10. **Blandina (died, AD 177):** Slave-girl. Martyred in Lyon alongside the city's leading pastor.

**4 TERMS you should know**

1. **Anno Domini:** Latin for "the Lord's Year," usually abbreviated AD. Refers to the number of years since Christ's birth. Dionysius Exiguus, a sixth-century monk, was the first to date history by the life of Christ. His calculations were off by between one and five years. So, Jesus may have been four or five years old in AD 1!

2. **Century:** One hundred years. The first century extended from AD 1 to 100; the second century, from AD 101 to 200; the third, from AD 201 to 300, and so on.

3. **Yahweh:** Hebrew name for God. The name means "I AM" (see Exodus 3:13-14).

4. **Apostolic Fathers:** Influential first-century Christians, such as Ignatius, Polycarp, and Papias. A few later theologians—such as Augustine—are known as *church fathers*.

# CHAPTER 1

# The Gospels, the Apostles, Then ... What?

## IN THIS CHAPTER
## AD 64 – AD 177

Emperor Nero
Peter and Paul Martyred
Destruction of Temple
Martyrdom of Polycarp
Justin Martyr

# Who were the Christians, anyway?

What is a "Christian"? If someone asked you that question, you could probably come up with a response without much thought. Chances are, you would say something like, "It's someone who has trusted Jesus as Savior and Lord." But what if you lived in a world in which only a small percentage of the population had even heard about Jesus?

In the first few decades of Christian faith, followers of Jesus struggled to help people around them understand what it really meant to be Christian. From the Roman perspective, Christians were simply one more Jewish sect (Acts 16:20). The Jewish faith was recognized throughout the Roman Empire, so this association protected Christians in many areas. Yet, according to some Jewish leaders, Christians were renegades who had abandoned the ancient and venerable Jewish faith. Christians claimed that their

*Paul's missionary journeys spread Christianity through Asia Minor and the western Roman Empire. Believers were first called Christians in Antioch, in modern Turkey. (The Chora Monastery, Istanbul)*

faith fulfilled the Jewish Law, even calling themselves "the Israel of God" (Galatians 6:16). At the same time, as Christianity expanded among non-Jews, Christians' practices increasingly separated them from the Jewish faith that Jesus and his first apostles had practiced.

By AD 100, the Christian and Jewish faiths were recognized as two separate groups. Jewish synagogues had excluded Christians, and the Roman Empire had engaged in widespread persecution of Christians. How did those who claimed Jesus as their Messiah come to constitute a distinct group? The answer can't be confined to any one event. Yet two fires—one in Jerusalem, one in Rome—contributed to this separation in a critical way.

## Rome burns, but Nero doesn't fiddle

In midsummer, AD 64, Rome burned. Flames ravaged the city for six days. When the smoke cleared, ten of Rome's fourteen districts had been reduced to charred rubbish.

Nero, the Roman emperor, was several miles away when the fire began. When he heard the news, Nero rushed back to Rome. During the fire, he organized fire-fighting efforts. After the fire, thousands of refugees stayed in his gardens. Yet, as the rebuilding

**Nero**

the web

To take a virtual tour of ancient Rome:
www.romereborn.virginia.edu/

Check out the dates and historical contexts of New Testament events:
www.beliefnet.com/gallery/TheFinalInquiry.html

of Rome began, many citizens blamed Nero for the tragedy.

According to one rumor, Nero had ordered his servants to start the fire. Nero torched Rome—the rumor claimed—so he could rebuild the city according to his own whims. Later rumors even insisted that Nero had played his harp while Rome burned. In fact, the fire probably began by accident in an oil warehouse—but this probable fact was quickly lost amid raging gossip and rumors.

*Roman imperial coin of Claudius*
*AD 41 to 54*

Nero responded to the rumors by lavishing gifts on the citizens of Rome. Nothing helped. In desperation, Nero blamed the fire on an unpopular minority group—the Christians. Nero became the first emperor to recognize publicly that Christianity was a different religion, and he began immediately to persecute this faith. One Roman historian described the persecution in this way, "Some were dressed in furs and killed by dogs. Others were crucified, or burned alive, to light the night."

The apostle Peter was martyred in Rome during Nero's persecution. According to ancient tradition, Peter didn't believe he was worthy to die like his Savior, so the big fisherman asked to be crucified upside down. Roman authorities also arrested the apostle Paul. Since it was illegal to crucify a Roman citizen, Paul probably died by the sword.

In some ways, Nero's false accusation made sense. Christians *did* claim that a great inferno would accompany the end of the world (Revelation 20:9). Some overly eager Christians may have seen a certain sign of Christ's return in Rome's reduction to rubble. Yet Christians were—according to a pagan writer—"hated for their abominations" *before* the fire. What made Christian faith so unpopular?

## Christians rejected all other gods

Christians believed in only one God—the God of Israel, revealed in Jesus Christ (Deuteronomy 6:4; 1 Timothy 2:5). This belief seemed arrogant to the Romans. Most Romans covered all their spiritual bases by sacrificing to many gods, known and

WORDS from the **ones** who were there
*Anonymous pagan writer who misunderstood the Lord's Supper:* "An infant is covered with dough, to deceive the innocent. The infant is placed before the person who is to be stained with their rites. The young pupil slays the infant. Thirstily, they lick up its blood! Eagerly, they tear apart its limbs. After much feasting, they extinguish [the lights]. Then, the connections of depraved lust involve them in an uncertain fate."
Quoted by Minucius Felix, *Octavius 9*

**THINK** about **it...**

Early Christians refused to share in cultural customs that devalued human life, such as abandoning unwanted infants. What cultural customs should Christians avoid today?

unknown (Acts 17:23). They even offered incense to dead emperors. (As one emperor died, he joked, "I think I'm becoming a god now!") Yet Romans didn't sacrifice simply for their own sakes. They sacrificed for the sake of their empire. Numerous sacrifices, they believed, secured divine assistance for their government. To deny the existence of any divinity was, at best, unpatriotic and, at worst, perilous to the security of their empire.

## Christian customs were widely misunderstood

When they described their worship, Christians talked about consuming the "body" and "blood" of Christ at their "love-feasts" (John 6:53-56; 1 Corinthians 10:16; 11:23-27; Jude 1:12). Believers called one another "brothers and sisters"— terms used in Egypt to refer to sexual partners.

Alone, either of these practices might have struck the Romans as odd. Combined with the Christian conviction that Christians followed the only true God, such practices convinced many citizens that

*Many scholars believe that a group of Jews hid their sacred scrolls in these caves near the Dead Sea. When the Dead Sea Scrolls were found in the late 1940s, they confirmed the reliability of the Hebrew Bible.*

Christianity was a dangerous cult. Romans couldn't quell their concerns by attending a church service. When early Christians shared the Lord's Supper, they wouldn't even let nonbelievers watch. Without firsthand information, Romans began to accuse Christians falsely of cannibalism and incest.

## Christians challenged the social order

Paul had declared, "There is neither Jew nor Greek, there is neither slave nor free, there is neither male nor female" (Galatians 3:28). In other words, every person matters, whatever his or her social status. Early Christians lived out Paul's words. The results offended the Romans.

The church challenged the entire structure of Roman society by welcoming the lower classes and by valuing every human life. The laws of Rome prevented slaves from inheriting property; the customs of the empire treated women as lesser beings. If a Roman father didn't want his child, he left the infant alone in a field, to die. Christians defied such social structures by adopting unwanted infants and by welcoming slaves and women as equal inheritors of God's grace.

# The World of the First Christians

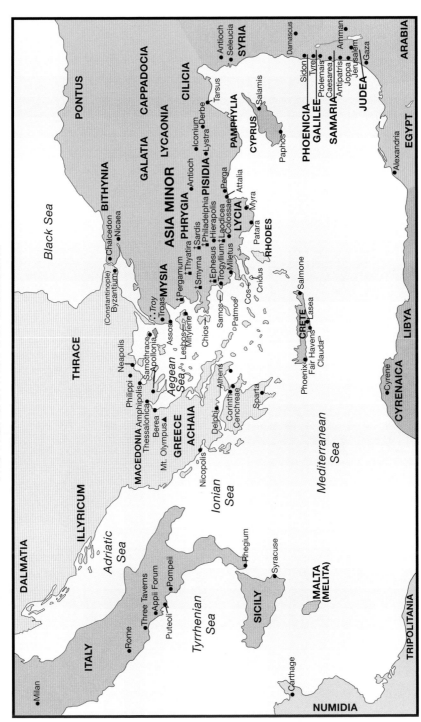

From *Deluxe Then and Now Bible Map Book* (692X)  Rose Publishing, Torrance, California.

### Christianity was a new religion

New and improved products seem to fascinate people today. The trend in ancient Roman society was precisely the opposite: It seemed better to them to choose an old, proven product than to fall for a new, improved gimmick. Romans tolerated the Jews' belief in one God partly because the Jewish faith was so ancient. One thousand years before Rome was founded, Abraham had encountered Yahweh [YAH-way] in the desert.

*Trajan's market in Rome*

To be sure, Christians claimed that their religion reached back, beyond Abraham (John 8:58). Still, from the Romans' viewpoint, the church was very new. What's more, unlike the Jews, Christians had no sacrifices, no temples, no sacred city. As a result, Christians seemed unusual, unsafe, and unpleasant to their Roman neighbors.

The first fire—the one that ravaged Rome in 64—highlighted habits of life and faith that caused Christianity to be unpopular among the Romans. There was another fire, this time in Jerusalem, that helped to solidify the distinction between Christian and Jewish faiths.

**THINK** about **it...**

A few years earlier, Nero had abused the Christians in Rome. Yet Christians refused to partake in the revolt against Rome in AD 70. What does this tell you about the church's relationship to the state? Read 1 Peter 2:13-17.

### Jerusalem burns and bleeds

The Romans tolerated the Jewish faith because of its ancient roots, but the Romans rarely showed any real respect for the Jewish people. Around AD 50, for example, thousands of Jews were celebrating their sacred Passover. A Roman fortress towered over the Jewish temple in Jerusalem. Suddenly, one guard "lifted up his robe and bent over indecently. He turned his backside toward the Jews and"—in the words of the Jewish-Roman historian Josephus— "made a noise as indecent as his posture." In the riot that followed, as many as 30,000 women and men may have died.

A new Roman ruler, a man named Florus, arrived in Judea in AD 64. For two years,

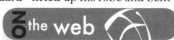

**ON** the web

Read Josephus's account of the Jewish rebellion in Book 7 of The Jewish Wars:

www.ccel.org/ccel/josephus/works/files/works.html

See a model of the temple before its destruction:

www.bible-history.com/jewishtemple/

Take a video tour of Masada:

www.360cities.net/image/masada

AD **64** – AD **177**

Florus flagrantly insulted the Jews. When several Jewish leaders demanded that Florus stop stealing from the temple, Florus sent his soldiers into the market. Their orders? Slaughter and steal. Before the day ended, 3,600 Jews were dead.

ON the web

Read Pliny's original letter to Emperor Trajan:

www.tyrannus.com/pliny_let.html

Seeds of anger toward Rome had germinated for years. Now, they blossomed into open revolt. In a few weeks, bands of Jewish rebels violently overwhelmed Roman strongholds in Jerusalem and Galilee.

Emperor Nero knew that, to maintain his hold on this corner of the Roman Empire, it was necessary to stop the rebellion. He provided 60,000 soldiers to a Roman general named Vespasian [ves-PAY-see-unn]. Vespasian's mission was to regain the Galilean and Judean provinces at any cost. Vespasian's campaign began in Galilee, destroying Jewish communities as he moved southward. Thousands of Jews fled to Jerusalem in the face of the advancing legions. As Vespasian prepared to attack Jerusalem, he received an unexpected message: Nero had committed suicide. This provided Vespasian with a chance to seize the throne for himself.

In the end, Vespasian did rule the Roman Empire, but he never forgot his previous task. As soon as his position was relatively secure, Vespasian sent an army to besiege Jerusalem. On August 5, AD 70, Jerusalem fell. The rebels were massacred. The sacred city was plundered. The survivors were sold as slaves. The temple was burned to the ground. Only one wall of the temple mount—a segment known today as the "Wailing Wall"—remained. Within a few years, every rebel stronghold had fallen to the Romans. The Jewish defenders of the final fortress —Masada, near the Dead Sea—chose mass-suicide instead of surrender. The revolt was over.

*The siege ramp (circled) was built by the Roman army at Masada, the Jewish rebels' last stronghold.*

After the revolt, the religious landscape of the Roman Empire shifted. Many people wanted to make certain that they weren't associated with odd religious sects. During the last half of the first century AD, this shift would lead eventually to rejection and widespread persecution of Christians.

AD 64 – AD 177

# What should we do with all the Christians?

## "I won't wait to be a god!"

For a few years—from around AD 70 until the early 80s—Roman emperors ignored Christianity. Then, Vespasian's son, Domitian [do-MEE-shan], became emperor. Previous emperors had waited until death to be declared divine. Domitian didn't want to wait, though. He demanded the title "Lord and God" throughout his reign. Domitian also decreed that, since the Jewish temple was gone, Jews should send their religious tithes to Rome. Some Jews refused.

*Colosseum, Rome, Italy*

Domitian reacted by enacting laws against all "Jewish practices." His sweeping sentence included Christian worship. For the first time, persecution spread beyond the Italian province.

Persecution continued even after a new emperor, Trajan, took the throne. Pliny, a governor in northern Asia Minor—the region now known as Turkey—wrote a letter to Emperor Trajan. Pliny described how he treated Christians. He gave alleged followers of Jesus three chances to recant. All who cursed Christ, he released. Roman citizens who refused to curse Christ went to Rome to await their trial. Common persons who refused to curse Christ were executed immediately. Emperor Trajan applauded Pliny's procedures.

Pliny had interrogated two deacons from a nearby church to find out what Christians believed. He reported that he learned nothing from them but "outlandish superstitions."

And indeed, that's precisely what Christianity seemed like to the cultured people of the Roman Empire. Christians were even accused of "atheism," because they rejected the reality of the Roman gods and goddesses.

on the web

Do you want to learn more about Justin Martyr?

www.earlychristianwritings. com/justin.html

## "We're not outlaws!"

In the mid-100s Christian scholars began to answer the charges that critics hurled at them. These scholars were called "apologists" [a-PAW-lo-jists]. Apologists didn't try to convert the Romans. They simply wanted to prove that Christians weren't criminals.

One of the most famous apologists was Justin. Unlike some Christians, Justin embraced Greek philosophy. Why? According to Justin, the pagan philosophers had discovered dim shadows of God's cosmic Word. In Jesus, this cosmic order "became flesh" (John 1:14). As a result, even in pagan philosophy, there was a point of contact with Christian faith.

In his attempts to show the connections between Christian faith and pagan philosophy, Justin sometimes seems to have conformed biblical concepts to his own Greek world-view. Yet Justin clearly recognized the distinction between faith in Jesus and faith in the pagan religions. When forced to choose between Jesus and the Roman gods, the apologist chose Jesus without hesitation and without apology. Around AD 165 he was beheaded for his faith. He soon became known as "Justin Martyr."

*The Celsus Library ruins in Ephesus, a few miles south of the city Smyrna where Polycarp served as pastor*

It wasn't only philosophers that found themselves facing such fates. Polycarp [PAW-lee-karp] of Smyrna was a prominent pastor who had personally known John the apostolic elder. When several Christians were executed at the arena in Smyrna—a city in modern Turkey, known in modern times as Izmir—the crowd began to chant, "Away with the atheists! Find Polycarp!" The authorities tortured one of Polycarp's stewards until they learned Polycarp's hiding place. When confronted, the elderly pastor surrendered peacefully.

At the judgment seat, the Roman governor said, "Have respect for your old age. Say, 'Away with the atheists!'" Polycarp slowly surveyed the throng that surrounded him. Pointing to the very people who considered him to be an atheist because he rejected the Roman gods, Polycarp said, "Away with the atheists!" Turning back to the governor, Polycarp declared, "Eighty-six years, I have served Christ, and he has done me no wrong. How can I blaspheme my king, the one who has saved me?" Polycarp was burned alive.

# Why did the churches grow?

Find biographies of hundreds of ancient martyrs:

www.catholic.org/saints

## "Outlandish superstitions"

That's what Pliny called the core Christian beliefs that he heard from two tortured deacons. Viewed from the perspective of cultured Romans, that's the sole function Christian faith seemed to serve. Why, then, did people continue to become Christians, even when Christian faith could cost them their lives?

To be sure, the church grew because God's Spirit was working. Still, God uses human factors—and sometimes even human failings—to prepare

AD 64 – AD 177

people to receive God's truth. To draw first-century Romans to trust in Jesus, God used their longings for moral guidance, for personal value, and for personal relationship with the divine.

## Christianity provided moral guidelines

By the mid-100s, the moral depravity of the ancient Roman Empire repulsed not only Jews and Christians but also many Gentiles who had never heard God's moral law. (The word "Gentile" refers to any person who is not a Jew.) Some Romans turned to the loving-yet-righteous God of Israel. Yet, because of the painful custom of circumcision, Gentile men were often hesitant to commit themselves fully to the Jewish faith. Many of these men were content to attend the synagogues and to support them financially. These Gentiles received a title of respect from the Jewish people— "God-fearers" (see Acts 10:2; 13:26). Christianity appealed to these Gentiles. Gentiles could embrace a relationship with the God of Israel without submitting to the ritual of circumcision that God had ordained to signify his eternal covenant with the Jewish people.

## Christianity offered equality and respect

The Christian view of women differed deeply from the view of many Romans. One pagan writer depicted the role of women in this way: "We have courtesans for pleasurable sex, young female slaves for day-by-day physical usage, and wives to produce legitimate children and to serve us faithfully by managing our houses."

Christians not only encouraged women to become followers of Jesus; Christians embraced and respected women as equal heirs of God's salvation (see Galatians 3:28). The church's acceptance of women and slaves provided ammunition for many pagan writers who wanted to ridicule Christian faith. Celsus, an anti-Christian writer, put it this way: "Because Christians admit that ignorant people are worthy of their God, Christians show that they want and can convert only foolish, dishonorable, stupid people, and only slaves, women, and little children."

Why did Christians treat women with respect? For starters, they were following the example of Jesus! During his ministry on planet earth, Jesus talked to women. He taught women. It was to women that he first entrusted the news of his resurrection. In the early church, Philip's four daughters served as prophets (Acts 21:9). The apostle Paul may have referred to a woman named Junias as a person whom the apostles found to be noteworthy (Romans 16:7). Phoebe may have served as a deaconess in the early church. (The word translated "servant" in Romans 16:1 in many Bibles is the word rendered "deacon" in passages such as Philippians 1:1.)

AD **64** – AD **177**

## Christianity offered a personal relationship with God

Among many Romans, the ancient gods and goddesses seemed increasingly impotent and inadequate. The Christian faiths, as well as mystery cults imported from Eastern provinces, claimed to provide a pathway to direct fellowship with the divine realm. Yet Christianity offered more than fellowship with the divine. Christians claimed that they worshiped a deity who became flesh and whose life had intersected human history (John 1:14-18). This deity not only embraced human flesh but also experienced human suffering (Isaiah 53:3-7; Hebrews 2:17-18).

The knowledge of Christ's sufferings strengthened thousands of early martyrs. In the city of Lyon in the region known today as France, nearly fifty Christians died in one bloody massacre, during the early August festivities that celebrated the greatness of the Roman emperors.

Years earlier, Polycarp had personally sent Pothinus [poh-THEE-nuss] to establish a church in Lyon. Pothinus the pastor of Lyon, now 92 years old, was tortured and imprisoned in a cell that was about the size of a small refrigerator. Two days after he was confined to his cell, Pothinus died. The deacon Sanctus had red-hot plates of steel pressed against his groin before being placed on the rack. It was later said that, as death claimed Sanctus, it was seen that "nothing is fearful where the Father's love is found, and nothing is painful so long as the glory of Christ is near."

Others were tormented in the amphitheater to entertain the crowds. From dawn until evening, Blandina [blahn-DEE-nah], a physically challenged slave, was tortured. Still, she refused to offer incense to the emperor. In the arena, Blandina's tormentors hanged her naked body on a cross. Wild beasts were released to devour the girl, but they did not touch her. Blandina was stripped from the cross and scourged. Still refusing to offer incense, Blandina was

thrown on a red-hot grill. Finally, a bull gored her twisted body and tossed her to the ground. There, she died. As fellow-Christians watched her, it was said that "they saw in the form of their sister"—an eyewitness recalled—"him who was crucified for them." They glimpsed a reflection of the One who understood their sorrow.

*The Martrydom of Blandina From the Martyrs Mirror,*
*this is an etching by Jan Luyken (1649-1712)*

## 4 EVENTS you should know

**1. Gnostic Controversy (AD 90-150):** The Gnostics' false teachings first surfaced in the first century. By AD 140, Gnostics outnumbered Christians in some areas.

**2. Second Jewish Rebellion (AD 132-135):** Simon Bar Kokhba, claiming to be the Messiah, revolted against the Romans. Jerusalem was destroyed again.

**3. Montanist Movement (AD 156-220):** Montanists—also known as "New Prophets"—tried to return churches to the New Testament's emphasis on dynamic acts of the Spirit. Their harsh moral standards and failed prophecies led many Christians to reject the movement.

**4. Books of the New Testament Recognized (before AD 190):** The Muratorian Canon acknowledged every New Testament book with the exception of Hebrews, James, and Peter's epistles; decades passed before these texts were universally acknowledged.

## 10 NAMES you should know

**1. Marcion (died AD 160):** Proponent of Gnostic ideas. Rejected the Old Testament and tried to remove sixteen books from the texts that Christians recognized as apostolic.

**2. Montanus (died AD 175?):** Earliest leader of the New Prophets (also known as "Montanists").

**3. Maximilla (died AD 190?):** Leader of the New Prophets.

**4. Prisca (died AD 190?):** Leader of the New Prophets, predicted Jesus would return to Phrygia.

**5. Victor (died AD 198):** Overseer of Rome. Excommunicated Christians in the eastern part of the Empire who celebrated Easter during Passover. Fourteenth pope, for Roman Catholics.

**6. Irenaeus (AD 130-200):** Church father. Defended eastern Christians during Easter controversy.

**7. Felicity (died AD 203):** North African slave girl and Christian, probably a Montanist. Martyred with Perpetua, a fellow Christian. Felicity bore a child in prison. Their captor scoffed, "You're in such pain now! What will you do when you're thrown to the beasts?" She replied, "Now, I suffer alone. Then, there will be another in me. He will suffer for me, for I am about to suffer for him."

**8. Tertullian (AD 160-225):** North African church father. Attacked "modalism" (the belief that the Father, Son, and Spirit are not distinct in any way). Became a Montanist near the end of his life.

**9. Hippolytus (AD 170-236):** Roman theologian. Recorded the *Apostolike Paradosis* (Apostolic Tradition), which includes an early form of the Apostles' Creed.

**10. Origen (AD 184-254):** Educator in Alexandria. Encouraged allegorical interpretation of Scripture.

## 4 TERMS you should know

**1. Heresy:** Any teaching that directly contradicts an essential New Testament teaching.

**2. Gnosticism:** From the Greek, *gnosis* ("knowledge"), the belief that the physical world is evil and that only secret, spiritual knowledge can free persons from the physical world.

**3. Docetism:** From the Greek, *docein* ("to seem"), the belief that Jesus only seemed to possess a physical body. Most Gnostics were also Docetists.

**4. Rule of Faith:** A series of statements that tested a new believer's understanding of essential Christian doctrines, known today as "the Apostles' Creed."

# CHAPTER 2

# Balancing the Past with the Present

# IN THIS CHAPTER
## AD 90 — AD 250

Gnosticism
Marcion
Origen
Montanism

The Christmas rush had ended. Rayann and I were wandering the supermarket's deserted aisles; six months or so had passed since our wedding.

"And, of course," Rayann suddenly commented, "we have to buy black-eyed peas."

My nose wrinkled, "We have to buy what?"

Peas with optical complications have never appealed to me.

"Black-eyed peas," Rayann repeated. "You always eat black-eyed peas on New Year's Eve!"

The Madaba map depicts several rectangular-shaped churches ("basilicas") built by Christians in Jerusalem in the 200s.

About then, she realized I'd never heard of welcoming the new year with a plate of peas. And, once again, we faced the dilemma that every couple deals with during those first few years of marriage: "How do we balance our past traditions with our present circumstances?"

In the end, I did—against my own more prudent preferences—eat visually-challenged vegetables on New Year's Eve. The problem wasn't with Rayann's past or with mine, though. The problem had to do with how we balanced past traditions with present expectations.

Throughout the second and third centuries, Christians dealt with the same sort of question. Christians were forced to ask themselves, "How do we deal with our present needs in ways that remain faithful to God's past works?" As Christians struggled to answer this question, the church's structure shifted, a canon of Scripture emerged, and the issues that emerged in the aftermath of these changes became far too complex to be solved by a plate of peas.

## Changes in the empire, changes in the church

Among the earliest Christians, "elder" (or "presbyter" from the Greek *presbyteros*) and "overseer" (or "bishop" from the Greek *episkopos*) apparently referred to the same role. A group of equal elders guided each church; Christians gathered in homes; and people were baptized soon after they declared their intention to follow Jesus.

By the third century, Christians were organizing themselves above the local level. In most cities, one elder—the "overseer" or "bishop"—directed the other elders. Congregations built and maintained their own buildings. In some

AD 90 – AD 250

areas, new believers received three years of training before baptism. An increasing number of churches baptized infants. Others still urged parents to wait until their children trusted Christ for themselves. Yet neither group seems to have condemned the other.

Why had the church's structure changed? During the second century a twisted version of Christianity—the Secret Knowledge Movement, also known as *Gnosticism* [NAW-sti-sizm]—had threatened the survival of some of the most essential tenets of Christian faith. Powerful overseers, centralized meeting-places, and careful training emerged to help Christians confront the Gnostic [NAW-stik] worldview.

*Ancient Ruins at Ephesus in Turkey*

# The secret knowledge movement

## What did Gnostics believe?

From the perspective of the Gnostics, everything physical was corrupt; only spiritual things were pure. In this, the Gnostics drew heavily from Greek philosophers such as Plato. Certain persons could—the Gnostics claimed—experience secret knowledge of God. This knowledge transported these persons into a higher realm, beyond the limitations of their flesh.

Because they detested everything physical, Gnostics rejected or reinterpreted verses like John 1:14: "The Word became flesh and dwelt among us." According to many Gnostics, Jesus Christ never became flesh; instead, Christ was a *spirit* that temporarily possessed an ordinary human being named Jesus.

The apostles had, however, repeatedly affirmed Christ's humanity. The apostle Paul even commanded Christians to honor God with their bodies—an impossible request from the Gnostic perspective! (1 Corinthians 6:19-20).

And why was it so important, from Paul's perspective, for Christians to glorify God with their bodies? *For Christians, salvation isn't a spiritual retreat from the physical realm; it is a renewal that unites and restores both realms.*

from the **ones** who were there

*Hymn, written to combat Gnosticism, AD 190:*

*"The great Creator of the worlds,*
*The sovereign God of heav'n,*
*A holy and immortal truth*
*To us on earth has giv'n.*
*A holy and immortal truth*
*To us on earth has giv'n!"*

*"God sent Christ down as sending God;*
*One man for humankind;*
*As one with us*
*Christ dwelt with us,*
*And died and lives on high.*
*As one with us*
*Christ dwelt with us,*
*And died and lives on high!"*

*"God sent no angel of the host*
*To bear this mighty Word.*
*But Christ through whom the worlds were made*
*The everlasting Lord.*
*Yes, Christ through whom the worlds were made*
*The everlasting Lord!"*
                    —Epistle of Diognetus.

You can sing this song to the tune of "All Hail the Pow'r." (Coronation).

It wasn't merely the immorality of ancient Rome that drove people toward Gnosticism, though: In the late first century, several natural disasters shook the Roman Empire. In AD 79, a volcano destroyed the cities of Pompeii and Herculaneum. In the mid-80s, as many as 10,000 people died every day during an Empire-wide plague. Amid such tragedies, Gnosticism's negative perspective on the physical world appealed to more than a few people.

## A troublesome preacher's kid

One prominent Gnostic sect began with a preacher's kid. His name? Marcion [MARR-see-un or MARR-kee-un]. His father was an overseer or elder in a city on the southern coast of the Black Sea. At first Marcion followed a different path from his father. He became a ship-owner, sailing passengers and cargo throughout the Roman Empire. During his travels, Marcion developed a distaste for the physical world and a theology that mingled this distaste with a heretical form of Christian faith.

**Browse Marcion's writings:**
www.earlychristianwritings.
com/marcion.html

Around AD 140, Marcion's father's church excluded the young ship-owner from fellowship. According to some reports, Marcion had seduced an unmarried girl who belonged to his father's church. While this is possible, the problem was more likely with Marcion's theology. Whatever the reason for his exclusion from his father's church, Marcion fled to Rome, where no churches knew about his past. The church in Rome quickly accepted the ship-owner—a process that may have been hastened by his donation to the church of more than two million dollars, by modern monetary reckoning.

While a member of the church in Rome, Marcion developed his heretical ideas into a full-fledged system. Even though Marcion didn't proclaim full-fledged Gnosticism, his heresy did borrow freely from the Gnostic world-view. According to Marcion, the wrathful God of the Jewish Scriptures was not the same deity as the Father of Jesus. The God of the Jewish people was, Marcion claimed, a lower deity, the Creator of the physical world. The supreme God of the universe was the all-loving Father of Christ—a deity who would never punish anyone or resurrect anyone's physical body. Marcion even reduced the Savior to a spirit; according to Marcion, Christ only *seemed* human. This belief later became known as *Docetism*.

Because they believed the earth was evil, Marcion's followers denied every earthly desire. When they celebrated the Lord's Supper, Marcion's followers drank only water. Why? Drinking the fruit of the vine might incite physical pleasure. They banned all sexual relations—even between spouses.

As he proclaimed this perspective on life, Marcion perceived a problem: Some portions of the apostles' writings challenged his teachings. And what was his solution? Marcion created the earliest known list of authoritative writings for

Christians. Only eleven books made Marcion's list—an edited version of Luke's Gospel and ten of Paul's letters. The good news was that, in Marcion's Sunday school, learning the books of the Bible was easy. The bad news was that Marcion had rejected the God of Israel—the very God that, according to the earliest eyewitnesses of Jesus, had been revealed in Jesus Christ. This placed Marcion's beliefs far beyond the boundaries of faith that had been passed down through the apostles.

In 144 the Roman church returned the money Marcion had donated. Several Christians, including Polycarp of Smyrna, tried to turn Marcion away from his wayward teachings. In the end, Marcion refused, and he was removed from the church's fellowship. He responded by forming his own congregations in Italy and Asia Minor.

## How did Gnosticism affect Christianity?

Most Gnostics eventually withdrew from the churches. Still, the Greek philosophy that undergirded Gnosticism left a mark on the Christian faith, especially through Origen [ORR-i-jenn] of Alexandria. During a local persecution in AD 202, Origen's father had died for his faith. Origen begged to offer himself as a martyr, but his mother hid his clothes. The sixteen-year-old was reluctant to become a streaker, and so his life was spared. The Alexandrian church soon noticed Origen's teaching skills. Two years after his father's death, the young man, now fully clothed, was directing a church-school for new disciples.

Origen preached against the Gnostics. Yet he borrowed freely from the same Greek philosophies that had fed the Gnostic movement. According to Origen, God's original creation had been spiritual. Only after the Fall did God form a physical world. Eventually, Origen taught, God will restore all creation—even Satan—to a sinless, spiritual state.

Like the followers of Marcion, Origen renounced physical comforts. Origen drank only water and wore no shoes. In literal obedience to Matthew 19:12, he castrated himself.

Christians had refused to accept the idea that some believers possessed secret knowledge. Yet many teachers, influenced by teachers like Origen, continued to deal with difficult texts by looking for hidden spiritual or allegorical meanings. First-century Christians had refused to renounce God's gift of sex (see 1 Corinthians 7:3-5). Yet, by the third century, many Christians viewed marriage as an acceptable but less holy alternative to lifelong virginity.

AD 90 – AD 250

**Origen**

Examine parts of early New Testament manuscripts:

www.xmission.com/~research/gospel

## How did Christians respond to the Gnostics?

So what were the long-term effects of Gnosticism? The Gnostic challenge compelled second-century Christians to ask themselves anew, "How do we remain faithful to the testimony of the apostolic eyewitnesses who heard and saw Jesus?" Most believers found their answers in a canon of writings, a Rule of Faith, and a priesthood of overseers.

### Which writings do we obey?

**IN CASE you're confused**

Three questions that Christians seem to have asked about the church's authoritative writings were: (1) Is the book reliably connected to an apostle? (2) Do churches throughout the known world value this writing? (3) Does this writing agree with what we already know about God? Look at your New Testament. Does each book conform to the three questions? These facts may help: Mark traveled with Peter and translated his accounts of Jesus' life. Luke traveled with Paul. Timothy, Paul's protege, is mentioned in Hebrews 13:23. James and Jude–Jesus' half-brothers– were likely viewed as apostles (Galatians 1:19).

Against Marcion, Christians throughout the Roman Empire agreed that it was Yahweh—the "I AM" of the Hebrew Scriptures—who Jesus Christ revealed (John 8:58). As such, they accepted the Hebrew Scriptures as God's inspired words.

But on which *Christian* writings should God's people rely?

It wasn't as if second-century believers could head to their local bookstore and pick up a copy of the New Testament from the shelf next to *Christian History Made Easy.* For these believers, the authoritative texts for their faith were the writings that literate Christians read aloud each week in times of worship. But how did churches decide *which* writings to read? After all, some Gnostics claimed to possess authoritative oracles from Jesus—sayings that, in some cases, directly contradicted the core beliefs of the earliest Christians.

Although no one put this criterion into writing, the basic standard in the churches ran something like this: *Among early Christians, testimony that could be connected to eyewitnesses of the risen Lord was considered to be uniquely authoritative.* Even while the New Testament books were being written, the words of people who saw and followed the risen Lord—especially words from apostolic eyewitnesses—carried special authority in the churches (see Acts 1:21-26; 15:6–16:5; 1 Corinthians 4–5; 9:1-12; Galatians 1:1-12; 1 Thessalonians 5:26-27).

This standard was followed in the churches even during the time of Marcion. When someone in the Roman church in the middle of the second century AD considered which Christian writings should be considered authoritative, here's what he wrote regarding a popular book, known as *The Shepherd,* that some Christians wanted to read alongside the writings of apostolic eyewitnesses:

AD 90 – AD 250

*"The Shepherd* was composed quite recently, in our times. So, ... it cannot be read publicly for the church, because it is counted neither among the prophets (for their number has been completed) nor among the apostolic eyewitnesses (for it is after their time)."

The logic behind this standard was simple: The people most likely to tell the truth about Jesus were either eyewitnesses who had encountered Jesus personally or close associates of these witnesses. Two other standards followed the logic of this one: An authoritative writing couldn't contradict other writings that were known to represent eyewitness testimony to the truth (after all, if two eyewitness testimonies both testified to the truth, they shouldn't contradict each other), and the writing had to be recognized by Christians throughout the world.

Although the emergence of the canon can seem confusing and even a bit unsettling, here's one of the most important facts about this process: There were twenty or so books that, from the very beginning, were known beyond any doubt to have their roots in eyewitnesses testimony—and these are the writings that reflect some of the most essential truths about Jesus. From the very beginning, Christians embraced the four Gospels, Acts, the letters of Paul, and at least one letter from John.

**IN CASE you're confused**

The word "canon" means "measuring stick." For Christians, the word refers to the books that God inspired to form the church's faith. These books are called a canon because they measure the boundaries of the church's beliefs.

Arguments about a small handful of writings—including Hebrews, James, the letters of Peter, John's second and third letters, and the letters of James and Jude—persisted past the second century. Still, from the first century onward, Christians universally recognized twenty or so books as authoritative, and—by the fourth century AD—God had led churches throughout the Empire to recognize one basic canon of texts that could be traced to eyewitnesses of the risen Lord or to close associates of these eyewitnesses. Not only did Christians trust in the living Word and Spirit, their faith was also shaped by a canon of written words.

## What must Christians believe?

When baptizing a new believer, most pastors ask the person, "Have you trusted Jesus as your Lord?" or some similar question. Asking questions before baptism isn't a new custom. The practice is deeply rooted in the Christian Scriptures and in the church's traditions. Scattered throughout the apostles' writings are statements of faith, like "Jesus Christ is Lord" (Philippians 2:11). In many cases, these confessions were probably based on questions that Christians were asked at their baptism.

After Marcion left the Roman church, the baptismal questions became a bit longer and more detailed. These baptismal questions became known as the "Rule of

AD **90** – AD **250**

Faith." And why did the baptismal questions become more detailed? Christian leaders wanted new believers to understand how their faith differed from Marcion's false teachings. Marcion had argued that Christ's Father had nothing to do with the physical world; the Rule of Faith called God "Ruler of all." Marcion claimed that Jesus Christ wasn't truly human; the Rule clearly affirmed the birth and death of Christ. Marcion said the human body was beyond redemption; the Rule emphasized "the resurrection of the flesh."

Every authentic believer in Jesus Christ could accept the Rule of Faith. Why? Every line was drawn from the teachings of apostolic eyewitnesses to the risen Lord. The Rule was the church's answer to the question, "What must a Christian believe?" The Rule is still used today, in a slightly altered form. It's known by most Christians as "the Apostles' Creed."

**WORDS from the ones who were there**

**The Rule of Faith**

*"Do you believe in God the Father, Ruler of all? Do you believe in Christ Jesus, God's Son, who was born by the Holy Spirit through the virgin Mary, was crucified under Pontius Pilate, died and was buried, and rose again on the third day, alive from the dead, and ascended into heaven, sat at the Father's right hand, and will come again to judge the living and the dead? Do you believe in the Holy Spirit, the holy church, and the resurrection of the flesh?"*
—Apostolike Paradosis, 21

## Who should protect our teachings?

Gnostics and other heretical teachers often tried to trace their traditions back to an apostle. (No fewer than three heretical tracts were supposedly written by Thomas!) With so many false claims circulating, how could Christians protect the apostles' true teachings? In an attempt to protect authentic apostolic traditions, some overseers began tracing their beliefs back to apostles who may have lived in or passed through their cities.

By the third century, not only were the overseers' *teachings* traced to the apostles, but overseers also traced their *authority* back to the apostles. Overseers became, in some sense, the official trustees of the apostles' teachings. As a result, overseers' powers expanded rapidly, especially in larger cities. Since city overseers nurtured God's children throughout entire regions, they began calling one another "popes"—Latin for "fathers."

In the early second century, the church father Polycarp had urged *every* believer in Jesus Christ to protect the apostles' teachings. Eighty years later, one of Polycarp's pupils wrote, "The tradition ... is protected by the successions of elders." A priesthood of church leaders was beginning to supplant the priesthood of all believers.

In AD 110, Polycarp urged every believer to protect the apostles' teaching.

AD **90** – AD **250**

*Ichthus, the ancient Christian symbol, on a seventh century cave chapel in Pittenweem, Fife, Scotland*

The priesthood of overseers probably did help to preserve Christian truth. Increased power can, however, create increased problems. During the controversies over Marcion's teachings, Christians were also arguing about another issue: *When should we celebrate Easter?* Believers who lived in the eastern regions of the Roman Empire—including Polycarp, who tried to convince Marcion to change his mind—celebrated the resurrection of Jesus *during* the Jewish Passover. In the western Empire, Christians waited until the Sunday *after* Passover to celebrate the resurrection. Both groups celebrated Easter with the ancient equivalent of a potluck dinner. So, each spring, some Christians found themselves feasting while others were fasting.

Polycarp and Anicetus [ah-nee-SAY-tuss], the overseer of the Roman church, discussed and disagreed about the Easter issue. Yet Polycarp left Rome at peace with Anicetus.

After Polycarp's death, the bishops or overseers of the Roman church began to secure more powerful roles. In some ways, this made sense: Rome was the capital of civilization. As Roman citizens, people looked to the Roman Empire for direction. It was only normal for Christians to look to the Roman church—a church that could trace its lineage to two leading apostles, Peter and Paul—for direction.

**IN CASE you're confused**

Uncertain about how to locate the eastern and western regions of the Empire? The province of Illyricum marked the division between east and west.

Thirty years after Polycarp visited Rome, the Easter dispute arose again. Victor was the new Roman overseer. At Victor's request, churches around Jerusalem began to observe the Roman pattern, but other eastern Christians kept following their earlier customs. Victor responded by cutting off eastern Christians from fellowship with believers in Rome.

Many church leaders protested Victor's actions. One overseer pled with him, "The elders who led the Roman church before you didn't observe the Asian custom; still, they maintained peace with churches in Asia. The very fact that we can fast at different times proves the unity of our faith!" In a letter to Victor, another leader in the eastern churches insisted that the apostles Philip and John had followed the eastern custom of celebrating Easter during the Jewish Passover. Still, Victor refused to back down. From his viewpoint, God had cursed the eastern churches. After Victor's death, most Christians ignored his rejection of the eastern churches. Today, churches whose heritage is rooted in the eastern Roman Empire still celebrate Easter during the Jewish Passover.

**did YOU know?**

The fish became an early symbol of Christian faith. Why? Each letter of the Greek word for fish— ΙΧΘΥΣ (ichthus)—could be used to remember an aspect of Christ's life.

Ι = Iesous (Jesus)
Χ = Christos (Christ)
Θ = Theou (God's)
Υ = Uios (Son)
Σ = Soter (Savior)

AD 90 – AD 250

# The new prophecy movement

How do we balance God's past truths with God's present workings?

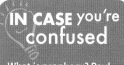

**IN CASE you're confused**

What is prophecy? Paul connected prophecy with public prayer and encouragement (Acts 15:32; 1 Corinthians 11:4-5; 14:3).

With stronger overseers, a Rule of Faith, and a growing consensus about the canon, it became easier to identify which beliefs represented the ancient, apostolic testimony about Jesus. At the same time, many Christians were asking, "What about the miraculous acts of the Spirit that saturated the book of Acts? What about God's promise, 'I will pour out my Spirit on all flesh. Your sons and daughters will prophesy'?" (Joel 2:28-29; Acts 2:17-18).

## The New Prophets call for renewal

In the mid 100s, a renewed emphasis on the Holy Spirit and personal holiness swept through churches in Asia Minor. The movement began in Phrygia [FRI-jee-yah] (now central Turkey). Around AD 160, three Phrygian believers—two women and one man—began prophesying. Prisca[PRISS-kah], Maximilla[maks-i-MILL-ah], and Montanus[MONT-ah-nuss] called fellow Christians to embrace radical self-denial.

Powerful church leaders in Rome and Asia Minor denounced the so-called "New Prophets" or "Montanists." The divide between the New Prophets and other Christians became so great that once, when Roman Christians and New Prophets were martyred in the same arena, they died for the same Lord but they tried to avoid being eaten by the same beasts!

Still, not everyone agreed with the decision to denounce the New Prophets. One overseer even argued that by denouncing all New Prophets the church was pushing out both true and false prophets. Many Christians rejoiced in the New Prophets' renewed emphasis on the Holy Spirit. The movement's strict moral standards attracted others.

Why, then, did the churches regard the Montanists as a heretical sect? Some persons claimed that the New Prophets relied on their personal prophecies instead of Scripture. Whether or not the New Prophets actually placed their prophecies above Scripture isn't certain. Two facts *are* certain, though:

**from the ones who were there**

**WORDS**

*Tertullian, convert to Montanism, describing their worship:*

"We have among us a sister who has received manifold gifts of revelation. She experiences these through ecstatic visions given during the sacred ceremonies."
—*De Anima, 9*

➤ **The New Prophets did make some false predictions.** *Montanus and Prisca prophesied that the New Jerusalem would soon arrive in Pepuza, a back-woods village in the Phrygian desert. Since the New Jerusalem never did pay a visit to Pepuza, many Christians concluded that God hadn't inspired the New Prophets (compare Deuteronomy 13:1-5).*

➤ **The New Prophets called for stricter moral standards than the Scriptures.** *Marriage was banned among New Prophets. Frequent fasts were required. To prepare themselves for Christ's return, the New Prophets required adherents to deny physical pleasures and to focus on the spiritual realm.*

# What makes the church holy?

To guard essential teachings, church leaders had created a chain of command directed by overseers. Yet some leaders went beyond guarding the church's essential beliefs. Overseers like Victor moved beyond the Scriptures by attempting to enforce nonessential beliefs. As the power of overseers or bishops increased, some Christians even began to view the overseer as the channel of the Spirit's work. For them, the church's holiness resided in the overseer. The church, like Noah's ark, contained clean and unclean creatures. Yet, as long as persons remained united to their overseer, they remained united to God's Spirit.

Other Christians understood that every believer is a channel of God's Spirit. The New Prophets or Montanists, for example, rooted their understanding of God's work in the spiritual experiences and righteous lives of individual believers. They reasoned that, if unholy persons were allowed in the churches, the church could not be Christ's holy bride. Yet the New Prophets also moved beyond the Scriptures, proclaiming prophecies that turned out to be false and calling for moral standards that went far beyond the standards of Scripture.

What some persons in both groups seem to have missed is that the sacredness and vitality of the church flows neither from the church's overseers nor from the experiences of individual members. The church's unity with the mission of Jesus Christ in this world is rooted in the church's faithfulness to the apostolic testimony about Jesus Christ, a testimony that has been preserved for God's people today in the pages of Holy Scripture.

The church is, the apostle Peter wrote, "made a holy people by [God's] Spirit"— but this Spirit will never lead God's people in ways that are contrary to Scripture (1 Peter 1:2, *Good News Bible*). It was, after all, this very Spirit who inspired the writers of Scripture, and it is this same Holy Spirit who guides the people of God in every present circumstance—always renewing God's people, always calling us to deeper devotion to Jesus Christ, always leading us in ways that faithfully reflect the Scriptures that he inspired so long ago.

**KEY concept**

God's people must learn to view God's present activities in the light of God's past revelation of himself in the pages of Holy Scripture.

AD **90** – AD **250**

**5 EVENTS you should know**

**1. Era of Martyrs (AD 303-305):** Emperor Diocletian issued a series of edicts that led to the harshest Roman persecution of the church.

**2. Edict of Milan (AD 313):** Emperors Constantine and Licinius affirmed Galerius' decision to legalize Christianity.

**3. Arian Controversy (AD 320-364):** The Arian heresy remained popular until the late 300s. In AD 350, Arians outnumbered Christians in some areas of the Eastern Empire.

**4. The Council of Nicaea (AD 325):** Emperor Constantine invited every overseer in the Roman Empire to deal with the Arian heresy. The Creed of Nicaea confessed the church's belief in the Trinity and in the full deity of Jesus Christ. The Council of Nicaea was later recognized as the first general council of the church.

**5. Athanasius' Easter Letter (AD 367):** For members of churches under his guidance, Athanasius made a list of authoritative Christian writings, including the same 27 books that appear in New Testaments today. In AD 397, the Synod of Carthage confirmed Athanasius' list.

**8 NAMES you should know**

**1. Cyprian (died AD 258):** Overseer of Carthage, North Africa. Allowed Christians who faltered during persecution to return to their churches.

**2. Helena (AD 255-330):** Devout Christian and mother of Emperor Constantine. In 326 she visited the Holy Land and had churches built in Bethlehem and on the Mount of Olives.

**3. Eusebius of Caesarea (AD 263-339):** Wrote the earliest surviving history of Christianity.

**4. Pachomius (AD 292-346):** Founder of communal (or cenobitic) monasticism in the Western Empire. His sister Mary founded religious communities for women.

**5. Basil of Caesarea (AD 329-379):** One of the Great Cappadocians, opposed Arianism.

**6. Gregory Nazianzus (AD 329-389):** One of the Great Cappadocians, opposed Arianism.

**7. Gregory Nyssa (AD 330-394):** One of the Great Cappadocians, Basil's brother.

**8. Jerome (AD 345-420):** Monk and scholar, translated the Vulgate.

**5 TERMS you should know**

**1. Eastern and Western Empires:** Diocletian divided the empire into two halves in 292. Rome remained the capital of the Western Empire until AD 476. Constantine placed the capital of the Eastern Empire in Byzantium, later renamed "Constantinople."

**2. The Great Cappadocians:** The Eastern theologians who helped Christians recognize Arianism as a false teaching. All of them were born in the imperial province of Cappadocia.

**3. Donatism:** The belief that—if an overseer ever faltered under persecution—all ordinances and ceremonies that the overseer had performed were invalid. Donatism (named after Donatus, an early leader) split North African churches from AD 311 until the fifth century.

**4. Arianism:** The belief that Jesus is not fully God; Jesus is, rather, God's foremost creation. Arianism (named after the movement's leader) was denounced by the Council of Nicaea.

**5. Vulgate:** From Latin *vulgaris* ("common"), Jerome's translation of the Bible into ordinary Latin. The Vulgate was the official Bible of the Roman Catholic Church for 1,000 years.

# CHAPTER 3

# The Church Wins ... and Loses

## IN THIS CHAPTER
### AD 247— AD 420
Emperor Diocletian
Emperor Constantine
Arius of Alexandria
Athanasius of Alexandria
Paula and Jerome

When I wrote the first edition of this book, I was the pastor of a small church—a *really* small church in a *really* small town, to be exact. Some Sundays, I was tempted to enroll the Father, Son, and Holy Spirit in Sunday school and count their attendance, just so the numbers would sound better. During my first few years in that context, the addition of the three persons of the Trinity would have constituted quite a significant increase in attendance!

As such, the postcards that clogged my mailbox on Monday mornings did tempt me: "Make your church more user-friendly!" "Double your worship attendance in thirty days or less." "You can be the pastor of a mega-church wherever you are!" Between my mailbox and the wastebasket, it was difficult not to do some speculating: *Would our church grow more if only my message could be more exciting? Would more people show up if only this church became more user-friendly? Could we attract more people if only I changed the worship services ... again?*

What I forgot more often than I care to admit was this simple truth: *What matters most isn't always the growth that I am able to count; it's whether I'm faithful wherever God has placed me.* Sometimes growth is good, but growth alone doesn't guarantee that God is being glorified.

I have a feeling that some Christians in the second and third centuries played an "if only" game too. I suspect that some of them said at some points, *If only we could be free from persecution ... if only the Roman emperor would listen to us ... if only we could worship without fear.*

In the early fourth century, these "if only's" came true. The churches gained political favor. Congregations grew numerically. Church treasuries expanded exponentially. Yet even with so much growth that could be counted so easily, the outcome wasn't all good.

## The empire strikes back

### The birthday party the church didn't attend

Few nations—and even fewer people—ever reach their thousandth birthday. Yet, in AD 247, the city of Rome turned one thousand years old. Citizens celebrated in the streets for three days and nights. I wasn't there, but I suspect that the party was something like New Year's Eve and Mardi Gras mixed into one wild celebration. Because the party celebrated Rome's pagan state religion, Christians refused to take part in the party.

This probably wouldn't have been a problem—after all, the fewer Christians at the party, the more hors d'oeuvres for everyone else, right?—if it hadn't been for what happened immediately after the party. Soon after the party ended, a plague ravaged Rome. Many Romans wondered if the Christians had angered the gods by refusing to take part in the festivities.

To regain the gods' good will, Emperor Decius [DEE-see-uss] launched an empire-wide persecution. People who were willing to sacrifice to the pagan gods received sacrifice certificates. And what about people who didn't have certificates? They were to be imprisoned and tortured. Many prominent overseers, including Origen, died from the injuries they received in prison. (If you can't recall Origen's origins, glance back at Chapter Two.) Emperor Decius died in 251; so, the hardship was short-lived. Still, the persecution led to some problems that lasted for decades.

## How sorry do we have to be?

To escape persecution, many Christians had sacrificed to the pagan gods or forged sacrifice certificates. When the persecution ended, some church members who had sacrificed to the gods wanted to re-enter their churches. This forced the churches to face a serious question: How could churches re-admit repentant Christians without also receiving false believers? After all, these people had lived a lie to escape persecution while their Christian brothers and sisters endured confinement and torture.

That was the question that confronted Cyprian [SIPP-ree-yun] of Carthage, an overseer or bishop in North Africa. When the persecution began, Cyprian believed that God was calling him to flee into hiding. When Cyprian returned, his congregation was in chaos.

Cyprian urged churches to re-admit Christians who had obtained forged sacrifice certificates. Before being admitted, however, these Christians had to show outward signs of sorrow. How? Prayer and fasting. In Cyprian's mind, true believers would want to show their repentance outwardly.

from the **ones** who were there
*Sacrifice Certificate, AD 251*

"To: The Sacrifice Commission

"From: Diogenes, aged 72 years, with a scar over my right eyebrow.

"I've always sacrificed to the gods. Now, in obedience to the emperor, I've sacrificed again, poured out a drink offering, and eaten meat offered to the gods. Please certify this below."

"I, Syrus, saw Diogenes and his son sacrificing."

*Paraphrased from Harvard Theological Review, 16 (1923): 363-365*

**on the web**

Christians often met in the catacombs, a series of tunnels beneath Rome—but not to hide from their persecutors! They gathered there to remember deceased Christians who were buried there.

Explore the catacombs:

www.catacombe.roma.it

Not everyone agreed with Cyprian's approach, though. Many North Africans thought that anyone who had tried to avoid martyrdom had never authentically trusted Jesus Christ. At the very least—this group believed—any overseer who had cooperated with the persecutors must have professed Christ falsely. According to these more strict believers, this meant that every ceremony of

AD 247 – AD 420

ordination, baptism, or communion performed by these false bishops ought to be considered invalid. These believers became known as the Donatists [DAW-na-tists], after a prominent leader named Donatus. The Donatist division continued to cause dissension in the churches for several decades.

Seven years after the first wave of persecution, another persecution spilled across the Empire. This time, God chose not to spare Cyprian's life. A judge commanded Cyprian to sacrifice. The overseer refused. He died on a Roman chopping-block.

## The last Roman persecution

Diocletian [DY-o-KLEE-shan] seized the imperial throne in Rome in AD 284. To avoid spreading his power too thinly, Emperor Diocletian divided his Empire. Diocletian became emperor of the Eastern Empire. A co-emperor governed the Western Empire. To avoid bloody battles over who would succeed the emperors, Diocletian chose two assistants. When one emperor retired, his assistant would replace him. Diocletian was a brilliant ruler in every way … except in his treatment of Christians. Diocletian's assistant was Galerius [gah-LAY-ree-uss]. As an army officer, Galerius had noticed that Christian soldiers were more loyal to Jesus than to their human commanders. Urged by Galerius, Diocletian lashed out against the church. The torment worsened when Diocletian retired.

Emperor Galerius wanted to rule not only his domain but also his co-emperor's. So, he abducted his co-emperor's son, Constantine [KAHN-stann-TEEN]. In 305 Constantine's father became deathly ill. Galerius released Constantine to visit his father, the co-emperor.

**did YOU know?**

Constantine moved his capital from Rome to a small village in Asia Minor, called Byzantium. He renamed the village "Constantinople." After Constantine's move, the Empire's strength shifted from the Western Empire to the Eastern Empire, also known as "the Byzantine Empire."

*Statue of of the Roman Emperor Constantine*

When his father died, Constantine demanded that Galerius recognize him as the new co-emperor. Galerius might have fought Constantine, but a fatal sickness struck Galerius. On his deathbed, Galerius realized his program of persecution had failed. Instead of returning to the Roman gods, church members usually continued to worship Christ or worshiped no god at all. As he died, Galerius issued a decree that allowed persons to follow Jesus "as long as they don't disturb the public order."

AD 247 – AD 420

By 312 two power-hungry soldiers, Constantine the new co-emperor and Maxentius [maks-ENN-she-uss], were fighting to control the Empire. Maxentius retreated to Rome, the capital of the Western Empire. As Constantine's army approached Rome, something happened. No one knows exactly what, but the church's relationship with the Empire would never be the same.

# Milvian Bridge is falling down, falling down

**Emperor Constantine**

## The sign in the sky

The day before his battle with Maxentius, Constantine prayed, probably to the Sun-God. As he looked at the sun, Constantine saw a cross. According to one legend, he also saw the words, "By this sign, you will win." That night, Constantine dreamed that Christ himself commanded him to place a Christian symbol on his shields. In Greek, the first letters of Christ's name look like the English letters *XP*. Constantine's soldiers chalked these letters on their shields the next morning. Constantine may even have added a cross to his personal battle-flag.

Maxentius was nearly invincible inside Rome's walls, but he was also unpopular with the people. If he stayed in the city, citizens might revolt during the battle, forcing him to fight both citizens within the city and Constantine outside the city. Maxentius left the city to position himself for battle. To keep Constantine out of Rome, Maxentius destroyed the Milvian Bridge. He replaced the bridge by tying together a column of boats, in case he needed to withdraw.

*Although many people understood it as a reference to Christ, Constantine's symbol was also a pagan monogram that meant "high quality." Within a century, the pagan meaning had been forgotten, however. Christians today still use the symbol, now known as the "chiron," as an abbreviation for "Christ."*

A few miles north of the river, Constantine forced Maxentius to retreat. Maxentius' troops fled across the boat-bridge, back into Rome. As Maxentius crossed the river, the boats broke. Several hundred soldiers, including Maxentius, drowned.

Constantine marched triumphantly into Rome, beneath the symbol of the cross. For the first time in history, the cross was smeared with the blood of a battle for human power.

AD **247** – AD **420**

*Emperor Constantine*
*—AD 337*

## Christianity's new corporate sponsor

The next year, Constantine and his co-emperor, Licinius [ly-SEE-nee-uss], issued the Edict of Milan [me-LAWN]. "Our purpose," they decreed, "is to allow Christians and all others to worship as they desire, so that whatever Divinity lives in the heavens will be kind to us."

In Constantine's mind, Christ was now his personal patron. The cross, once an emblem of Christ's death, began to function as a charm, confirming Constantine's power. Constantine granted church leaders—now commonly called "priests"—widespread favors. Constantine sincerely believed he was a Christian. Yet he seems to have worshiped Jesus as the Sun-God. In some ways, his confusion made sense. Didn't Christians call Jesus the "sun of righteousness" (Malachi 4:2). And wasn't Jesus the "light of the world"? (John 8:12). Christians even worshiped on *Sun*-Day!

A squabble in Africa quickly dashed Constantine's hopes that Christianity might unite his empire. Around 312, the Donatists in North Africa asked Constantine to settle the dispute about who could ordain an overseer. Constantine decided against the Donatists.

*The Arch of Constantine was built in honor of his victory over Maxentius.*

A momentous change had occurred—a change far more significant than anyone involved in the Donatist controversy could have imagined. For nearly 300 years the empire and the churches had remained separate. Now, a church had asked the emperor to sponsor its beliefs. Twelve hundred years would pass before a church completely severed its ties with the state again.

## The Council of Nicaea

Constantine's largest church squabble began with Arius [AIR-ee-uss], an elder in Alexandria, Egypt. Like many fourth-century Christians, Arius didn't believe God experienced emotions. Yet, if Jesus was fully divine, God did—through Jesus—feel sorrow and pain. The dominant perspective on this issue was that, in some way that transcends human understanding, God the Son had experienced emotions in his human nature but that God, in his essence, did *not* feel emotions, at least not in the same way that humans do.

Arius chose a different option: He taught that Jesus was *not* eternal God; Jesus was, instead, the first being that God created. "Once," Arius claimed, "the

Son did not exist." Arius knew the power of music; so, he put his theological ideas to a catchy tune. Within weeks Alexandrians were singing in the streets, "Once the Son did not exist!"

Church members who rejected Arius' ideas responded with a chorus that Christians still sing—a hymn that's known today as *Gloria Patri*: "Glory be to the Father, and to the Son, and to the Holy Ghost; As it was in the beginning, is now, and ever shall be, world without end."

Constantine probably didn't care whether Jesus was God. He did, however, care about a united Empire. To restore unity, he invited every overseer in the known world to Nicaea, a village in northern Asia Minor that is now part of the city of Iznik, in Turkey. On July 4, AD 325, three hundred overseers arrived in Nicaea with two thousand elders and deacons. It was the Fourth of July, but fireworks hadn't yet made it to Asia Minor. As such, the opening ceremonies consisted of Constantine, having proclaimed himself an overseer and apostle, calling the council to order.

In the crowded hall, one group denounced Arius in no uncertain terms, because Arius denied the unique deity of Christ. Another group applauded Arius. Most representatives didn't understand Arius. They only wanted peace … until an overseer who supported Arius explained the elder's ideas. When the overseer suggested that Christ had been created instead of having existed eternally, the fireworks

began. One overseer screamed, "Blasphemy!" Another overseer ripped Arius' notes into pieces. Suddenly, nearly everyone agreed that the council should condemn Arius.

**THINK about it…** Arius (like Mormons and Jehovah's Witnesses today) used Colossians 1:15 and Hebrews 1:5-6 to try to prove that God created Jesus and, therefore, Jesus is not God. List three reasons why these texts do not teach that Jesus was created.

One overseer suggested a statement of faith that might exclude Arius' ideas. With a few changes, his statement became the Creed of Nicaea. The key change was the added phrase "of one essence with the Father." Even though Eastern Christians worshiped Jesus as God, the phrase "one essence with the Father" bothered many of them. Why? Some Eastern Christians felt the phrase could mean

AD 247 – AD 420

that the Son and the Father were somehow *not* distinct. Despite this difficulty, only two overseers refused to sign the creed. The council excluded both overseers—as well as Arius—from fellowship in their churches. Constantine wasn't content with the exclusion alone, though. Everyone who refused to sign the creed, he exiled.

After the council, the emperor's concern for peace, even at the expense of truth, became clear. By 327 most churches were calmly cooperating again; so, Constantine tried to restore Arius. Few voices protested the emperor's actions. One very loud voice *did* rise in protest, though. This very loud protest came from a surprisingly small man—Athanasius of Alexandria.

*Constantine and the first Council of Nicaea*

# Athanasius of Alexandria

Athanasius [AH-tha-NAY-shee-uss] was short and dark-skinned—so short and dark that his enemies called him "Black Dwarf." As a child, he had served the devout Christian hermits—also known as "monks"—who lived alone in the Egyptian desert. (The word *monk* simply means "alone.") As an adult, he retained a deep respect for the monks.

### "I don't want to be an overseer!"

Athanasius was present at the Council of Nicaea as a deacon, serving his overseer. After the council, the Alexandrian overseer fell fatally ill. The overseer asked Athanasius to replace him, but Athanasius wanted to serve people, not lead them. He fled to his friends, the desert monks. After weeks of running, Athanasius emerged. The church promptly ordained him as an overseer, in spite of his protests.

Athanasius and Constantine quickly clashed with each other. Despite Constantine's commands to the contrary, Athanasius refused to restore Arius as a church member, because Arius still denied Jesus' unique deity. Constantine threatened Athanasius, "If I hear that you've kept anyone from becoming a church member, I'll banish you." After five years of threats, Constantine exiled Athanasius on a false charge of treason.

In 337 Emperor Constantine died. At Constantine's deathbed, a follower of Arius baptized Constantine. (In the fourth century, many people believed that God did not forgive sins committed after baptism; so deathbed baptisms were common among persons who hadn't been baptized as children.) Ironically, Constantine, who did so much to weaken

## THINK about it...

The story of Julian should alarm every Christian. Why? He might have had a positive perspective on Christianity had it not been for the Christians he knew. People who called themselves Christians killed his family, imprisoned him, and forced him to learn the Scriptures until nothing could relieve his hatred of Christianity.

the pagan gods, was declared a pagan god after his death. The Roman Senate passed a resolution identifying Constantine as "divine."

## A pagan emperor— but no persecution

By AD 362 Athanasius had returned to Alexandria. The new emperor was Contantine's nephew, Julian. Julian hated Christianity—with good reason, at least from a human perspective. When Julian was six years old, Constantine's son had slaughtered Julian's family without a trial. Julian's childhood was spent alone, in constant fear of Constantine's sons.

When Julian became emperor, he revoked the civil privileges that Constantine had extended to Christian clergy. Julian also canceled all overseers' exiles—whether they were orthodox or heretical—hoping to create turmoil in the churches.

**on the web**

Intrigued by Athanasius?

www.earlychurch.org.uk/athanasius.php

And how did the churches do without political support?

At first, chaos ensued. Yet, one year into Julian's reign, Eastern and Western churches began cooperating with each other again.

Athanasius asked both supporters and opponents of the Creed of Nicaea to come to a meeting (or "synod") in Alexandria. Together, they rejected Arius' ideas. A few Western overseers finally saw why Eastern churches didn't like the phrase "one essence with the Father." Both groups at the Synod of Alexandria agreed that the Father, Son, and Spirit are three persons who share the same essence.

Emperor Julian feared Athanasius' ability to unite the churches. So "Black Dwarf" fled to the desert again. When Julian's soldiers found Athanasius, he was sailing up the Nile. The imperial ship drifted behind Athanasius' slower boat. A soldier shouted, "Have you seen Athanasius?" The overseer answered truthfully, "Yes! He is just ahead of you, and if you hurry you shall overtake him." Soon the ship passed by and left Athanasius behind. Desert monks hid Athanasius until Julian's death. A decade later, Athanasius died in Alexandria.

# The ones who got away from it all— for a lifetime

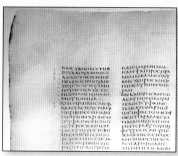

**Sinaiticus Text**

*Fourth-century Christians copied the oldest known complete copies of the Christian Scriptures—Sinaiticus and Vaticanus codices—in fine leather (vellum) books.*

## The desert monks

For years Christians—influenced a little by the apostle Paul and a lot by Greek philosophy—had revered persons who rejected physical pleasures. Athanasius even wrote a book about a desert monk named Anthony. The biography became wildly popular in the churches—sort of the ancient equivalent of *The Purpose-Driven Life*—and the desert became a refuge for Christians who disliked the church's newfound power. Desert monks lived in extreme poverty, eating only enough to stay alive. Alone for years, many monks endured horrible visions. Extreme sexual urges haunted others.

Some monks began to see the truth behind Genesis 2:18: People weren't created to live alone. These monks founded "monasteries"—communities for monks. Women had already founded their own religious communities. (*Nonnus* is the feminine form of *monk*; so these women became known as "nuns.") These communities for women became known as "convents" (Latin for "gathering-place").

Some women joined convents because they believed that God was calling them to lives of meditation. Others became nuns to avoid distasteful arranged marriages. Still others became nuns against their wills; fathers sometimes forced their daughters to join convents to avoid paying for their weddings.

## Jerome and Paula

Perhaps the most intriguing monk was a guilt-wracked Christian named Jerome. Before retreating to the desert, Jerome felt ashamed because he admired pagan authors. After his retreat, he battled physical longings and memories of nude dancers in Rome.

Jerome's hatred of everything physical led to some unusual habits and teachings. It was Jerome who first defended the idea that Jesus' mother remained a virgin throughout her life. Jerome also refused to wash his body, claiming that Christ had cleansed him once for all. Still, he could not escape his physical longings.

In a final effort to rid his mind of everything but God, Jerome began to learn Hebrew.

Even Hebrew couldn't quite take care of Jerome's urges, though.

After two tortured years, Jerome realized God had not called him to live alone. He returned to Rome. The overseer of Rome suggested a project to occupy his mind—a reliable, Latin translation of the Scriptures.

A wealthy Roman widow named Marcella [marr-SELL-ah] financed the project. Marcella was a brilliant biblical scholar who had committed herself to remain unmarried. Even after he left Rome, Jerome was known to refer pastors who were struggling with unclear biblical texts to Marcella.

In Marcella's mansion, Jerome met the person who would become his closest companion—a woman named Paula. In Paula, Jerome found someone with whom he could discuss his hopes and fears, his questions and dreams. She became an outstanding scholar, quickly matching Jerome's abilities in Hebrew. Soon, Paula and Marcella embraced the same sort of self-denial as Jerome, even to the point of refusing to bathe.

did **you** know**?**

At first, people didn't like Jerome's Latin translation. Why not? Jerome didn't translate from the old Greek text of the Jewish Scriptures. He translated the Jewish Scriptures directly from Hebrew. Also, his version used easily understood words that some church members didn't like. People called his translation "Vulgate" (Latin for "Common" or "Vulgar"). Even so, within a few years, the Vulgate became everyone's favorite version. Even after people didn't understand its outdated language anymore, churches still used Jerome's Bible.

With three people boycotting the bathtubs for life, that mansion *must* have reeked after a few years. Despite the odors around him, Jerome completed his Latin translation of the Bible in 405. But deep pain tempered his joy: Paula had passed away a few months before he completed the project. Fifteen years later, Jerome died.

*Jerome finished translating the Old and New Testaments into Latin after 22 years of work.*

AD 247 – AD 420

## The Great Cappadocians

After Athanasius' death, four Eastern Christians became the most vocal supporters of the Creed of Nicaea. They were Basil, his sister Macrina [mah-KREEN-ah], their brother Gregory, and a close family friend, also named Gregory. They lived in Cappadocia, an area in contemporary Turkey.

Because they came from the region of Cappadocia, Basil, Gregory, and Gregory became known as the Great Cappadocians—which is certainly preferable to what they might have been called if they had lived after their homeland became known as Turkey. (After all, who could take a theologian seriously if he was known as one of "the Great Turkeys"?) The Great Cappadocians' support of the Creed of Nicaea helped to bring together Christian thinking in the Eastern and Western Empires.

*Basil, Gregory, and Chrysostom*

*Icon of the Three Holy Hierarchs from Lipie (XVII century, Historic Museum in Sanok, Poland)*

Macrina—and later Basil— founded the first Eastern communities for nuns and monks. Persons who joined their communities didn't spend all day meditating. They worked. While they worked, they sang psalms. They sold what they grew and made. Profits were used to help the poor. Unlike many nuns and monks, Macrina and Basil banned extreme fasting and self-punishment. Instead of withdrawing completely from the world, they founded convents and monasteries in cities. In these communities, nuns and monks taught and nursed thousands of city children.

# Is all growth healthy?

Between 300 and 400 Christians gained something they had never possessed before—earthly peace and power. Churches grew more rapidly than ever before. Still, not all growth is good. In God's kingdom, quality matters more than quantity. Many people joined the Christian movement to hedge their spiritual bets by gaining the good will of one more deity. Others joined churches to improve their social status. Some believers resisted the church's new status and spent their lives in exile. Others fled to communities in the desert.

Most Christians, however, welcomed their new-found acceptance. (After centuries of persecution, wouldn't you?) One result was that many church members began to identify Christianity with earthly institutions, instead of with the invisible community of all true believers. The institutional aspects of the church became overly important, and the gospel became diluted.

It's easy to become caught up in what we can count—sometimes even allowing human growth to determine our perspective on whether God is truly working. Sometimes growth is good, but growth alone doesn't guarantee that God is being glorified. What matters most isn't always the growth that we are able to count. What matters is whether we're faithful wherever God has placed us.

*From AD 300 until 1300, more than 400 churches could be found in Cappadocia— a region near the center of modern Turkey. Many of of these churches were concealed in the caves and underground cities. Rock churches still stand today in this region, full of frescoes portraying subjects from the Bible.*

AD **247** – AD **420**

**EVENTS you should know**

**5**

**1. First Council of Constantinople (381):** The church's second general council denounced Apollinarianism and approved the Nicene Creed.

**2. Emperor Theodosius Declared Christianity the Official Religion of the Empire (391).**

**3. Council of Ephesus (431):** The church's third general council accused Nestorius of teaching that Jesus was two separate persons, one human and one divine.

**4. Council of Chalcedon (451):** At the church's fourth general council more than 500 overseers condemned the One-Nature ("Monophysite") view of Christ. They agreed that, according to Scripture, Christ was one person with two natures (one human, one divine). This became known as the Two-Nature ("Dyophysite") view.

**5. Second Council of Constantinople (553):** Around 542, One-Nature theology became popular again. Justinian, emperor of the Eastern Empire, convened the church's fifth general council to end the controversy. The council denounced the *Three Chapters*—the writings of three Nestorians (all of whom were dead anyway). The council also declared that Jesus' mother remained a virgin throughout her life.

**NAMES you should know**

**7**

**1. Pelagius (died 420):** Monk who taught that humans have the natural ability to please God. Denounced by a local council in Carthage (418) and by the Council of Ephesus.

**2. Theodore of Mopsuestia (350-428):** Theologian from Antioch who held some Nestorian views. His writings were included in the *Three Chapters*.

**3. Augustine of Hippo (354-430):** North African overseer. Greatest theologian of his era.

**4. Benedict of Nursia (480-550):** Father of Western monasticism. Wrote *The Rule of Benedict*, a manual for monks. Founded religious communities near Monte Cassino, Italy, with his sister Scholastica.

**5. Columba (521-597):** Irish missionary, founder of Iona monastery.

**6. Gregory (540-604):** First Roman bishop to attain the status that would later be linked with the title "pope." The sixty-fourth pope for Roman Catholics.

**7. Augustine of Canterbury (died, 605):** Monk sent by Pope Gregory I to begin new churches in England after barbarians destroyed previous missionaries' work.

**TERMS you should know**

**5**

**1. General Council:** One of seven councils acknowledged by Eastern and Western Christians.

**2. Apollinarianism:** The belief that Jesus had no human mind. Named after Apollinarius, an early proponent. The First Council of Constantinople condemned Apollinarianism.

**3. Theotokos:** A Greek word meaning "God-bearer." Many Christians called Jesus' mother *theotokos*. Nestorius criticized the term, arguing that Mary didn't bear only a divine being; Mary bore the Lord Jesus Christ, who was fully human and fully divine.

**4. Nestorianism:** The belief that Jesus was two separate persons, one human and one divine. Named after Nestorius who was unfairly accused of teaching this view. This view is more properly termed "hyper-Dyophysitism" ("beyond two natures").

**5. Monophysitism:** From the Greek *monophysis* ("one-nature"). The belief that Jesus' divine nature fully absorbed his human nature. Also called "Eutychianism," after an early proponent.

# CHAPTER 4

# Servant-Leaders or Leaders of Servants?

# IN THIS CHAPTER
## 376 – 664
Ambrose of Milan
John Chrysostom
Augustine of Hippo
Cyril of Alexandria
Leo the Great • Patrick

Take a good look at your feet. What do you think? I think I can safely assume that your feet are not your body's most beautiful features, despite the ancient prophet's portrayal of them (Isaiah 52:7). They aren't always clean. And, after a hot day, they don't produce pleasant scents.

In modern times, shoes and sidewalks have removed much of the foot's foulness. In earlier times, feet were far more offensive. Sporadic baths and grimy streets combined to produce uncommonly powerful podiatric odors. Foot-washing was an act of servitude reserved for the lowest slaves.

Perhaps that's why Jesus reminded his disciples that no task should be beneath the men and women who lead his people—not even washing feet (John 13:1-17).

Or loving outcasts.

Or enduring ridicule and persecution.

Or dying on a cross.

"The Son of Man did not come to be served," Jesus said, "but to serve, and to give his life as a ransom for many" (Mark 10:44-45). That's why the leaders in God's kingdom aren't called primarily to stand above God's people and tell them how to live. Leaders in God's kingdom are called to kneel beside God's people and show them how to serve.

*Beginning between 400 and 600, monks and priests had the crowns of their heads shaved when they took their vows. This rite became known as the "tonsure." The practice was abolished in 1972 by Pope Paul VI.*

## How the power grew

As church leaders gained far-reaching powers, leaders of servants seem to have replaced servant-leaders in many areas. The powers associated with leadership in the church elevated church leaders above their people in many cases. The gap between laypeople and clergy became broader as increasing numbers of church leaders expected priests to remain unmarried.

One Christian who objected to this gap was a monk named Jovinian [jo-VIH-nee-ann]. He argued that, since sex wasn't sinful, faithful spouses and lifelong virgins would receive the same eternal reward. He also denied that Jesus' mother remained a virgin throughout her life. Yet Jovinian's ideas did not prevail. Twelve years before he died, church leaders excluded Jovinian from fellowship.

AD 376 – AD 664

During the fifth century Western church leaders gained even *more* political power, and the gap between clergy and laypeople widened. Why? Masses of migrating "barbarians" were weakening the Empire's ability to manage its provinces. As the Roman Empire began to fragment and falter, church leaders found themselves assuming the tasks that had once been shouldered by Roman governors and prefects.

**ON the web**

Read about one Roman's meal with a group of barbarian Huns:

www.fordham.edu/halsall/source/priscus1.asp

## "Southward, ho!"

Who were the so-called barbarians? They were tribes of nomads who had once lived on the edges of the Roman Empire. They were dubbed "barbarians" because, to the Romans, their language sounded like someone babbling "bar-*bar*-bar." Roman writers accused barbarians of all sorts of savagery. Admittedly, barbarians couldn't comprehend proper table manners. (Then again, neither can most middle-school students, and only their parents call them barbarians.) Yet, in truth, most so-called barbarians, including the Goths and the Vandals, were no more savage than the Romans. In some cases, the Huns—an Asian tribe that lacked more than table manners and definitely deserved the title "barbarian"—had forced the Goths and Vandals south, in search of farmland.

# The western predicament

During this turbulent time of barbarian migrations, Ambrose of Milan was one of the church's most powerful leaders. In the 370s Ambrose was the governor of Milan, in Italy. Even though he had never confessed Christ as Lord and Savior, Ambrose supported the Creed of Nicaea—perhaps, at least at first, for reasons that were as much political as personal.

**WORDS from the ones who were there**
"Before we are born we are infected with the contagion, and before we see the light of day we experience the injury of our origin."

—*Ambrose of Milan, describing humanity's sinful nature*

When the church overseer in the city of Milan died, tensions erupted between followers of Arius and supporters of the Creed of Nicaea. (If you don't remember what Arius believed, glance back at Chapter Three.) Each side was willing to fight to the death to gain the right to choose the new bishop.

Riots had recently claimed 137 lives when a new overseer was elected in the city of Rome. It seemed as if the same tragedy would strike in Milan.

In desperation, Governor Ambrose raised his voice to support the Nicenes in the city cathedral. Suddenly, a child cried, "Ambrose! Overseer!" The

AD **376** – AD **664**

crowd took up the chant. Ambrose protested. He was not even a Christian! How could he be an overseer of the church? The mob persisted. A week later, Ambrose the overseer, newly baptized and no longer a governor, launched an offensive against Arian theology.

## How human was Jesus?

Even as Milan stood on the brink of anarchy, Eastern Christians were dealing with their own problems. An Eastern church member named Apollinarius had taught that Jesus had a human body but no human mind. One of the Great Cappadocians (remember them from Chapter Three?) retorted, "If deity took the place of a human mind, how does that help me? Deity joined to flesh alone is not truly human!" (See Hebrews 4:15).

Theodosius [THE-uh-DO-see-us] was the emperor of the Eastern Empire. Wanting to settle this dispute, Theodosius convened a council in the city of Constantinople in AD 381. In Constantinople, more than 150 overseers expressed their agreement with a refined version of the Creed of Nicaea. This creed echoed the truths affirmed at the Council of Nicaea concerning Jesus' unique deity while clarifying the relationship of Jesus' two natures. This gathering became known as the Council of Constantinople. Their statement of faith became known as the Nicene Creed.

## Ambrose's challenge

Emperor Theodosius may have rallied the Christians in the Eastern Empire around the Nicene faith. Yet, in Milan, Ambrose the overseer openly defied Emperor Theodosius— and, surprisingly, survived.

The dispute arose when a mob of church members burned a synagogue. Theodosius justly and wisely ordered the arsonists to rebuild the Jewish place of worship.

"The burning of one building doesn't justify a commotion such as this!" Ambrose protested.

from the ones who were there

*The Council of Constantinople*

The Nicene Creed: "We believe in one God, the Father, the Almighty, maker of heaven and earth, of all that is seen and unseen. We believe in one Lord Jesus Christ, God's only Son, eternally begotten of the Father, God from God, Light from Light, true God from true God, begotten, not made, of the same essence as the Father. Through him all things were made. For us and for our salvation he came from heaven: by the power of the Holy Spirit he was born of the Virgin Mary and became human. For our sake he was crucified under Pontius Pilate, suffered, died, and was buried. On the third day he arose in fulfillment of the Scriptures; he ascended into heaven and is seated at the Father's right hand. He will come again in glory to judge the living and the dead. His kingdom will never end. We believe in the Holy Spirit, the Lord, the giver of life, who proceeds from the Father. With the Father and the Son he is worshiped and glorified. He has spoken through the prophets. We believe in one holy, universal, and apostolic church. We recognize one baptism unto the remission of sins and await the resurrection of the dead and the life of the coming world."

"It was only a synagogue, an abode of unbelief, a place cursed by God."

Theodosius backed down ... sort of. He commanded the church to raise funds to restore the synagogue. This was still too much for Ambrose of Milan. Ambrose threatened to exclude the emperor from the Lord's Supper unless he canceled all charges. Theodosius gave in.

Ambrose also excluded Theodosius from communion when the emperor encouraged his soldiers to slaughter 7,000 citizens after a riot. Only after Theodosius wore sackcloth and ashes for several weeks did Ambrose allow him to partake of the Lord's Supper.

*Cave church at Cappadocia*

After Theodosius reentered the church, he supported Ambrose's perspective on Christianity through the only means he knew: *force.* The church and empire grew closer together. Partly because of Ambrose's audacity in dealing with the emperor, the church remained the stronger partner in the Western Empire.

## The eastern situation

Someone else also defied Emperor Theodosius—but in a very different way than Ambrose of Milan. Olympias [oh-LIMM-pee-ahs] was her family's only heir. Two years after she married, her wealthy husband died. At the age of 25, she was one of the richest people in the empire.

To the chagrin of nearly everyone, Olympias chose not to remarry. She surrendered her life to Christ. She used her wealth to purchase slaves and set them free. Her church recognized her as a deaconess. At the same time, she attracted scores of suitors, including Theodosius's cousin.

When Olympias rejected his cousin, Theodosius seized her property. Olympias promptly thanked him. "Had I kept my property," she said, "I might have fallen prey to pride." Outfoxed, Theodosius returned her wealth. Again, Olympias gave it away. It was during these years of persistent philanthropy that she met an overseer named John.

John once served as a priest in Antioch, Syria. He learned public speaking in the Eastern Empire's finest schools. His eloquent sermons would later earn him the nickname "Chrysostom" [krih-SOSS-tom]—"Golden-Mouth."

AD **376** – AD **664**

*Inside the Hagia Sophia. The original church, built during Constantine's reign, was burned during the riots after the patriarch John Chrysostom was banished by Emperor Arcadius.*

Unlike many preachers in his era, John focused heavily on the original intent of biblical texts.

After Emperor Theodosius died, a power-hungry eunuch ruled the Eastern Empire through Theodosius' son. The eunuch had John Chrysostom ordained as Constantinople's overseer. The eunuch hoped that, since John owed his power to the eunuch, this eunuch could control the church through John. The plan flopped. John the overseer refused to listen to the eunuch. He further enraged the eunuch by living like a monk.

John Chrysostom demanded holiness. Many unmarried priests were living with so-called "spiritual sisters." John sarcastically noted that many "spiritual sisters" were somehow becoming "spiritual mothers." Under his leadership, unmarried priests couldn't live with women. John demanded holiness not only among priests but also among church members, even those who were powerful. At one point, he preached publicly against the sensual lifestyle of the royal empress. To silence him, the empress gave a costly gift to the church. John thanked her and continued preaching, just as he had before.

**IN CASE you're confused**

Two preaching methods arose in the early church. One method developed in Antioch, Syria; the other emerged in Alexandria, Egypt. Preachers from Antioch (like Chrysostom) searched the Bible for the messages that the authors intended.

Alexandrians (like Origen and Ambrose) had a tendency to search for allegorical meanings that were often unrelated to the text's original intent.

John's passion for biblical church discipline is clear in these words from one of his sermons: "It's beyond imagination that the sexually immoral or the blasphemer should eat from the Holy Table. Likewise, it's impossible that anyone who even has an enemy, who has any hatred, can enjoy Holy Communion. So, let no one who has an enemy come close to the Holy Table or receive the Lord's body! ... Do you have an enemy? ... First, be reconciled, and only then come close to touch what is holy! ... We are commanded to have one enemy: the Devil. Never be reconciled with him! But with a fellow believer, there must be no enmity in your heart."

In 403 the royal empress exiled John Chrysostom. That night, rioters who supported him burned several buildings. John's foes accused Olympias of arson and had her banished. John and Olympias both died in exile.

AD **376** – AD **664**

# Silver, gold, land, and … Pepper?

By the 400s many barbarians were frustrated with Roman rulers. The migrating barbarians wanted to live in the Empire and enjoy its benefits. Yet the Romans treated them as invaders. In 408 Alaric [ah-LAIR-ik] the Goth asked the Western emperor for farmland for his people, 18 tons of gold and silver, and one ton of pepper. (Whatever he was cooking, it must have been huge.) The emperor refused the request for land, though he seems to have been willing to come up with the gold, silver, and pepper.

**on the web**

Learn more about Olympias and John Chrysostom:

http://mb-soft.com/believe/txug/chryso11.htm

In AD 410, the city of Rome fell to Alaric and his Goths. The Goths pillaged the capital city for three days.

For the first time in eight centuries, Rome—once a symbol of the Empire's invincible power—had fallen. The ancient glory of the Roman Empire was rapidly fading. Even in the farthest reaches of the Roman Empire, Rome's fall shook people's souls. One man who helped them deal with their confusion was a North African who turned to Jesus Christ on a park bench near Milan.

## The park, the hippo, and the city of God

**did YOU know?**

Until the 400s, "Hadrian's Wall" kept the barbarians out of southern Britain. When the barbarians broke through the wall, a British battle-chief known as "King Arthur" won twelve battles against them.

The young man staggered through the park, a dismal and restless void gnawing at his innermost self. He dropped his

book on a bench and stumbled on. "Lord," he sobbed, "how long? How long?" Suddenly, he heard a child singing, "Pick up, read! Pick up, read!" He rushed back to the bench. When he opened his book, one passage seized his eyes: "Let us walk properly, as in the day, not in revelry and drunkenness ... Put on the Lord Jesus Christ, and make no provisions for the flesh" (Romans 13:13-14). "Instantly," the young man later wrote, "light ... entered my heart." The man's name? Augustine [aw-GUSS-tinn].

AD **376** – AD **664**

**Augustine of Hippo**

## Where the journey to faith began

Monica, Augustine's mother, was a Christian, "always in deep travail for [her son's] salvation." As a teen, Augustine had dismissed Christianity as crude and simplistic. He explored every possible path to find pleasure and truth. Then he associated himself with the Manichees [MANN-i-kees], a Gnostic-like sect. Augustine could not become a full Manichee unless he rejected sex, though—a request that Augustine found to be impossible.

"Lord," he prayed, "make me chaste."

"But," he quickly added, "not yet."

Soon Augustine decided to move to Italy. Monica begged God not to let her son go to Italy. She feared that he would drift further into sin. Little did she know that, in Italy, God would answer her prayers for her son's salvation. It was there that Augustine heard Ambrose of Milan for the first time. Ambrose preached in the Alexandrian style, treating the Bible as a vast and intricate allegory. This approach may seem odd to us, but it helped Augustine see that the Bible wasn't simplistic.

**THINK** about **it**...

It seems as if God denied the request of Monica's lips in order to give her the desire of her heart. Has that ever happened to you?

One problem lingered, though. Augustine was determined not be a halfhearted believer. If he became a Christian, he would become a monk. "But I can't be celibate!" he cried. In the end, the news of two unexpected conversions changed Augustine's outlook.

## Where the journey to faith led

Through a friend, Augustine heard about two powerful officials who read Athanasius's biography of Anthony and became monks. It was too much; Augustine could no longer deny his longing for God. He fled to the park and heard the voice of God in the song of a child. There, Augustine embraced the truth of Jesus Christ and became a monk.

Longing to grow closer to his newfound Savior, Augustine fled to the desert. His retreat was short-lived. When he visited a church at Hippo, the congregation ordained him as an elder. (No, no, no, this wasn't a church in a zoo; Hippo was a city in North Africa.) Six years later, Augustine became the overseer of Hippo.

AD **376** – AD **664**

*Painted dome in Chora Church, Istanbul, first built in the fifth century*

*Saint Augustine's statue— holding a burning heart in hand, Charles Bridge in Prague, Czech Republic.*

As Hippo's overseer, Augustine struggled against a pious but misguided monk named Pelagius [peh-LAY-jee-uss]. Throughout Rome, Pelagius had seen so-called Christians whose lives were far from holy.

To promote piety, Pelagius preached that salvation doesn't depend completely on God's grace. Instead, Pelagius claimed, every person naturally possesses the power to be holy. Pelagius even argued that no one is born with a sinful nature; instead, every human being is born in innocence. (Pelagius obviously never taught preschoolers.)

When Pelagius' teachings reached Hippo, Augustine responded harshly. Augustine argued that the first sin corrupted all humanity. This corruption is so radical that no one naturally desires to follow Jesus Christ. So far, Augustine's ideas seem to have conformed to the apostle Paul's writings.

Still, in some areas, Augustine seems to have parted with Paul. According to Augustine, sin was a sexually transmitted defect, and sex was inherently evil. Augustine also believed that infant baptism purged primal sin and prepared persons to receive God's grace.

## The City of God and the City of Mankind

So how did Augustine help Christians to deal with the aftermath of Rome's fall? After Rome was pillaged, Christians became targets of criticism. Non-Christians declared, "When we sacrificed to our gods, Rome prospered. Now sacrifices are banned, and look what's happening!" For years, some Christians had tied the power of the Roman Empire to the power of God, even arguing that Christ fought for Rome. Had God changed sides? Even believers such as Jerome wondered, "What is to become of the church now that Rome has fallen?"

In his book *The City of God,* Augustine responded that two realms exist on the earth—the City of God and the City of Mankind. Even though these cities seem to mingle, God's realm cannot ultimately be identified with any human regime; one day, the City of Mankind will fall and only God's reign in the hearts of his people will remain. "The earthly city will not be everlasting," Augustine declared, "for when it is condemned to the final punishment it will no longer be a city.... We have learned that there is a City of God: and we have longed to become citizens of that City with a love inspired by its founder."

AD **376** – AD **664**

*The Virgin and Child, a Byzantine mosaic in the interior of Hagia Sophia in Istanbul, Turkey.*

# What you said isn't always what others say you said

A few years ago, several baseball fans hung their coats on an outfield fence. The announcer immediately asked, "Would the fans along the outfield please remove their clothes?" The announcer said what he meant. But what he said could also mean something that he didn't mean at all.

That's sort of what happened to Nestorius [neh-STORR-ee-uss] of Antioch.

In 428 Nestorius moved to Constantinople to become the city's overseer. His tenure began with a blaze of something besides glory. He decided to deal with the heresy of Arius by torching an Arian chapel. The flames got out of hand and destroyed the whole block. Nestorius' less-than-laudable act of ecclesiastical arsonry earned him a nickname—"Fire-Brand."

Nestorius was not only a poor judge of where the winds might send the flames that he had started; he was also a poor judge of how people might take his words. Nestorius criticized a common title for Mary: *Theotokos* (or "God-Bearer"). What he probably intended people to understand was that Jesus Christ was not only God; Jesus was also fully human. So, Mary carried in her womb not only a divine being but also a human being. What some people understood Nestorius to mean was that Jesus was two completely separate persons—one human, one divine—and that Mary had only borne the human person.

## One nature or two?

Cyril [SI-rill], the overseer of Alexandria in Egypt, was a brilliant thinker. He was also ruthless and corrupt. In 415 Cyril had even approved the murder of a female philosopher named Hypatia. When Nestorius' teachings reached Alexandria, Cyril accused Nestorius of dividing Jesus into two separate persons. Controversy threatened to split the churches once again.

In 431 the emperor of the Eastern Empire convened a council in Ephesus. Cyril arrived first, convened the council, condemned Nestorius and his followers before any supporters of Nestorius arrived, then adjourned the council. When Nestorius' friends arrived, they convened the council—for the second time—and condemned Cyril. When the representatives of the Roman church arrived, they called the council to order—for the third time—and sided with Cyril. In the end, Nestorius was exiled.

A confusing chapter in the church's story had ended.

Or had it?

AD **376** – AD **664**

**THINK about it...**

Do the differences between One-Nature and Two-Nature thinkers seem trivial? They aren't! The divine nature is all-present. If Jesus' divine nature absorbed his humanity (as One-Nature Christians claimed), his body would have been all-present. How, then, was he born? But if his two natures were fully divided (as some Nestorians claimed), did God really become "flesh"? (John 1:14).

Cyril's successors took Cyril's ideas to the opposite extreme. They became known as "One-Nature" ("Monophysite") thinkers. They were eager to forsake the idea that Jesus was two separate persons—so eager that they began to claim that Christ's divine nature had consumed his humanity "like the ocean swallows a drop of wine."

One-Nature theology became popular, especially among the Egyptian Copts. Yet it seemed to many Christians that One-Nature thinking ignored Christ's humanity. Again, overseers throughout the world were invited to a council.

## Agreement at Last

Leo, the Roman overseer, received his invitation too late to attend the council. Instead, he sent a summary of his teaching, which became known as a "Tome." Leo, like Nestorius, believed Jesus had two natures, united in one person. The One-Nature party ignored Leo's *Tome* and mortally mauled the opposing spokesperson. Still, the matter did not end.

**on the web**

Check out the Coptic Church's web site:

www.coptic.net

In 451 a new emperor convened a council in the city of Chalcedon [KAL-se-DAWN or kal-SEE-dohn]. There, more than 500 overseers combined the Nicene Creed, Cyril's writings, and Leo's *Tome*.

The result? Despite the many political machinations that had preceded this council, what emerged was a beautiful, biblical portrayal of Christ: "Christ [is] ... recognized in two natures, without confusion, division, or separation ... but not as if Christ were parted into two persons." This understanding of Christ became known as the "Two-Nature" view or "Dyophysitism." At last, agreement had been reached. Nestorius—still exiled—said that the council had confessed what he had always intended.

After the Council of Chalcedon, some Christians in Egypt and Syria still supported One-Nature theology. These groups eventually pulled away from the Roman and Eastern churches. Today, these churches are known as Coptic Orthodox and Syrian Orthodox Churches; hundreds of years later, they remain committed to One-Nature theology. A few native Egyptian churches accepted the doctrinal statement of the Council of Chalcedon and remained in communion with churches in the Eastern Empire. These Egyptian churches became known as Imperial—or *Melkite*—Churches.

AD **376** – AD **664**

# Rome falls again ... and again

The *Tome* from the overseer of Rome had reshaped Christian theology. In the city of Rome, however, survival concerned the citizens far more than Leo's theology. It was Leo's boldness before the barbarians that won him the respect of Rome's citizens. Leo laid the foundations for what developed into the position of a Roman bishop who oversaw churches throughout the world. That's why some historians have classified Leo as "the first pope."

In 452 Attila the Hun attacked Italy. As the Huns approached Rome, nothing stood in their way. No emperor. No army. No one but Leo, the overseer or bishop of Rome. Leo met Attila on the road to Rome. Somehow, Leo persuaded the Huns to retreat. In 455 another barbarian tribe, the "Vandals," besieged Rome. This time, Leo could not convince them to retreat, but he did persuade them not to rape or kill. Instead, they looted and—true to their title—vandalized the city.

*The Meeting between Leo the Great and Attila*
*Raphael (1483-1520)*

Finally, in 476, a barbarian named Odovacer deposed the last Western emperor. The Western Empire had ceased to exist. Only the Eastern Empire remained, a dim echo of the ancient and glorious Roman Empire.

# The city of God endures

When reading about the early Middle Ages, it's easy to wonder, "Was anyone really a Christian?" Christian theology became a tool to unite and to divide empires. Kings claimed to be Christians, yet some of them mercilessly looted and slaughtered. Were people simply ignorant? Was their faith false? Truth be told, I can't judge the status of those people's souls. What I *do* know, though, is that God preserved a kingdom for God's own glory (the "City of God") amid the darkness of human failure and greed (the "City of Mankind"). One way that God preserved his people was by calling Christians to seek His glory in the context of religious communities.

## Scholastica and Benedict

Scholastica [sko-LASS-tih-kah] and her twin brother, Benedict [BEH-neh-dikt], were born in Italy. In 520 Benedict organized a religious community in a remote area. Even though Christianity had been the Empire's official religion for more than a century, a pagan altar still stood on one hill. Benedict smashed the altar and built a monastery on top of it. Scholastica founded a convent near the monastery.

One of Benedict's greatest gifts was his *Rule*, his guide for religious communities. Unlike many communities' rules, the demands of the *Rule of Benedict* were not extreme. The daily routine balanced Bible reading, prayer, and work. In 589 barbarians burned Benedict's monastery. The monks fled to Rome. There, a very important overseer named Gregory encountered Benedict's *Rule*.

### Gregory

Gregory had grown up in Rome. According to one account of his childhood, Gregory once had seen slaves from Angle-Land ("England") being unloaded at the docks.

*This distinct style of cross arose in the Celtic-Irish churches.*

"Where are they from?" Gregory asked.

"They are Anglos," someone responded.

"Angels, you say? Angels they may be," Gregory responded, "but who rules them?"

"King Aella," was the reply.

"Alleluia?" Gregory said, "Alleluia! In their land, God's name must be praised!"

did **YOU** know?

Previous overseers had possessed the title "pope" ("father"), but Gregory was the first Roman bishop to possess the power later achieved by his office. Some persons have referred to Gregory as "the first pope."

God's name *had* been praised in Britain as early as AD 300. In the fifth century, though, Anglo-Saxon barbarians had migrated into Britain and destroyed these churches. The burden to see these barbarians turn from their pagan gods followed Gregory throughout his life.

As an adult, Gregory became a powerful and successful politician. Then, in 573, God changed his career plans: Gregory gave everything away and became a monk. Soon afterward, a plague ravaged Rome. Unlike many monks, Gregory refused to stay in his monastery. He left his monastery to serve the sick. His kindness earned him an honored place in people's hearts. When the Roman overseer became fatally ill, it was Gregory who succeeded him.

When Benedict's monks arrived in Rome, their *Rule* pleased Gregory. In AD 599 Gregory sent 41 reluctant Benedictine monks to England to evangelize the Anglo-Saxons. One of the monks would become known as Augustine of Canterbury.

Despite the monks' initial reluctance, 10,000 Anglo-Saxons—including the king of Kent—had been baptized by Christmas of 599. Canterbury, the capital city of Kent, became the center of English Christianity.

As Gregory worked among the citizens of Rome, he wrote about theology and pastoral

on the web

Read more about Gregorian chants:
www.ccwatershed.org/kyriale

AD **376** – AD **664**

care. He depended deeply—perhaps too deeply at times—on Augustine of Hippo. For example, Augustine had wondered if there might be a place where God purged the unconfessed sins of Christians who died. From this, Gregory developed the foundations of a doctrine of "purgatory," a place between death and heaven where God removes any barriers to total enjoyment of God's presence. Gregory also taught that God's forgiveness sometimes requires specific works of penance.

One of Gregory's most familiar legacies flowed from his concern for the church's music. Remembering his concern for the music of the church, one form of Roman plainsong—the "Gregorian chant"—was named after Gregory after his death.

## Patrick

When many people think of St. Patrick, the first things that come to mind are shamrocks, leprechauns, and maybe pinches for people who don't wear green. What's easy to miss in these celebrations of St. Patrick's Day is the fact that the real Patrick was a devout Christian and a missionary.

Patrick was a Roman Briton, born to wealthy parents. His father was a deacon, but Patrick wasn't particularly religious. Around the year 430, when Patrick was sixteen, Irish raiders kidnapped him. Patrick became a slave, watching his Irish master's sheep. In his loneliness, he turned to the God of his father and entrusted his life to Jesus Christ.

*Stained glass image of St. Patrick*

Six years later, Patrick escaped from the Irish and returned to his family—but soon afterward, a dream changed his destiny. He saw an angel, and the heavenly messenger told him to go back to Ireland.

For fifteen years Patrick studied theology and Scripture; then he returned to Ireland not as a slave but as a missionary. He used familiar Irish symbols to explain Christian theology—the three-leafed shamrock, for example, became a metaphor for the Trinity. According to tradition, Patrick died on March 17, 493.

## Hilda of Whitby

The Anglo-Saxon migrations did not reach the Celtic-Irish churches and religious communities in Ireland and some northern regions of Britain. After the migrations, Celtic-Irish Christians found themselves cut off from Roman and Eastern churches. So, they developed their own unique patterns of administration and worship. Celtic-Irish congregations were not ruled by overseers. Monks and nuns guided Celtic-Irish churches. Celtic-Irish Christians also didn't observe Easter on the same day as Roman Christians. As Roman Christianity spread throughout the British Isles, tensions emerged between the two groups. In 664 Celtic-Irish and Roman Christians met to resolve

*Irish Castle*

AD **376** – AD **664**

their problems. In honor of an English Christian woman named Hilda, they met in Whitby.

After Hilda gave her life to Christ, an overseer noticed her leadership talents and gave her a position of leadership in two religious communities. In 657 Hilda founded a community in Whitby. There she trained hundreds of nuns and even some monks—five of whom later became overseers.

At the Synod of Whitby, in 664, only Hilda and one overseer defended the Celtic-Irish Christians' right to follow their traditions. In the end, Celtic-Irish churches became Roman churches. The power of the Roman church and the Roman overseer had now extended throughout most of Europe.

## How's your serve?

Sometimes, pastors sin. Sometimes, pastors even sin in areas about which they have recently preached. (I know, I know, that's difficult for some of you to believe—but bear with me for a moment.) When I was a pastor and that happened to me, my wife sometimes reminded me that she had actually listened to my sermon.

*Jesus washing Peter's feet at the Last Supper, Ford Madox Brown (1821-1893)*

"Why are you so worried?" she might ask. "On Sunday morning, you said, 'Stop worrying! God has a plan, even when you don't have a clue.'" (It sounded so much less convicting when I was the one *speaking* the message instead of *hearing* it.)

And once again I would find myself reminded that, if my messages reflected God's truth, I too was obligated to obey them. Servant-leaders cannot stand above God's people and proclaim God's truth unless they are also ready to kneel among God's people and live God's truth.

When ministers persistently stand above God's people, they end up as administrators and managers instead of shepherds and servants. That's what seems to have happened in the early Middle Ages. In a society that was falling apart, church leaders found themselves shouldering political and social powers. In the process, many of them became leaders of servants instead of servant-leaders.

Jesus told his followers, "Whoever wants to become great among you must be your servant" (Mark 10:43-44). If every Christian is a servant, every Christian is equal. If every Christian is equal, every Christian—whether layperson or bishop, pastor or janitor— is equally responsible to reflect God's truth. Live as if you are called to be a servant-leader wherever you are. Then live as if one servant-leader can change the world. Why? He has, you are, and you can.

AD 376 – AD 664

**5 EVENTS** you should know

**1. Third Council of Constantinople (681):** The church's sixth general council denounced Monotheletism (see below) and reaffirmed the beliefs of the Council of Chalcedon.

**2. Pepin's Donation (754):** Pepin III, a Frankish battle-chief, gave part of Italy (the "papal states") to the pope. In return, the pope granted Pepin the church's approval and a royal title.

**3. Second Council of Nicaea (787):** The church's seventh and last general council denounced Adoptionism, the idea that Jesus was not God's Son by nature. The council also allowed Christians to revere—but not worship—icons.

**4. Overseer of the Roman Church Excommunicated Eastern Christians (1054).**

**5. Investiture Dispute (1076–1123):** In 1076 Emperor Henry IV claimed the right to invest bishops with their authority; Pope Gregory VII (Hildebrand) forced him to beg forgiveness for three days. In 1122 a concordat signed in Worms, Germany, allowed emperors to be present at bishops' ordinations, but church leaders controlled the selection. The First Lateran Council confirmed the Concordat of Worms in 1123.

**5 NAMES** you should know

**1. Clotilde (474-545):** Frankish queen. Led her husband, Clovis, to become a Christian.

**2. Charles Martel (690-741):** Frankish battle-chief. Stopped Muslims from conquering central Europe.

**3. Alcuin of York (740-804):** Monk. Major contributor, with Theodulf of Orleans, to the "Carolingian Renaissance," Charlemagne's effort to decrease illiteracy and preserve ancient texts.

**4. Godfrey of Bouillon (died, 1100):** First king of Crusaders' Latin (Roman) Kingdom in Palestine which lasted until 1291 when Muslims conquered the port of Acre.

**5. Pope Innocent III (1161-1216):** One of the most powerful bishops of Rome. Claimed power over all secular rulers (1201). Initiated the Fourth Lateran Council (1215).

**5 TERMS** you should know

**1. Monotheletism:** From the Greek *monothelos* ("One-Will"). One-Will thinkers taught that Jesus had two natures, but only his divine nature could make choices. In AD 681 the Third Council of Constantinople affirmed that Jesus had two wills—one human, one divine. But, they added, his two wills never disagreed.

**2. The Donation of Constantine:** A document, forged around AD 800, which claimed Constantine gave the pope power over all other bishops, as well as large portions of Italy.

**3. Holy Roman Emperor:** The title which, in theory, made someone the heir of the ancient Roman emperors and the ruler of the Western Empire. In reality, Holy Roman Emperors only ruled portions of central Europe. German kings possessed the title from AD 962 until 1806, when Napoleon abolished it.

**4. Albigensians:** Heretical sect, named after Albi, the French town where they arose. Also called "Cathars" ("Pure Ones"). Condemned by the Fourth Lateran Council for their Gnostic teachings.

**5. Transubstantiation:** Roman Catholic and Eastern Orthodox belief that the Lord's Supper elements become Jesus' body and blood, even though their outer appearance never changes.

# CHAPTER 5

# From Multiplication to Division

## IN THIS CHAPTER
## 496 – 1291

Muhammad

Charlemagne

Photius of Constantinople

The Crusades

Pope Leo IX (Bruno)

R emember the comic strip *Calvin and Hobbes*? Years after Bill Watterson drew the child in the striped shirt and his stuffed tiger for the last time, *Calvin and Hobbes* remains one of my favorite strips of all time. In one strip, Calvin begins a school report with these words: "In the Middle Ages lords and vassals lived in a futile system." Hobbes, that feline fountain of wisdom, remarks, "That's '*feudal*' system." Concern clouds Calvin's face. He sighs, "Just when I thought this junk was beginning to make sense."[1]

Calvin may have misunderstood his readings of medieval history, but there *is* some truth to be found even in Calvin's error. In the Middle Ages a feudal system did restore some order in Europe, but the attempt ultimately proved futile. In the aftermath of this "futile system," the heirs of the barbarians and the Romans fumbled their way toward a new society—a society of countries, united by common cultures, instead of one vast empire. You and I live in that society today.

*Remains of a medieval manor*

## The wobbling west

Imagine a land with no central government. Imagine cities without police officers. Imagine children without schools. Imagine an empire with no army.

What you've just imagined is the former Western Empire in the Middle Ages. With no central government to mint coins or to determine weights and measures, land became the key form of wealth. Landowners ("lords") set up self-sufficient plantations ("manors"). To protect their manors, lords maintained mounted bands of knights. In one area several lords might even unite their knights under one powerful lord or king.

Without land of their own, peasants could not provide food or protection for themselves. In exchange for the promise of such provisions, peasants could become a lord's "vassals." They farmed part of their lord's land. In return, they received enough to survive, but nothing more. This was the "feudal system"—or in Calvin's parlance, the "futile system."

Lords paid priests to serve their manors. Unfortunately, since kings and lords chose their own priests, obedience to earthly lords could easily supplant obedience to the heavenly Lord.

### ON the web

Want to learn more about medieval churches?

www.netserf.org

AD 496 – AD 1291

Few people could read. Priests relied on statues, stained glass, and plays to teach their people about God. Church buildings became "Bibles in stone" as images and architecture replaced the preached and written Word.

# An empire in search of survival

Efforts to maintain order in the Eastern Empire didn't take the form of a feudal system. Yet Eastern efforts to preserve order were nearly as futile as Western attempts. In the seventh century a "storm" from the south nearly brought the East to its knees.

## The firestorm from the south

Muhammad [mou-HAHM-mahd] lived in Mecca, a small Arabian trading post. In the year 610, Muhammad claimed that the angel Gabriel had entrusted him with a message from Allah, the only true God. Muhammad quickly began to preach against the idols that surrounded him. At first, no one minded his message. But around 622, angry idol-peddlers forced Muhammad to flee. By the time he returned to Mecca, Muhammad had gathered an army of followers. He called his followers Muslims ("those who submit [to Allah]"). Their religion became known as Islam ("submission").

*The Golden Dome of the Rock, Jerusalem, Israel*
*Muslims believe Muhammad ascended to Allah from the Temple Mount in Jerusalem. Around 690, the Dome of the Rock was built over the stone from which Muhammad was said to have ascended.*

After Muhammad's death, his followers conquered Arabia, Syria, and North Africa. In 638 Jerusalem fell to the Muslims. By 711 Muslim troops had invaded Europe, conquering Portugal and Spain. How did the Muslims make such unbelievable progress? Of course, the skill of Muslim military leaders and soldiers contributed to the campaign's success—but a couple of other factors helped the Muslims to solidify their control in Africa and Europe.

➤ *In the first place, Muslims did allow a small measure of religious freedom. They forced Christians to wear distinct clothes and pay higher taxes. In some areas Christians had to wear heavy crosses around their necks. Yet all religions that had holy writings—including the Jewish and Christian faiths—were provided with some protection.*

➤ *The Eastern church had already rejected North African Christians—especially the Copts—because of their One-Nature (or Monophysite) theology. As a result, some North Africans willingly transformed their churches into Muslim mosques.*

AD **496** – AD **1291**

**IN CASE** you're **confused**

Eastern Christians often kiss icons as they enter their church buildings. Why? They are recognizing that past saints still surround them today (see Hebrews 12:1). By kissing icons, they believe that they are welcoming these saints into their worship.

## Smashers and kissers

Paintings of Jesus and the saints had provided a backdrop for Christian worship for many years. Yet when do these "icons" become idols? That's the question that confronted Christians in the eighth century. Because Christians used icons in their worship, some Muslims called them "idol-worshipers"—and, in some cases, it seems that the Muslims may have been correct. As pagans, people had worshiped idols. As Christians, some of them worshiped images of Jesus and the saints.

All of this set the stage for a controversy in the eighth century between "Smashers" and "Kissers." Here's how the controversy began: In 725, a volcano rocked Constantinople. Fearing that the volcano had resulted from God's fury against idol-worship, the newly crowned emperor of the Eastern Empire acted against the "Icon-Kissers" (or "Iconodules").

The city's grandest icon was a golden image of Christ, set above the palace doors. The emperor sent a crew of soldiers to destroy it. The soldiers' initial attempt to obey the emperor was thwarted when a mob of women, armed with pots and pans, kicked a scaffold from under the crew. Angry citizens labeled the emperor an "Icon-Smasher" (or "Iconoclast"), and a bloody struggle between "Kissers" and "Smashers" began.

*Mosaic details from St. Sophia*

*Eastern icons look 'flat' because Eastern Christians strictly observe the Second Council of Nicaea's ban on three-dimensional images.*

By 780 icon disputes had raged for 61 years. That's when a woman named Irene seized the throne of the Eastern Empire. It was Empress Irene who called the seventh church-wide (or "general") council. In 787 more than 350 overseers gathered in Nicaea to end the icon disputes. The Second Council of Nicaea denounced the "Smashers." Yet the council did not allow Christians to idolize icons. The delegates clearly banned icon-worship, as well as three-dimensional depictions of Jesus and the saints. What they promoted was not *icon-worship* but *icon-reverence*.

**ON the web**

To learn more about icons try:

www.goarch.org/en/resources/clipart

# Franks become the top dogs

In the early Middle Ages, the pagan Franks had emerged as the prime political power in the areas that once comprised the Western Empire. The Franks had originated in the area now known as western Germany. Around 496, Clovis, the Frankish battle-chief, led his people to turn to the Christian God. Clovis even accepted the Nicene Creed. As a result, when the Franks began their conquest of the former Western Empire, many Christians accepted their rule. By AD 600, the Franks ruled large portions of central Europe. As the Franks' power increased, so did their support of the Roman church. In 754, King Pepin III of the Franks even handed over most of central Italy to the Roman church.

*Statue depicting the baptism of Clovis*

*In 496, the Frankish battle-chief Clovis accepted the Christian God and the Nicene Creed.*

## How the West was won (or, at least, baptized)

Near the end of the eighth century, King Charles, the son of King Pepin III, launched evangelistic campaigns against his enemies. When Charles mastered a tribe, he forced everyone to be baptized or die. Not surprisingly, more than ninety percent of his subjects reacted positively to his invitation. Whether or not they really became Christians is another question—one that God alone can answer.

When one German tribe refused to be baptized, Charles slashed off 4,500 heads in a single day. Then he returned to his camp to celebrate Christmas. By the beginning of the ninth century, Charles controlled the lands now known as Germany and France, and the people of these lands viewed themselves as Christians in communion with the Roman church.

## A frightened friar flees to the Franks

During Charles's conquests, a forged document surfaced. Known as *The Donation of Constantine*, this document claimed that Emperor Constantine had given central Italy to the Roman church hundreds of years earlier, in the fourth century. Most people accepted this document as authentic. The results of the church's possessions weren't always pleasant, though.

In 799 several Italian nobles wanted to control the Roman church so that they could benefit from the church's ever-growing wealth. Unfortunately for their plans, their candidate for the overseer of Rome was rejected in favor of a priest

AD **496** – AD **1291**

who took the name Leo III. The nobles were pretty determined, though: To force Leo III to think twice about his calling, they hired thugs to gouge out his tongue. Some Franks who were loyal to the Roman church brought the tongueless overseer to Charles's palace.

King Charles warmly welcomed Pope Leo III. Yet there was a problem: The nobles who had assaulted Leo III had also sent letters to Charles. The letters charged Leo III with embezzling church funds. Normally, Leo III would have spoken to the emperor, but he didn't have a tongue anymore. He might have written a letter to the emperor instead, but even that was problematic, at least from Leo III's perspective: The West no longer had an emperor, and Empress Irene ruled the Eastern Empire. Leo III refused to let a woman judge him. How, then, could he clear his name? By *creating* an emperor.

### The Frankish Privilege

On December 23, 800, King Charles declared Pope Leo III innocent of all charges. Two days later, amid the candles of the Christmas communion service, Leo III solved the problem of not having anyone to whom he could appeal. A crown was placed on Charles's head and the Frankish king was dubbed "Charles Augustus, crowned by God as supreme and peaceful Emperor." For the first time in history, the church had created an emperor. Later generations would call this emperor "Charlemagne" [SHARR-le-mayn], French for "Charles the Great."

**Charlemagne, the first Holy Roman Emperor**

As the newly dubbed "Holy Roman Emperor," Charlemagne viewed himself as the guardian of the Roman church. He founded monasteries to preserve ancient texts and to increase literacy. He appointed the church's bishops. He ensured the Roman church's control of central Italy.

What Charlemagne revived wasn't simply the power of the Roman church, though. He revived people's hopes for a renewed Western Roman Empire. Even after Emperor Charlemagne's death, the dream of a revived Western Empire refused to die. It lived on under a new name, "the Holy Roman Empire."

AD 496 – AD 1291

# Holy church, unholy leaders

Between 880 and 980 the position of Roman overseer or bishop—once held by godly men like Pope Gregory—slipped into the hands of several not-so-noble nobles.

**on the web**

View illuminations of Charlemagne and Leo III:

http://expositions.bnf.fr/carolingiens/expo_us/salle3/index.htm

One Italian heiress, Marozia [mah-RO-zee-ah], controlled the bishops of Rome for 60 years. During those years, she was one bishop's mother, another's murderer, and another's mistress. In 955 her grandson, John XII, became the new pope. John XII celebrated his impending election as pope with a toast to the devil. His election did nothing to diminish his devilish lifestyle.

Even after Pope John XII died, corruption continued to disgrace the Roman bishop's place in the church. The Roman church desperately needed reform. Eventually, the reforms came, but—alongside the reforms—there also came division.

# The church does the splits

Eastern and Roman church members had quarreled for centuries. Still, they viewed themselves as one body. This unity did not last, though. Between the ninth and thirteenth centuries, three separate blows split Christianity into two separate fellowships.

## Somebody's messing with my creed!

Do you recall the Nicene Creed? (If you can't recall the content of this creed, glance back at Chapter Four.) Ninth-century Christians remembered the creed too, but there was a serious problem: *Roman and Eastern Christians remembered the creed differently.*

**THINK** about **it**...

Read John 14:26; 15:26; 16:7; and Galatians 4:6. Which view of the Trinity seems more biblical? Roman or Eastern? A good case can probably be made for either view.

Here's what seems to have happened: A church in Spain added one Latin word to the Nicene Creed. The original creed had confessed, "[The Spirit] proceeds from the Father." The revised creed claimed, "[The Spirit] proceeds from the Father and the Son." The Roman church soon adopted the revised Nicene Creed. Now, contemporary Christians might respond, "So what? It's only a slight difference!" Why did the addition matter so much?

➤ In the first place, both Eastern and Roman Christians, believing that they had been led by the Scriptures and the Holy Spirit, had approved the Nicene Creed. At the Councils of Ephesus and Chalcedon, they had committed themselves never to change the creed.

➤ Both groups agreed that God is one being in three persons. Yet each group envisioned the Trinity differently. Roman theologians believed that the divine being dwelt equally in the Father, Son, and Spirit. According to Eastern thinkers, one being can dwell in only one person. In their view, divinity dwells only in the Father. The Father shares this divine being with the Son and Spirit. This does not, however, decrease the deity of the Son or the Spirit. As a result, Eastern Christians could state that "[the Spirit] proceeds from the Father through the Son." But they could not confess that

AD **496** – AD **1291**

*Photius, Bishop of Constantinople*

the Spirit "proceeds from the Father and the Son." If the Spirit arose from "the Father and the Son," the Son would be sharing divine being—which could come only from God the Father—with the Holy Spirit.

In 867 Photius [FO-shee-uss or FO-tee-uss], the bishop of Constantinople in the Eastern Empire, denounced the added phrase. Five years later, the pope offered to drop "and the Son" from the Nicene Creed. But there was a condition: Eastern churches had to accept the pope's absolute supremacy over all churches throughout the world. Photius declined. A narrow crack pierced the church's unity.

## A Roman bull gores the East

One day in AD 1048, three shoeless pilgrims—Bruno, Humbert, and Hildebrand [HILL-de-BRAND]—walked together through the gates of Rome. Each one would, in his own way, transform the Roman church.

In Rome, Bruno was acclaimed as Pope Leo IX. Immediately, Bruno launched a program of moral and theological reform in the Roman church. To prevent priests from passing positions to their children, Bruno banned all priests from marrying. Bruno didn't want powerful nobles to exploit the church. So he fought to free the Roman church from all outside controls.

**IN CASE you're confused**

Ever since the tenth century, popes have assumed new names at their elections.

Bruno and his successors sincerely believed that God had given the pope authority over all Christians. Their sincere belief contributed to a church-wide split that still exists today.

Michael Cerularius, the new bishop of Constantinople, refused to recognize Bruno as pope. Michael closed every church in Constantinople that was loyal to the Roman bishop. Bruno sent envoys to Constantinople to restore peace. Bruno's chief envoy was his friend Humbert.

*Ruins from the Church of Holy Wisdom (Hagia Sophia) where Humbert laid the bull of excommunication in 1054.*

Before leaving Rome, Humbert wrote a brash bull. (No, no, no, he didn't scrawl on a male bovine's flank. A bull is a notice written in the pope's name. The English word "bulletin" comes from the Latin "bull.") Humbert arrived in Constantinople, with his bull in hand, in the summer of 1054.

On July 16, 1054, Humbert marched into the Church of Holy Wisdom in Constantinople, during the Lord's Supper. Humbert's notice was, well, a lot like a Texas longhorn: It had a point here, a point there, and lots of bull in between. According to the notice, Eastern Christians:

from the **ones**
**who** were there
*Humbert*
**"Let Michael Cerularius and his followers be damned at the Lord's coming, with ... all other heretics, yes, even with the devil and the devil's angels."**

➤ *... allowed priests to marry. (True, but so had the Roman church, for several centuries.)*

➤ *... refused to recognize baptism performed in Roman churches. (Untrue in most cases.)*

➤ *... had deleted "and the Son" from the Nicene Creed. (Completely opposite of the truth!)*

Humbert flung the bull on the communion table and turned his back on the priest. At the door, he brushed dust from his sandals and bellowed, "Let God look and judge!" An Eastern deacon grabbed the bull and chased Humbert. He begged Humbert to take the bull back. Humbert refused.

Two blows—an altered creed and a brash bull—had divided Roman and Eastern Christians. Had it not been for a third blow, the gash might have healed. The final blow was the Crusades.

**on the web**

For an Eastern Orthodox perspective on the schism, check out:

www.goarch.org/en/ourfaith/

or

www.saintignatiuschurch.org/timeline.html

## The Crusades

Many medieval people believed they could prove their desire to turn from sin by going on a "pilgrimage." Pilgrims typically traveled to local shrines, but there was a greater pilgrimage, undertaken by many sincere believers. The supreme pilgrimage led to Jerusalem. To impede a pilgrim's journey was, from the medieval church's perspective, to imperil that person's salvation. Since about AD 638, Muslims had controlled Jerusalem and the roads that led to Jerusalem. On the roads to Jerusalem, Muslim converts (also known as "Turks") began to force Christian pilgrims to pay vast tariffs.

In 1095, Pope Urban II reacted to this practice by preaching one of history's most influential sermons. "Your Eastern brothers have asked for your help!" he proclaimed in a field in Clermont, France. "Turks and Arabs have conquered their territories. I—or, rather, the Lord—beg you ... destroy that vile race from their lands!"

The response astounded Urban II. The crowd began to chant, "God wills it!" Lords and fools, ruffians and serfs joined together, sewing cloth crosses on their tunics. Their campaign would be, as they saw it, both a pilgrimage to

AD **496** – AD **1291**

**from the ones who were there**

Pope Urban II

"If anyone out of devotion alone ... sets out for Jerusalem to free God's church, the journey shall be the equivalent of penance ... All who die ... shall have immediate forgiveness."

—*Gesta Dei per Francos, 1:382 Mansi, 20:816*

Jerusalem and a war against "the infidels." The pilgrims agreed to gather in Constantinople. The First Crusade was underway.

It wasn't only the people who heard the pope's sermon that headed to Constantinople, though. There were also the peasants that followed a monk known as Peter the Hermit. Of all the Crusaders, Peter the Hermit probably possessed the strongest scent. The swarthy monk had not bathed in decades. He rode a burro that, according to several eyewitnesses, bore a remarkable resemblance to its rider. Peter's preaching seems to have been even more powerful than his odor. In nine months, he gathered 20,000 Western peasants to fight the Muslims.

Peter's peasants caused immediate chaos when they arrived in Constantinople. Complaints of robbery poured into the emperor's office. The emperor knew that the untrained peasants were no match for the Muslims, but he couldn't let them linger in his city. So the peasants were ferried across the river.

On the other side of the river, Peter's peasants began pillaging the homes of Eastern Christians, straining relations between the Eastern and Roman churches. Two months later, these peasants marched straight into a Muslim ambush. Peter—who was in Constantinople at the time, begging for supplies—was the sole survivor. Here's how the venerable Huckleberry Finn described the Crusades: "As near as I can make it out, most of the folks that shook farming to go crusading had a mighty rocky time of it"[2]—and, at least in the case of these peasants, Huck got it right. Peter the Hermit joined another army, led by European princes and lords. These Crusaders clashed with the Muslims in Antioch and then continued to Jerusalem.

On July 15, 1099, Jerusalem fell to the royal Crusaders. On the Temple Mount, Muslim blood flowed ankle-deep. Newborns were thrown against walls. Crusaders torched a synagogue and burned the Jews inside alive. Still today, this wholesale slaughter in Christ's name affects how Jews and Muslims perceive the Christian gospel.

**IN CASE you're confused**

In the aftermath of a Second Crusade, Muslims retook Jerusalem. Three kings led a Third Crusade. Only Richard Lion-Heart's army reached Jerusalem. The Robin Hood legends supposedly occurred while Richard was gone on the Third Crusade.

# The Fourth Crusade

In 1198 a noble known as Innocent III became the bishop of Rome. It was Pope Innocent III who inspired the Fourth Crusade, the crusade that would finally divide Eastern and Roman Christians.

The intent of Innocent III was simply to destroy a Muslim army base in Egypt. The merchants of Venice agreed to supply the Crusaders with ships at the cost of 84,000 silver coins. In the summer of 1202, the Crusaders arrived in Venice expecting to sail to Egypt. But there was a problem: Only one-third of the expected number of Crusaders showed up, and they came up with only 50,000 silver coins.

An Eastern prince offered to finance the crusade under one condition: The Crusaders had to sail to Constantinople and dethrone the current Eastern emperor before heading to Egypt. Pope Innocent III forbade the attack, but no one seemed to care.

**Words from the ones who were there**

Nicetas of Constantinople
"How shall I tell of the deeds done by these vicious men!... Couldn't they at least have spared the decent wives and young women, and the virgins who were devoted to God?...
In alleys, streets, temples ... shrieks of wounds, rape, captivity sounded."

*Reenactment of a Crusade battle.*

On July 5, 1203, the Crusaders arrived in the capital city of the Eastern Empire. Not surprisingly, Constantinople's citizens did not relish the intrusion into their affairs. The citizens revolted and installed an anti-Crusader emperor on the Eastern Empire's throne.

The Crusaders were furious. They had set out to destroy the Muslims. Now, they were stranded in Constantinople. The crusade leaders decided to plunder Constantinople. One priest proclaimed—without the pope's approval—"If you rightly intend to conquer this land and bring it under Roman obedience, all who die . . . partake in the pope's indulgence." To partake in an indulgence was to be freed from enduring the earthly punishment—that is, performing the penance—for one's sins. From the perspective of many Crusaders, this proclamation provided a license to do whatever they pleased in Constantinople.

On Good Friday, 1204, the Crusaders, with red crosses on their tunics, sacked Constantinople. For three days, they raped and killed Christians in the name of Christ. The city's statues were hacked to pieces and melted down. The Church of Holy Wisdom (the "Hagia Sophia") was stripped of its gold vessels. A harlot performed sensual dances on the Lord's Table, singing vile

AD **496** – AD **1291**

Hagia Sophia in Istanbul, Turkey
Built between 532-537

drinking songs. One Eastern writer lamented, "Muslims are merciful compared with these men who bear Christ's cross on their shoulders."

Neither the Eastern Empire nor the Eastern church ever recovered from those three days. For 60 years Crusaders from the Roman church ruled what was once the Eastern Empire. The Eastern emperor established an Empire southeast of Constantinople, in Nicaea. Rather than embrace Roman customs, many Eastern Christians fled to Nicaea. There they remained until 1261, when an Eastern ruler retook the city of Constantinople.

Pope Innocent III had tried to prevent the fall of Constantinople, but no one had listened. Afterward, he attempted to reunite the churches, but it was too late. After the Fourth Crusade, the church was shattered into two communions—Roman Catholic and Eastern Orthodox.

# Separate churches, separate paths

## The shaping of Roman Catholicism

The most lasting achievement of Pope Innocent III was a council that molded Roman Catholic theology for more than three centuries. The council convened in the Lateran palace in Rome. Three earlier councils had also gathered at the Lateran palace. So this council became known as the Fourth Lateran Council. In 1215 the Fourth Lateran Council:

➤ Declared that in the Lord's Supper the observable features of the bread and wine never change. But, at an unseen level, the elements actually become Jesus' body and blood. This is known as transubstantiation. The bishops at the council explained transubstantiation this way: "[Christ's] body and blood are contained in the sacraments under the outward forms of bread and wine; the bread being transubstantiated by God's power into the body, and the wine into the blood."

➤ Formed the groundwork for the Inquisition, a court to uproot ideas that defied the church's understanding of Scripture. Around 1231 the Inquisition became a systematic tool to destroy heretics. At first, the Inquisition focused on the Gnostic-like Albigensians, then expanded to affect other groups, including Muslims and Jews.

AD 496 – AD 1291

# How do Roman Catholicism and Eastern Orthodoxy differ?

## A look at ourselves

It's easy to try to dismiss medieval Christianity as empty and corrupt. Yet, when we allow ourselves to dismiss medieval church members in this way, we are guilty of the same misdeed as many people in the Middle Ages. We have

*The Hagia Sophia in Constantinople was one target of the Crusaders' greed.*

become like Charlemagne, celebrating Christmas while 4,500 German widows mourned their spouses ... like Humbert hurling his notice of excommunication on an Eastern communion table ... like a horde of crusaders flooding the streets of Constantinople with innocent blood. How? We also have condemned before seeking to comprehend.

did **you** know **?**

In Latin, the farewell phrase of the communion service is "missa est"— "Go forth." Among Catholics, communion became known as "missa" or "Mass."

For every devilish pope or crusader, there were thousands of bishops, priests, and common people who sincerely believed they were following Christ. Some lived out their faith as farmers and merchants. Others lived out their faith as lords and kings. Some were probably Christians; others were not.

Nothing can excuse any offense undertaken in Christ's name. At the same time, instead of flinging my own notice of excommunication on the communion tables of the Middle Ages, I must remember that it is not my blameless deeds or my denomination's theology that guards me against the same failures. It is grace and only grace.

**KEY** concept

Be critical only after you've tried to comprehend. Even then, speak with compassion.

1. Bill Watterson, *Attack of the Deranged Mutant Killer Monster Snow Goons* (Kansas City: Andrews and McMeel, 1992) 56.

2. Mark Twain, *Tom Sawyer Abroad* (Aerie, [n.d.]) 10.

AD **496** – AD **1291**

## Roman Catholicism

**Name**
"Catholic" means "worldwide" or "universal."

**Structure**
The bishop or overseer of Rome is the father ("pope") over all churches. He represents Christ's leadership in the church. Overseers ("bishops") guide each region and are responsible directly to the pope. High overseers ("archbishops") are highly esteemed by other bishops, but they have no power outside their own regions. Since 1150, bishops and archbishops who advise the pope have been known as "cardinal" overseers.

**Authority**
Scripture as interpreted and expounded through church councils, church tradition, and bishops in union with the pope.

This timeline summarizes relations between Eastern and Roman Christians from the second century through the thirteenth century.

AD 496 – AD 1291

| 196 | 362 | 787 |
|---|---|---|
| Pope Victor excommunicates Eastern Christians for celebrating Easter during Passover. | At the Synod of Alexandria, Eastern and Roman Christians both accept the Creed of Nicaea. | Eastern and Roman Christians agree to revere but not to worship icons. |

### Eastern Orthodoxy

**Name**
"Orthodoxy" means "correct belief" or "correct worship" and implies faithfulness to the church's ancient teachings and traditions.

**Structure**
Today, the Orthodox Church consists of several self-ruling groups of churches. A metropolitan patriarch ("city father") guides each group of churches. Some patriarchs also serve as high overseers ("archbishops"). Orthodox Christians highly esteem the patriarch of Constantinople (modern Istanbul, Turkey). Yet he has little official authority beyond his own churches.

**Authority**
The teachings of the apostles as understood through the Scriptures, the first seven church-wide councils, and the ancient church fathers.

| 857 | 1054 | 1204 |
|---|---|---|
| Patriarch Photius clashes with the Pope. | Humbert excludes Patriarch Michael from fellowship with Roman Catholics. | Roman Crusaders sack Constantinople. |

AD 496 – AD 1291

**4 EVENTS you should know**

**1. Spread of Nestorianism (780-823):** Nestorian monks took the gospel into India, Turkestan, China, Persia, and Syria. Nearly 100,000 Nestorians remain in southwest Asia today.

**2. Children's Crusade (1212):** Nearly 20,000 children gathered around a shepherd-boy named Stephen to conquer the Holy Land. A merchant offered them free transportation, but then sold them into slavery.

**3. Second Council of Lyon (1274):** More than 500 bishops tried to unite Roman Catholicism and Eastern Orthodoxy under the pope's authority. Eastern Christians rejected the union.

**4. Kublai Khan's Request (1266):** Marco Polo's father met Kublai Khan in 1266. Christianity so intrigued Kublai that he asked for 100 monks to teach his people, the Mongols. Fewer than eight monks were willing to go. When the trip became severe, all of them turned back. When monks finally reached Mongolia in the late 1200s, it was too late. The Mongols had already converted to Islam.

**9 NAMES you should know**

**1. Caedmon (died 680):** Monk. First English Christian poet. Retold Bible stories in song.

**2. Bede the Venerable (673-735):** Christian scholar. Wrote a history of English Christianity.

**3. Anskar (801-865):** "The Apostle of the North." Missionary to Sweden and Denmark.

**4. Alfred the Great (849-899):** English king. Translated parts of the Bible into English.

**5. Odo (879-942):** Succeeded Berno as the abbot (leading monk) of Cluny monastery.

**6. Peter Abelard (1079-1143):** Professor of theology until his affair with a student named Heloise. Heloise's uncle attacked Abelard and had him castrated. Afterward, Abelard retired to a monastery where he wrote several important doctrinal treatises.

**7. Bernard of Clairvaux (1090-1153):** Powerful abbot of Clairvaux monastery. In 1128 he obtained approval for the Knights Templar, an order of crusader monks based at the Temple Mount in Jerusalem.

**8. Bonaventure (1217-1274):** Franciscan theologian. Francis of Assisi's biographer.

**9. Thomas Aquinas (1225-1274):** Scholastic theologian. Applied Aristotle's philosophy to Christian doctrine. "Angelic Doctor" of Roman Catholic Church.

**4 TERMS you should know**

**1. Cistercians:** Roman Catholic monastic order. Also known as "White Monks" (because of their undyed robes) or the "Sacred Order of Citeaux." Named after Cistertium-Citeaux, the French town where Robert Molesme founded the order.

**2. Waldensians:** Group of lay-preachers. Also known as the "Vaudois." Named after Waldo (Valdes), their founder. Condemned at the Third and Fourth Lateran Councils. They survived until the 1600s, when they joined the Protestant movement.

**3. Franciscans:** Roman Catholic monastic order. Also known as the "Order of Friars, Minor." Many leading Scholastic scholars, including William of Ockham, were Franciscans.

**4. Dominicans:** Roman Catholic monastic order. Named after Dominic, their founder. Also known as "Black Friars" (because of their black robes) or the "Order of Friars, Preachers."

# CHAPTER 6

# God Never Stops Working

## IN THIS CHAPTER
## 673 – 1295

Cluny Monasteries
John Damascus • Cyril of Moravia
Hildegard of Bingen
Francis of Assisi • Thomas Aquinas
Anselm of Canterbury

When reading about the medieval church, it's easy to ask, "Which church did the real Christians belong to?" Many contemporary Christians simply can't picture "real Christians" worshiping alongside crusaders and corrupt clergy. When Christians today disagree with their church, the most frequent response is to join another church—or even to start a new church!

**KEY** concept

Even in the least likely places, God is working.

did **YOU** know?

Lioba and Boniface were English missionaries to Germany. According to tradition, Boniface began to chop down a German god's sacred tree. With his ax's first blow, a wind-gust felled the oak. The Germans immediately gave up their old gods. From the tree, Boniface built a chapel. When Boniface needed help, his sister Lioba convinced eleven nuns and monks to follow her across the English Channel. While the monks farmed and preached, Lioba's nuns ran hospitals and trained new converts.

But remember this: Medieval Christians could not imagine starting their own congregations. To be a Christian was to belong to "one, holy, apostolic church"—which implied, in the minds of many medieval believers, remaining unified with the established church. That's why medieval congregations in one area might include customs that one finds spread throughout several denominations today. Yet, with rare exceptions, these church members saw themselves as members of the same church.

In this chapter, you will read about a dozen Christians. They—just like Charlemagne and the crusaders—were counted as members of the medieval church. Yet these Christians seem to have lived with their eyes on Augustine's "City of God." And they were not mere exceptions. They were part of the rule.

## The city of God among missionaries and monks

*Statue of Lioba in Schornsheim, Germany*

Much of the time, early medieval monasteries were vital missionary centers, especially among the English and Irish. Here's how the process sometimes worked: Monks and nuns started small communities in pagan areas. The religious communities' farming methods were far ahead of their time. Soon, natives asked about the community's top-quality crops. Conversations about crops led to curiosity about the Christian faith. Curiosity about Christianity often led to authentic conversions.

By the late 800s, however, these communities of monks and nuns needed to experience revival. Corrupt nobles controlled many monasteries. Vikings had sacked others. The missionary zeal that had once marked the monastic communities had faded.

## The duke who lost his dogs

In 909 Duke William III of Aquitaine, France, founded a new monastery. William, unlike many nobles, didn't want to control his community. He enlisted a godly monk named Berno [BERR-no] to lead the monastery. (Don't confuse *Berno* with *Bruno,* the bishop—also known as Pope Leo IX—who led the Roman church in the early 1000s.)

Berno brought Duke William some unwelcome news: The best place to build a monastery was Cluny, William's prime hunting ground. William objected, but Berno reminded him that providing for hunting dogs wouldn't lead to any eternal reward; providing for monks might.

> **from the ones who were there**
>
> Duke William III
>
> "I hand over to the apostles Peter and Paul the possessions that I now control in Cluny ... The monks there shall not be subject ... to any earthly power."
>
> —*Recueil des Chartes de L'Abbaye de Cluny.*

William freed his dogs and deeded his property to Peter, Paul, and the leading monk—not to be confused with Peter, Paul, and Mary, the much later group that had nothing to do with monks. According to the community's charter, neither William nor any bishop could meddle in the monastery's affairs. Only Cluny's leading monk (the "abbot") had any power in the community.

> **THINK about it...**
> Only the richest men hunted with dogs. To give up one's dogs was to give up one's status. What prized possession could you release to please God?

The monks at Cluny stressed perfect obedience to Scripture and to Benedict's *Rule.* Throughout Europe, people began to assess their priests and bishops according to the high ideals of the monks at Cluny. The hunger for holiness that people saw at Cluny influenced Bruno's radical reforms in the Roman bishop's office. And it all started when one duke traded his finest hunting dogs for a monastery full of monks.

## The maimed monk

John Damascus inherited a powerful political position in Damascus, Syria. He wasn't only a politician, though. He was the Eastern church's brightest thinker. He remained a committed Christian in the midst of a Muslim government. During the icon disputes, John sided with the iconodules (or "Icon-Kissers"). Most important, it was John who discerned the difference between *icon-worship* and *icon-reverence.*

In Orthodox church buildings, an iconostasis *(Greek for "icon stand") often divides the altar from the central sanctuary.*

AD **673** – AD **1295**

AD 673 – AD 1295

John's political career was, unfortunately, cut short by a lie. An anti-icon Eastern emperor sent a forged document, with John's signature, to a Muslim leader. His letter claimed to expose a plan to hand over the city of Damascus to a Christian army.

The Muslim court convicted John of treason. The first part of John's punishment—lifetime exile in a distant monastery—wasn't too harsh. The second part of his punishment was a bit more brutal; his right hand was to be chopped off.

In the monastery, John and his fellow monks wove baskets. They sold their baskets to help the poor. John also wrote hundreds of hymns. (Since John had been forced to leave his right hand in Damascus, I assume he wrote them left-handed.) But even there, John did not escape persecution. John's genius made his fellow monks jealous. They arranged to have the one-handed monk sent back to Damascus. John spent his last days selling baskets in the streets where he once lived as a lord.

## The magnificent Moravian failures

In 862, the king of Moravia—the region in Europe now known as the Czech Republic—asked the Eastern Empire to send missionaries to his people. Photius, Constantinople's patriarch, chose Cyril as his envoy to the Slavic people in Moravia. (Don't confuse Cyril the missionary to Moravia with the corrupt fifth-century bishop who also bore the name Cyril.) Cyril was a Slav from the city of Thessalonica. He had moved to Constantinople to study. Now he taught philosophy in the capital city.

*Cyril and Methodius are founders of the Slavic written language. Monument in Kiev*

Before he left home, Cyril created an alphabet, based on his native Slavic language, so he could translate the Bible into the Moravian language. This caused Roman missionaries to oppose Cyril's efforts: According to these missionaries, the Scriptures and the church's worship should be translated only into "holy languages," like Latin, not ordinary languages that native people could easily comprehend.

Faced with this controversy over languages, Cyril and his brother Methodius [meh-THO-dee-uss] traveled to Rome in 869 to appeal to the pope. The pope let Cyril translate the Scriptures into common languages under one condition: Cyril had to place his mission under the pope's control. Cyril accepted the pope's terms, but he died before he could return to Moravia to complete his mission.

Methodius, Cyril's brother, continued to work among the Moravians. Unfortunately, the Moravians struggled to understand Cyril's translations. In 895 Hungarian invaders forced Cyril's missionary successors to flee to Bulgaria. No trace remained of Cyril's mission. From a human viewpoint, Cyril and Methodius failed miserably in Moravia.

Even though Cyril's efforts failed in Moravia, they began to bear fruit in Bulgaria. Boris, the Bulgar prince, had accepted Christ before Cyril's successors arrived. When Cyril's successors fled to Bulgaria, Boris' people began to embrace the gospel, too. Cyril's successors refined their master's missionary methods. They preached and worshiped in the people's language. They even adapted Cyril's original alphabet to the Bulgarian tongue.

By 900 Bulgaria stood as the center of Slavic Christianity. "Cyrillic" became—and remains to this day—the common way of writing in southeast Europe and Russia. When Cyril and his brother died, they were fruitless failures. Years later, God transformed their failure into success.

## The city of God among the mystics

What image enters your mind when you hear the word "mystic"? Mysterious mantras? Unexplainable enigmas? What may not enter your mind is devotion to Christ—and for good reason. Much of the time, mysticism becomes self-centered instead of God-centered. Yet mysticism became a significant influence in some areas of the church during the Middle Ages.

Why did mystics multiply in the Middle Ages? Every source of an encounter with God—the Scriptures, sermons, baptism, communion—was channeled through the churches. It's possible that mysticism became a pathway for medieval believers to experiencing God in more direct ways. Regardless of the reasons for the rise of mysticism, medieval mystics such as Bernard of Clairvaux and Hildegard of Bingen profoundly influenced many people's faith during the Middle Ages.

**THINK** about **it**...

Is mysticism helpful or harmful? This may help you decide.

*positively*

1. God commands Christians to love God with their whole beings, including their feelings (Mark 12:30).

2. Paul and John described mystical experiences (2 Corinthians 12:1-9; Revelation 1:9-11; 4:1-11).

*negatively*

1. Mystics may give their experiences equal authority with Scripture or with their church's collective wisdom.

2. Christian faith must depend on more than feelings. It must also engage one's mind.

AD **673** – AD **1295**

from the **ones** who were there

*Bernard of Clairvaux*
"Some seek knowledge for the sake of knowledge. That is curiosity. Some seek knowledge to be known by others. That is vanity. Some seek knowledge to serve. That is love."

## St. Bernard—no, not the dog, the monk!

Remember the reforms that blossomed in the monastic communities of Cluny? A few years after those reforms, the Cluny communities became so well known that every noble in France wanted to sponsor them. By the early 1000s, the monks and nuns at Cluny no longer labored or cared for the poor as they had before. Gold and jewels plastered their chapel walls.

In 1098 twenty-one monks from Cluny decided to return to Benedict's emphasis on poverty and labor. They founded a new religious community near Cistertium-Citeaux, France. They became known as Cistercian [siss-TAYR-see-ann] monks. So strict was the Cistercian rule that, to avoid any appearance of wealth, the monks even refused to dye their robes. Still today, Cistercians wear white robes.

*Stained glass window of Saint Bernard*

By 1112, there was a problem among the Cistercian monks, though: No one was joining their community. The lifestyle was simply too strict. The dispirited abbot was preparing to quit when someone knocked at the gate. When the abbot arrived at the gate, he was awestruck. Not one ... not five ... not ten ... but *thirty-one* men stood at the gate! All of them wanted to become monks. One of them was Bernard of Clairvaux, the man who would become one of the mightiest monks of the Middle Ages. What's more, an entire breed of canines would become his namesake!

Bernard never became a bishop. Yet, in some sense, he ruled the Roman church for three decades. He criticized Cluny's lavish lifestyle. When two bishops—Anacletus II and Innocent II—both claimed to be the rightful pope, it was Bernard who declared Pope Innocent II to be the true bishop of Rome. How did Bernard become so powerful? His poverty endeared him to peasants. His passion unnerved popes. His focus on God's love touched even the hardest hearts. "The reason for our loving God is God," Bernard once preached. "Yet every soul that seeks God ... has already been anticipated by him. He sought you before you began to seek him." According to Bernard, to love God is to be drawn into the love that flows eternally between Father, Son, and Spirit. This encounter mystically unites a Christian with God.

**THINK** about **it**...
After Bernard, Roman Christians focused on Jesus' humanity. Devotion to Mary and to Jesus' sufferings increased. Do you think this devotion was wholesome? Why or why not?

One of the long-term effects of Bernard's emphasis on love had to do with medieval art. Early medieval

icons portrayed Jesus as an angry judge. How could people love such fearful images? To help people to learn to love God, Bernard stressed Jesus' human weakness. Soon, pictures of the infant Jesus and the crucified Christ replaced the older icons.

## A Renaissance woman in the Middle Ages

Hildegard of Bingen

She was a musician and mystic, artist and author, proclaimer of truth and prophet of reform. Popes and emperors praised her. Only Bernard surpassed her prestige. She was Hildegard [HILL-de-GARD] of Bingen.

When she was five, Hildegard began to experience mystic visions. When she was eight, she entered a religious community. Three decades later, she became the leader (the "abbess") of a convent near Bingen, Germany. In 1151 she published her visions in a book, *Know the Way.*

**on the web**

Listen to the music of Hildegard:
www.last.fm/music/
Hildegard+von+Bingen

When Hildegard was nearly 80, the bishop of Mainz denounced her visions, and her convent was excluded from the church's fellowship. Yet Hildegard's devotion outlasted the bishop's condemnation. By 1400 the Roman Catholic Church had forgotten the bishop's charges. Hildegard was officially listed as a saint.

# The city of God among the mendicants

By the late 1100s the barbarian invasions no longer threatened Europe. People's loyalties were shifting from local lords to larger systems, like shared cultures and kings. In the cities, a class of mobile merchants emerged between serfs and nobles. Members of this "middle class" traded goods and services for cash. Mobile people needed mobile clergy. So a new type of preacher appeared—the "mendicant" [MENN-dih-kant]. Mendicants traveled from town to town, preaching to merchants and peasants who flocked to the growing metropolises.

AD **673** – AD **1295**

## Where's Waldo?

In 1173 a street-corner singer staged a play about a nobleman who gave away his wealth. The play so impressed a French merchant named Waldo (or "Valdes") that he committed himself and his wealth to Christ. He funded a French translation of the Bible and became a mendicant preacher.

Waldo became disturbed as he studied the Scriptures. And what disturbed Waldo? He found no references to purgatory in the Bible, even though he had been taught that this place definitely existed. More disturbing, he found no references to the pope's supreme power. As a result, Waldo rejected both ideas.

Waldo's fresh focus on Scripture soon attracted a band of followers. They called themselves the "Poor Folk of Lyon." All Poor Folk, including women, learned the Scriptures and shared the gospel in the language of the common people. Within four years, the so-called "Waldensians" or "Vaudois" could be found throughout France.

Waldo asked the pope to approve his movement. The pope agreed ... with one condition. Poor Folk could preach only when a bishop asked them to preach. Three years later, Waldo preached in Lyon with no invitation. The Poor Folk were thrown out of Lyon. A few returned to the Roman church. The remaining Waldensians ignored the church's condemnation and kept preaching.

When he died, Waldo remained under the condemnation of the Roman Catholic Church. At the Fourth Lateran Council, Innocent III reiterated the excommunication. By the mid 1200s the Inquisition began working to destroy the Waldensians. Hundreds of Poor Folk were executed by Crusaders. The remaining Poor Folk fled to Germany and Spain.

## The knight who stripped in front of a bishop

Not every band of mendicants endured condemnation, though. One mendicant founded a group that would become the Roman Catholic Church's largest religious order.

It all began in 1204. The knights of Assisi, Italy, marched against a rival city. A twenty-two-year-old cloth merchant's son was among them. The young man's name was Francis. As he traveled to the battle, he had a vision of the

*Basilica of Saint Francis in Assisi*

crucified Christ. He returned home utterly transformed. Francis rollicked through the city streets.

"Why are you so happy?" a friend asked Francis.

"Because," Francis exulted, "I have been married. I have married Lady Poverty!"

Francis kissed lepers and sold some of his father's cloth to repair a chapel. Francis' angry father dragged him to the bishop's office.

**THINK** about it...

Before his conversion, Francis despised lepers. Afterward, he forced himself to greet them with a kiss. God transformed his feelings from loathing to love. What group of people would you prefer to ignore? How can you offer them "a kiss of peace"?

*St. Francis*
*Francisco de*
*Zurbarán (1598-1664)*

Before the bishop, Francis stripped off the lavish clothes that identified him as the son of a wealthy merchant.

"Until today," Francis remarked, handing the clothes to his father, "I called you father. Now, I can say honestly, 'Our Father in heaven....' In him alone I place my faith." As he left the bishop's office, Francis chalked a cross on a tattered brown tunic. He secured the tunic around his waist with a rope that he filched from a farmer's scarecrow.

"Grant me, Jesus," he prayed, "that I may never own under heaven anything of my own."

On February 24, 1208, the lectionary text was Matthew 10:8-10. Francis applied Jesus' words directly to himself and his band of followers. A year later, Francis asked Pope Innocent III to approve his movement. Francis didn't want his order to become wealthy, as the order at Cluny had. Each Franciscan "friar" ("brother") could own two tunics— nothing more. The tunics would be simple and brown, secured with a rope like the one that Francis had taken from the scarecrow. Innocent III thought that the rules were too harsh, but he approved them anyway.

In 1214 Pope Innocent III allowed a nun named Clare to take up the Franciscan lifestyle. While the friars preached, Clare's nuns nursed the sick. After Francis died, the pope declared that Clare and her nuns could no longer listen to the monks' preaching. Neither could they embrace poverty. Clare was furious. As long as the pope withheld her "spiritual food," Clare refused physical food. In short, she went on a hunger strike. The pope backed down. In 1247 while Clare lay on her deathbed, Pope Gregory IX approved her rules for the community of "Poor Clares."

**On the web**

Learn more about Francis and Clare:

www.mgc.org/021.htm

AD **673** – AD **1295**

# The city of God among the Scholastics

In the early Middle Ages, survival concerned most folk far more than schooling. When European society became more stable in the late 1100s, merchants and mendicants weren't the only ones who crisscrossed Europe. Scholars also migrated from town to town. In many towns, small groups of scholars instructed circles of promising students. Mendicants and mystics had emphasized practical experiences. The migrant scholars urged people to question their experiences in the light of reason. Yet could reason work together with human experience and with God's revelation? That was the question that confronted the new thinkers—the Scholastics.

## The Scholastics' exiled ancestor

In 1093 an abbot from Normandy, France, became the archbishop of Canterbury, England. His name was Anselm [ANN-selm]. Anselm knew that he and the king would clash. Why? King William II of France wanted to control the English churches, but Anselm would not conform to the king's agenda. As a result, Anselm spent one-third of his career in exile. The works that he wrote before and during his exile earned him the title "Father of the Scholastics."

In the 1000s God's power so obsessed some Christians that they believed God could contradict logic. God might, for example, create square circles, change the past, or design a car that lasts until it's paid off—things that are, from a human perspective, utterly illogical. Anselm affirmed that no one can completely grasp God's actions. Yet he denied that God contradicted logic; to the contrary, logic reflected the order and design of creation, and this orderliness pointed to the glory and power of God. "I do not try to understand you so I can trust you," Anselm prayed. "I trust you so I can understand you." As a confirmation of the undergirding logic of faith, Anselm composed a logical expression of God's nature—the "ontological argument."

Anselm was also a compassionate Christian. Once, an abbot asked Anselm, "What should we do with the boys in the monastery? We whip them constantly and they keep acting worse!" Anselm replied, "If you planted a tree and hemmed it in on all sides, what would result?" "A useless tree," the abbot replied. "So you," Anselm retorted, "have hemmed in the boys. They fill their minds with twisted thoughts because they sense no mercy in you!"

## From dumb ox to doctor of the church

"Stupid." "Scum!" "Nerd." Everyone knows the sting of a degrading name. Perhaps more than anyone else in church history, Thomas Aquinas [ah-KWI-nass] knew what it felt like to endure ridicule.

Thomas was quiet, clumsy, and overweight. When he was 20, he decided to join the Dominicans, a group of black-robed mendicant monks. Thomas' parents had other plans, though. They wanted him to become an archbishop, not a wandering preacher. So his brothers kidnaped him. It was later claimed that, for fifteen months, they tempted Thomas with prostitutes and prestigious positions. Thomas remained unmoved.

*Statue of Thomas Aquinas at the Pincio (Rome)*

In 1245 Thomas escaped his family's castle and fled to the University of Paris. In college, students usually move beyond name-calling. Thomas' classmates didn't. They dubbed the shy Dominican "Dumb Ox." No one suspected that this ox's bellow would soon resound throughout the world.

Eleven years later, Thomas Aquinas was teaching in the university. Thomas' teachings transformed Christian theology. He integrated the logic of a pagan philosopher named Aristotle with God's revelation. Many monks had treated philosophy and the physical world as Satan's domain. For Thomas, philosophy and the physical world were full of signs that pointed to the Creator.

In 1266 Thomas Aquinas began his masterpiece—the *Summation of Theology* or *Summa Theologica*. Thomas worked on his summation for seven years. The English translation of his labors fills over 4,000 pages. Yet Thomas chose not to finish his supreme work. On December 6, 1273, Thomas attended an observance of the Lord's Supper. During that worship service, something happened. When he left the chapel, the famed Scholastic said, "All that I have written seems to me nothing but straw, compared to what I have seen and what has been revealed to me." Thomas never wrote another word. Three months later, he died. In 1567 he was declared a respected teacher, a "Doctor" of the Roman Catholic Church.

## Caution! God working ahead!

"My Father is always at his work," Jesus once commented (John 5:17). Do you grasp what Jesus was saying? God never stops working! Not when greed corrupts church leaders. Not when the church becomes a political power. Not even when the church loses sight of the cross. Somewhere, there is always a missionary who wants to tell someone about Jesus, a wealthy noble who is willing to give up his prestige for the sake of the gospel, or an ordinary Christian whom God is inviting to join in an extraordinary work.

Look around your church, your school, your job. Somewhere, Christ is calling someone to join in God's work. Then get ready. That someone could be you.

AD **673** – AD **1295**

## 3 EVENTS you should know

**1. Council of Vienne (1311-1312):** Pope Clement V convened this council to disband the order of crusader monks known as the Knights Templar and to give their property to the king of France.

**2. Council of Constance (1414-1418):** Pope John XXIII summoned this council to end the Great Schism and to reform the Catholic Church. The council elected a new pope and declared that a church council "holds its power direct from Christ; everyone ... is bound to obey it." This view became known as *conciliarism*.

**3. Council of Florence (1438-1445):** This council technically reunited Catholic and Orthodox Churches. However, Orthodox laypeople rejected the reunion. The council also claimed—against the Council of Constance—that the pope was superior to church councils. The council recognized seven sacraments to guide Christians from womb to tomb—baptism, communion, confirmation, confession, marriage, ordination, and last rites.

## 7 NAMES you should know

**1. Meister Eckhart (1260-1328):** Dominican monk and mystic. Sought "the unspeakable basis of all reality"—a point at which the soul becomes united with God. Accused of heresy for his unorthodox views in 1326.

**2. Marsilius (Marsiglio) of Padua (1275-1342):** Wrote that the church derives its power from the state and that church councils are superior to the pope. Condemned as a heretic.

**3. Jan Hus (1372-1415):** Czech priest and reformer. Burned at the Council of Constance.

**4. Julian of Norwich (1342-1417):** Famous English nun and mystic.

**5. Valla (1406-1457):** Italian humanist. Proved *The Donation of Constantine* was a forgery.

**6. Girolamo Savonarola (1452-1498):** Dominican preacher. Introduced moral reforms in Florence, Italy. Defended Catholicism but became entangled in a political conflict with the pope. Hanged as a heretic in 1498.

**7. Desiderius Erasmus of Rotterdam (1469?-1536):** Renaissance scholar and Roman Catholic priest. Compiled *Textus Receptus* Greek New Testament.

## 4 TERMS you should know

**1. Conciliarism:** The belief that a church council has authority over all church members, including the pope. The Councils of Constance and Pisa were triumphs for conciliarism.

**2. Ottoman Empire:** Muslim empire, founded by the fourteenth-century warrior, Othman. The Ottoman "Turks" eventually ruled the area now known as Turkey. In 1453, they conquered Constantinople, the Eastern Empire's last stronghold. The Eastern scholars who fled to Europe from Constantinople helped to trigger the Renaissance.

**3. Renaissance Humanism:** The Renaissance was a fifteenth-century revival of interest in ancient languages and in the humanities. Renaissance writers were called "humanists" because they focused on practical human actions instead of Scholastic logic.

**4. Spanish Inquisition:** This tribunal—formed in 1479 by King Ferdinand V and Queen Isabella—tortured, burned, and exiled thousands of Jews, Muslims, and heretics. Contemporary Roman Catholics have condemned the Inquisitors' methods.

# CHAPTER 7

# Everything Falls Apart

# IN THIS CHAPTER
## 1294 – 1517

Bubonic Plague
John Wycliffe
Jan Hus • Thomas A'Kempis
Joan of Arc • Gutenberg Bible

The lesson was a masterpiece. If you doubted such high praise, you could have asked the meek and modest freshman college student who also happened to be the teacher that week ... me. I had presented the finest lesson on God's sovereignty since Paul wrote Romans 9:11, or so I thought.

To fill the last few moments of class, I asked, "Does anyone have any questions?" (Of course, I knew that no one would have any questions. How could they? I had already answered every conceivable query!)

To my surprise, one woman raised her hand. She asked calmly, "If that's true, why did my daughter and son-in-law die last month in a car wreck? How could God let my grandchildren grow up without parents? How does God's sovereignty fit with that tragedy?"

I don't recall what I said—but my answer was empty. And looking back on that moment, I'm fairly certain that everyone except me knew it. I recited an answer that would have received high marks on a theology examination, defending and explicating the bounds of divine sovereignty. Yet I spoke no words of comfort for her in her circumstances.

Paul's teachings about divine sovereignty weren't the problem; in fact, I believe those teachings more strongly now than I did then. The problem was that I had lost sight of a fellow believer's needs. This woman needed a soothing awareness of God's sovereign love, even in her pain; instead of offering her comfort, I unloaded Systematic Theology 101. I spoke the truth with pristine logic. Yet I failed to speak "the truth in love" (Ephesians 4:15). Love is, after all, sensitive to the needs of God's people (1 Corinthians 13:5), and in that moment, I was not.

Between 1200 and 1500, the Middle Ages faded, and the world was wracked with war, plague, and political upheaval. What many church members needed was a renewed relationship with the living God. What the established church offered them included inquisitions, indulgences, and division. When it came to the people's real needs, many of the church's answers were as empty as my reply to the woman in that Sunday school class. And almost everyone knew it.

# Stumbling downward: The fateful fourteenth century

## The pope who couldn't

In 1294 the cardinal bishops in Rome chose Celestine [se-LESS-teen] V, a Franciscan monk, as their pope. Previous popes had ridden into

AD 1294 – AD 1517

from the **ones who** were **there**
*Pope Boniface VIII*
"The true faith compels us to believe that there is one holy, universal, apostolic church.... Outside of her, there is no salvation.... Both swords—the spiritual and the temporal—are in the church's power."
*Unam Sanctum*

Rome on grand horses. Celestine V meandered into Rome barefoot, with a worn-out donkey.

Celestine V was an aged pastor who loved the common people. Unfortunately, the Roman bishop's duties were no longer common or pastoral. Popes lived in palaces and shaped royal policies. The plain, pious monk simply couldn't play the political games.

Five disastrous months into his papacy, Pope Celestine V met with the cardinals and shed his rich robes. Clad in his brown tunic, he sat on the floor and resigned.

did **YOU** know**?**

Indulgences were certificates that freed their owners from performing the acts of penance that the church required to show sorrow for certain sins. The money paid for an indulgence was supposed to express a person's inner desire to turn from sin. In the latter years of the Middle Ages and the early Renaissance, many priests and popes distorted the original intent of indulgences.

*Pope Boniface VIII*
*Museo dell'Opera del Duomo in Florenz*

A ruthless politician dubbed Pope Boniface VIII replaced Celestine V. Pope Boniface VIII believed that the Roman bishop should rule all of Western society. In 1302 Boniface VIII issued a bull entitled "One Holy Church" (*Unam Sanctum*). The notice claimed that the pope possessed power over all of Europe's kings. The French king disagreed so strongly that he had the pope kidnaped. One month later, Boniface VIII and his lofty claims of supreme power were both dead.

Boniface VIII's successor fared no better; he was forced to flee Rome soon after his election. In exile, he endured a fruitless reign and a very "fruitful" death. He died soon after someone served him a plate of poisoned figs.

So what was happening in Europe and the Roman Catholic Church? A momentous change was emerging in the social order: Never again would popes or emperors rule entire civilizations. That would become the task of kings and lords, ruling smaller nations and ethnic groups. A Holy Roman Emperor— who was neither holy nor Roman nor an emperor, but who claimed to be all three—*did* possess some power in central Europe. He was, however, little more than a German king.

The next pope had the good sense at least to flee to a place where he could find personal safety. Unable to trust bulls, kings, or plates of fruit, the next pope retreated to Avignon [AH-veeg-NON], a village on the border of France.

AD 1294 – AD 1517

For 72 years, popes lived it up in Avignon. Bishops openly sold positions of leadership in the churches. Friars freely hawked indulgences. Celibate priests became a pious memory. In a bit of literature known as *The Canterbury Tales,* the indulgence seller sighed to a woman who was skeptical about her need for an indulgence, "[Your husband] knows that, for a certainty, / You've bedded down a priest, or two, or three." No one challenged his estimate.

This era of political and moral turmoil later became known as the "Babylonian Captivity" of the Roman Catholic Church. Just as the ancient Israelites were removed from the Promised Land and exiled to Babylon, so the church's dignity was removed from Rome and imprisoned in Avignon.

The Babylonian Captivity was only one source of chaos in fourteenth-century Europe, though. In 1337 King Edward III of England—the nephew of a deceased French king—claimed that he was the rightful ruler of France. Thus began the Hundred Years' War—which actually lasted 116 years, suggesting that no mathematicians were involved in the naming of the conflict. In the midst of a corrupt church and a war that spanned several generations, another hardship struck Europe: The Black Plague.

**THINK** about **it**...

Some popes and priests failed to help victims of the plague. To what sort of people do today's churches fail to minister? People whose skin is a different color? Prisoners? Unwed mothers? Bedridden elderly? AIDS victims?

## "And no bells tolled"

In October, 1347, an unwelcome passenger scurried unnoticed aboard a cargo ship. It was a rat with a disease-laden flea fixed on its hide. Weeks later, the ship's sailors brought home something more costly than their cargo. Dark spots swelled between their legs and beneath their arms. The blots oozed black blood and putrid pus. All of them died, but not before their disease began to race across Europe. For four years, "Black Death" ruled Europe and Asia Minor.

In Constantinople the plague killed 88 percent of the population.

In Paris, 800 people died daily.

In London, corpses rotted in the streets, unburied and unblessed.

"And no bells tolled," one man wrote,

The Black Plague
*Engraving by Gustave Dore*

AD **1294** – AD **1517**

**IN CASE** you're confused

By law, church members couldn't charge interest. Many Jews—excluded from the land-based feudal system—became bankers. In the 1300s society shifted from a land-based system to a cash-based system. Jewish bankers became wealthy, and envy arose among church members. Too often, envy erupted into senseless savagery.

"and nobody wept, no matter what his loss, because almost everyone expected death." Flushed circles ("rings") formed on victims' cheeks ("rosies"). As victims died, they often experienced breathing fits that sounded like sneezes. Folk filled their pockets with flowers ("posies") to mask the stench of death around them. So, parents sang to their children: "Ring around the rosie, pockets full of posies./Achoo! Achoo! We all fall down."

In most regions, popes and priests alike failed to respond to their people's needs. Many religious leaders retreated into luxuriant manors, hoping to escape the death that surrounded them.

And how did the people respond? Some threw themselves into unbridled parties. Others, believing that the plague was a punishment from God, begged for God's pardon in "penance parades." A few desperate church members even blamed the Jewish people and responded by butchering and burning entire Jewish communities. Still, the plague didn't stop.

In city squares people flogged themselves and screamed to the heavens, "Spare us! Spare us!" The pope denounced their tactics. Slowly, the mobs faded. And finally, so did the plague.

Between 1347 and 1350, the Black Death took the lives of approximately 23,840,000 people—nearly one-third of Europe.

And no bells tolled.

## The church has double vision

Even the end of the bubonic plague didn't produce peace, though. The Hundred Years' War dragged on. Corruption reigned in the churches. Catherine of Sienna, an innocent Italian mystic, tried to return the pope to Rome, but even she could not restore the church's place in people's hearts.

*Catherine of Sienna, Italian mystic*

AD 1294 – AD 1517

When she was 16, Catherine had joined a community of Dominican nuns. After two years of prayer and fasting, Catherine had a vision. She believed that Christ had commanded her to help the poor. To avoid doctrinal errors, Catherine surrounded herself with a circle of Dominican scholars. Together, they nurtured the needy and preached to prisoners. Even when the Black Death erupted anew in Sienna, they refused to leave.

In 1370 Catherine experienced another vision. Her new mission? Convince the pope to return to Rome from Avignon. "Sweet papa," she wrote to the Pope, "respond to the Holy Spirit who is calling you!" Throughout Europe Catherine spoke publicly against the "stench of sin" in Avignon.

Catherine's dream came true in 1377. Pope Gregory XI rode into Rome. Yet the church's struggles weren't over. When the pope died, most of the cardinal bishops wanted a French pope. Outside the Vatican, the cardinals could hear the crowd's chant: "Roman! Roman! We want a Roman!" To distract the mob, the cardinals dressed a Roman in the pope's clothes. The trick didn't work. The chant changed to, "Death to the cardinals!" Finally, the cardinals compromised. They elected Pope Urban VI, an Italian (though not a Roman) pope.

When Pope Urban VI didn't support the pro-French cardinals, the cardinals withdrew their former decision. In Avignon, they replaced the Italian pope with a Frenchman. However, Pope Urban VI refused to be deposed. Now, the church wasn't only split between East and West. The "Great Papal Schism" split the Roman Catholic Church between Rome and Avignon.

> **IN CASE** you're **confused**
>
> Some bishops misused the power of a church council. Still, don't let their failures obscure the positive purpose of councils: Like the apostolic council in Acts 15, later councils were supposed to protect essential beliefs by properly interpreting and applying Scripture.

## Triple trouble at an Italian Pisa party

In 1409 the cardinals from Avignon and Rome decided that the schism must end. Their council—the Council of Pisa—decreed, "The Church's oneness does not depend on or come from the Pope's oneness." In other words, the church does not need one pope to make a unified decision; a church council can make unified decisions that become binding on the whole church.

The Council of Pisa rejected both the French and the Italian popes and elected a new Roman bishop. Unfortunately, the two previous popes refused to be dismissed. Two popes had been a problem, but three popes ... that was an even greater catastrophe! Each pope excommunicated the other popes' followers. Priests and laypeople throughout Europe became increasingly uncertain about where to find the true church.

## Where is the church?

One answer came from an unlikely source—John Wycliffe [WIKK-liff], a philosophy professor at Oxford University in England. According to the Roman Catholic Church's teachings, only the true church could correctly understand the Scriptures. Wycliffe agreed, but he derived his definition of the word "church" from the New Testament instead of church tradition.

Wycliffe claimed that the church wasn't built on popes, priests, or sacraments. The church consisted of every person called by God to faith in Jesus Christ. And how could people know if they had faith in Christ? A godly life provided the best evidence of a life truly committed to Christ (James 2:18).

Every church member should, Wycliffe taught, strive to understand the Bible. That's why Wycliffe's followers translated portions of the Scriptures into easy-to-read English. "Christ ... taught the people in the language that was best known to them," Wycliffe wrote. "Why should people today not do the same?" Some English people called Wycliffe a hero. Church leaders called him

**John Wycliffe**

a heretic. Twice, they tried to put him on trial. Political problems and natural disasters prevented both trials. Wycliffe died of a stroke in 1384, still in good standing with his church.

After he died, Wycliffe's followers finished his translation of the Bible.

*A statue of Czech theologian Jan Hus stands in the center of the square in Prague. Across from the Town Hall is the Tyn Church, once a center of the Hussite movement.*

Throughout England, they shared Wycliffe's message of reform. Their friends called them the "Poor Preachers." Their enemies called them "Lollards"—a word that means "mumblers" in Dutch, and "darnel weeds" in Latin. Mumbling weeds they may have seemed, but their mumblings would soon shake the world.

## Unhushable Hus

Wycliffe's words quickly traveled beyond England, crisscrossing Europe. Around 1400 his ideas began to take root in Bohemia, a region in the lands now known as the Czech Republic. Roman Catholic bishops in Bohemia banned Wycliffe's writings. But Jan Hus, a brilliant Bohemian professor and priest, had already embraced Wycliffe's ideas.

AD **1294** – AD **1517**

The encounter would cost Hus his life. Hus began to proclaim Wycliffe's understanding of the church and the Scriptures from a pulpit in Prague. In 1407 the church revoked his right to preach. Still, Hus refused to hush. He claimed that people should obey the church only when the church agreed with the Bible.

At first, the king of Bohemia defended Hus. Then the king needed the pope's support. With the king's protection withdrawn, Hus was forced to flee. In 1415 an imperial herald found Hus and asked him to defend himself at a church council in the German city of Constance. The Holy Roman Emperor promised to protect Hus on the way to and from the council. Hus accepted his offer. Unfortunately, the cardinals didn't keep the Holy Roman Emperor's promise. Hus was imprisoned in a castle in Constance. Still, he refused to retract his radical teachings. "I appeal to Jesus Christ," he replied, "since he will not base his judgment on false witnesses and erring councils but on truth and justice."

On July 6, 1415, the cardinals drew demons on a paper hat and jammed it on Hus' head. The church could not kill a heretic; only the government could undertake that task. So the cardinals handed Hus over to the king's soldiers. As soldiers tied him to a pole and prepared to burn him alive, Hus prayed: "Lord Jesus, please, have mercy on my enemies." He died singing psalms. Even though John Wycliffe had been dead for more than thirty years, the bishops also demanded that John Wycliffe's bones be unearthed and burned—which, I must admit, seems far preferable to being burned alive.

**THINK** about **it**...

Sacraments (or ordinances) are ceremonies that Christ ordained as ongoing parts of Christian worship. Orthodox and Catholic church members believe the sacraments themselves impart grace to believers. Other Christians view the sacraments as outward signs of grace that God has already given. These Christians recognize only two sacraments—baptism and communion. Some churches add foot-washing to communion. What sacraments do you believe the Bible commands?

The Council of Constance did help the Roman Catholic Church maintain order. After burning Hus while alive and Wycliffe while dead, the cardinals imprisoned the pope who had been appointed by the Council of Pisa, deposed the pope in Rome, retired the pope in Avignon, and selected a new pope, Pope Martin V. By 1450 the Great Papal Schism was over, but the movement toward more radical reforms was already well underway.

AD 1294 – AD 1517

## Looking inward: the mystical alternative

Not only had church leaders lost touch with people's needs; so had many Scholastic theologians. Anselm's use of logic had led him to love God and to serve others. Later Scholastics argued about questions that seemed irrelevant to common people—questions like, "How many angels can dance on a pinhead?" Many theologians wrote treatises about God's power, yet few seem to have experienced God's power in their lives.

Around 1374 several Dutch Christians looked past pinheads and empty power. A fresh form of faith arose among them—the Common Life Movement. Members of the Common Life Movement denounced corruption among priests and bishops. Yet they do not seem to have criticized the church itself. The Sisters and Brothers of the Common Life blended profound scholarship with mystical devotion to Christ. Their focus on personal devotion to Jesus Christ became known as *Devotio Moderna*—the Modern Devotion.

The most famous member of the Common Life movement was Thomas A'Kempis. Kempis organized the movement's ideas into a powerful devotional work, *The Imitation of Christ*. Today, people throughout the world still study Kempis' simple guide to imitating Jesus.

Mysticism also flourished outside the Common Life Movement. One young mystic placed her experiences in a politicized context; her interpretation of these experiences would cost her life. She would become known to future generations as Joan of Arc.

**Joan of Arc**

from the **ones** who were there

*Thomas A'Kempis*

"**Even if you know the whole Bible by heart and the sayings of the philosophers, what does it profit you unless you also love God?... Truly, humble farmers who serve God are greater than proud philosophers who neglect [their need for God] and work to understand how the heavens move.**"
—*Imitatio Christi*

**ON the web**

Read more of *The Imitation of Christ*:

www.ccel.org/k/kempis/ imitation/imitation.html

In 1415 King Henry V of England conquered northern France by defeating the French at the Battle of Agincourt. Ten years later, a French peasant named Joan had a vision. She believed that Michael the archangel and two saints commanded her to throw the English out of France.

The peasant girl convinced a French prince to allow her to lead an attack on the English. United under Joan's command, the prince's troops reclaimed Orleans, France. The French prince was crowned as king. Joan wanted to return home, but the king forced her to continue fighting.

AD 1294 – AD 1517

The English desperately needed to disprove Joan's claims about her supernatural visions. Why? The English claimed that God was on their side. If Joan's claims were true, God was fighting for France, not England.

In May, 1430, Joan was wounded and captured near the French border. It embarrassed the French king to admit that he owed his crown to a peasant girl, so he refused to ransom her. A pro-English bishop bought Joan and confined her in a dungeon with brutal male convicts. Even though she recanted once, the bishops returned her to the dungeon. Finally, the Inquisition convicted her of heresy.

In May, 1431, the 19-year-old peasant declared that she had heard the saints' voices again. Soldiers

*Statue of Joan of Arc*

burned Joan of Arc alive. Like thousands of others in France and England, Joan was certain that Jesus somehow supported the political pursuits of her particular nation. Her savage torment and death was one sad sidelight within a vast, tragic misunderstanding of God's ways.

In 1456, Pope Calixtus III admitted that the Inquisition had unjustly condemned Joan. In 1920, Joan of Arc was recognized as a saint.

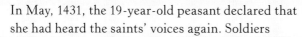

**THINK** about it...

Two people may disregard each other for decades. Yet, when tragedy strikes, they—like the Christians in Constantinople—forget their hatred. List three people that you dislike. Why wait for a tragedy? Why not forgive them now?

## Glancing backward: the humanist alternative

Emperor Constantine had founded Constantinople in AD 313. By 1453 Constantinople was all that remained of the ancient Eastern Empire. On May 28, 1453, the Ottoman Turks prepared for a final strike on that ancient capital city. That evening, the citizens gathered in the Church of Holy Wisdom (the "Hagia Sophia"). Several Roman bishops joined their Eastern Orthodox brothers and sisters amid the flickering candles. For a few moments, Roman and Eastern Christians forgot the ancient schism and shared the Lord's Supper. It was the last service of Christian worship that echoed in the church's sacred halls.

On May 29 the Muslim Ottomans conquered the city. When night fell, a Muslim teacher walked slowly into the Church of Holy Wisdom. "There is no God but Allah," he intoned from the altar, "and Muhammad is his prophet." The church building became a mosque. The building remained a

*Gutenberg Bible Page*

mosque until the 1930s. Today, it is a museum—known as "Aya Sofya"—in Istanbul, Turkey.

Hundreds of Eastern scholars fled west. They carried with them their most precious possessions: Ancient Greek manuscripts. For centuries, Roman Christians had neglected ancient Greek authors. The manuscripts from the East sparked a rebirth—a *Renaissance* [REH-na-SONSS]—of interest in ancient Greek rhetoric, art, and writing. Renaissance art, like ancient art, portrayed life from a human perspective. Renaissance scholars, like ancient orators, stressed practical language and actions. Poignant words became more important than precise logic. Because they focused on practical human actions, Renaissance scholars became known as "humanists."

Christian humanists applied this way of looking at life as they read the New Testament—a document that was originally written in Greek. They focused on the original intent and the original language of each biblical text. Their battle cry became, "Back to the sources!"

*German postage stamp commemorating Johannes Gutenberg*

*Johannes Gutenberg memorial in Mainz, Germany*

Much of the popularity of this rebirth was made possible through the work of a printer named Johann Gutenberg. In 1453 Gutenberg discovered how to mold movable metal type and incorporated this type into a printing press. For the first time, printers could mass-produce books. The price of books plummeted. Greek and Roman classics, as well as Bibles, flooded Europe.

The popes supported Renaissance art and the revival of classic texts. Yet most of them neglected one vital aspect of the Renaissance—the renewed focus on Scripture. Roman bishops became increasingly corrupt. Indulgences remained a booming business. The Spanish Inquisition exploited the church's power to persecute Muslims, Jews, and heretics. Reform became unavoidable.

AD 1294 – AD 1517

# Lurching forward

The first pope of the sixteenth century refused to accept a saint's name at his election. Instead, he took the name of the pagan caesar Julius. Today, many people remember Pope Julius II for his support of a young sculptor named Michelangelo. In the sixteenth century few people noticed this pope's art. No one could, however, ignore his military exploits. In 1507 his army forced every foreign soldier out of the church's lands in central Italy. Soon after resecuring the church's lands, Pope Julius II rode triumphantly into Bologna, Italy.

## Julius Caesar or Jesus Christ?

When Julius II rode into the city of Bologna, one young humanist didn't share Julius' joy. "Whose successor is this?" Desiderius Erasmus [eh-RASS-muss] muttered. "Julius Caesar's or Jesus Christ's?" Erasmus was the son of an unwed teenager and a prurient village priest. Erasmus' childhood school teachers had been Brothers of the Common Life. The Brothers had whetted Erasmus' taste for Greek.

As a teen, Erasmus longed to study Greek at a university, but he had no money. So he studied for the priesthood instead. Erasmus become more than a priest. He was also such a promising student that his bishop sent him to the University of Paris to study Greek.

*Erasmus 1466-1536*
*His work on the New Testament allowed the Word of God to speak to both simple people and scholars.*

Soon the budding humanist was studying Greek throughout Europe. It was during his travels that Erasmus witnessed Julius II's grand entrance into Bologna. After he saw Christ's representative leading an earthly army, Erasmus demanded changes in his church. He ridiculed Scholastic speculation: "Paul provides the finest example of love (1 Cor. 13). Yet he neither divides it nor defines it according to logical rules!" He even attacked the concept of a crusade. "Isn't the Turk also a human being?" he asked.

Despite such scathing charges against his church, Erasmus wanted to transform Christ's body—not split it. Nevertheless, it was this loyal Roman Catholic who created the tool that would lead to radical reforms. In 1516 Erasmus published an edition of the Greek New Testament that later became known as *Textus Receptus* or "Received Text." Now Christians could read the apostles' words in their original language.

*Pope Leo X*
*Santa Maria in Aracoeli in Rome*

## IN CASE you're confused

What concepts do you connect with humanism? Atheism? Aimless evolution? That's secular humanism. Be sure that you know the difference between *secular humanism* and *Renaissance humanism*. Renaissance writers were called "humanists" because they focused on practical human actions and human-oriented arts (the "humanities") instead of Scholastic logic.

## Calm before the storm

In 1517 calm settled on the Roman Catholic Church. Julius II was dead. Pope Leo X began his reign with the pronouncement, "God has given us the papacy—now let us enjoy it!" But it was too late. Wycliffe and Hus had packed a powder keg. Erasmus had woven a fuse. On October 31, 1517, a hotheaded monk lit the fuse and rocked all of Europe.

## KEY concept
When a church loses sight of people's needs, God raises fresh voices of repentance and reform.

AD 1294 – AD 1517

## 5 EVENTS you should know

**1. Moscow Claimed As Center of Orthodoxy (1500):** In 1448, Russian Orthodox Christians protested the Council of Florence by electing their own patriarch. After the Muslim Ottomans conquered Constantinople, Russians claimed that Moscow was the center of Orthodoxy.

**2. Fifth Lateran Council (1512-1517):** Reinterpreted the Council of Pisa's conciliar decrees. (If you can't define "conciliar" or "conciliarism," glance back at Chapter Seven.)

**3. Luther's 95 Theses (1517):** Martin Luther, a Roman Catholic monk, protested the sale of indulgences by publishing 95 topics for debate.

**4. Union of Brest-Litovsk (1596):** Several million Ukrainian Orthodox Christians entered into communion with the Roman Catholic Church. These Christians became known as Uniats.

**5. Rheims-Douay Bible Completed (1609):** Scholars from Douay College in England translated the Vulgate into English. The New Testament was published in Rheims, Germany. The Rheims-Douay was the standard Bible for English-speaking Roman Catholics for more than 300 years.

## 10 NAMES you should know

**1. Balthasar Hubmaier (1485-1528):** Anabaptist writer. He and his wife were killed for their faith.

**2. Oecolampadius (1482-1531):** First reformer to support laypeople's participation in church government. Defended Zwingli's view of the Lord's Supper at the Marburg Colloquy.

**3. William Tyndale (1494-1536):** English Bible translator. His Bible formed the basis for the King James Version.

**4. Carlstadt (1480-1541):** First reformer to observe communion in the people's language. Debated Eck at Leipzig.

**5. Johann Maier Eck (1486-1543):** Catholic theologian. Publicly criticized Luther's theology.

**6. Martin Luther (1483-1546):** German reformer. Emphasized justification by grace through faith.

**7. Martin Bucer (1491-1551):** German reformer. Tried to find a middle ground between Luther's and Zwingli's teachings about the Lord's Supper.

**8. John Calvin (1509-1564):** French theologian of the Protestant Reformation.

**9. Heinrich Bullinger (1504-1575):** Swiss reformer. Author of the Second Helvetic Confession, an important Calvinist statement of faith. Influenced the final form of the Heidelberg Catechism.

**10. Theodore Beza (1519-1605):** Succeeded Calvin as leader of the Genevan church.

## 5 TERMS you should know

**1. *Sola gratia, sola fide, sola scriptura:*** Latin for "grace alone, faith alone, Scripture alone." These words sum up the Protestant belief that justification is received by grace alone through faith alone and that the Bible should be the church's only authority.

**2. Reformed Churches:** Protestant churches, such as the Presbyterians, that were strongly influenced by Calvin and Knox.

**3. Consubstantiation:** Luther's belief that, after the prayer of consecration during communion, the body and blood of Christ coexist with the Lord's Supper elements.

**4. Heidelberg Catechism:** Reformed statement of faith, compiled in 1562. Widely used by Protestants for centuries.

**5. Uniats:** Christians in traditionally Orthodox areas who united with the Roman Catholic Church under the terms of the Union of Brest-Litovsk.

# CHAPTER 8

# Wild Pigs in a Dirty Vineyard

# IN THIS CHAPTER
## 1500 – 1609

Martin Luther

John Calvin

Anabaptists

King Henry VIII

Ignatius Loyola

Shyre was my first love. When I was the Lone Ranger, she was Tonto. When I was Luke Skywalker, she was Princess Leia. On June 14, 1979, I had to tell Shyre good-bye. We sat on the edge of her bed and cried together. Another man had stolen her heart, and I was a bit unsure about my role as the ring-bearer in their wedding.

I was six years old. My sister Shyre was 18. For the first time, I realized that division is never desirable. Yet, to build something better, division is sometimes necessary.

Few, if any, sixteenth-century Roman Catholics desired division. Yet reform was inevitable. Many people believed they could earn salvation through good works and indulgences. In many contexts, tradition had displaced Scripture as the church's supreme authority. The church's leadership was corrupt.

With the reforms came division. The division wasn't necessarily desirable, but the reformers were striving to build something better, both inside and outside the established church.

## All he wanted was peace

Martin Luther's translation of the Bible into German

### Lightning never strikes twice (once is enough)

A lawyer plodded along the rutted road. Suddenly, a summer shower blossomed into a raging thunderstorm. A lightning bolt struck a nearby tree and knocked the traveler to the ground. As he tumbled to the earth, he screamed, "Saint Anne, save me! I will become a monk!" The lawyer kept his promise, but his terror at the possibility of God's anger followed him to his monastery and beyond. The year was 1505. The lawyer was a German Saxon named Martin Luther.

By 1511 Martin's deep awareness of his own sin and of God's holiness drove him to the confessional for six hours at a time. Still, the guilt remained. "Love God?" the monk once wept, "I hate him!" Martin's monastery sent him to the University of Wittenberg to study. Yet no amount of study seemed to drive away Martin's anguish.

One man who tried to understand Martin was John Staupitz, a professor of biblical studies at the University of Wittenberg. Staupitz was an aged, godly mystic who was able to look beyond his church's corruption. "Perhaps," Staupitz

**Martin Luther**

seems to have thought, "if Martin explores the Scriptures more deeply, he will find peace." Beneath a pear tree, Staupitz told Martin his decision: Martin Luther would replace Staupitz as the university's Bible professor.

Still, one question haunted Martin Luther: How can anyone please a righteous God? When he considered the phrase "the righteousness of God" (Romans 1:17), the question tormented him even more deeply.

Martin found his answer in Erasmus's Greek New Testament. While reading Paul's epistles, Martin realized that the word "righteousness" means not only the *condition* of being righteous, but also the *act of declaring* someone to be righteous. God not only *is* righteous. God can also give righteousness to sinners, through faith in the righteous life and death of Jesus Christ! This righteousness is God's gift, given to every person who truly trusts Jesus.

> **WORDS from the ones who were there**
>
> *Martin Luther*
>
> "The righteousness of God is that righteousness by which through grace and mercy God justifies us by faith. I felt myself reborn!... The passage of Paul became my gate to heaven.... Works do not make one righteous. Righteousness creates good works."

"For in the gospel a righteousness from God is revealed," the apostle Paul had written, "a righteousness that is by faith from first to last, just as it is written: 'The righteous will live by faith'" (Romans 1:17). For years Martin had searched for peace. In the end, peace found him.

In 1517, Martin's peace in the truth grew into an explosive passion for the truth. The trigger was a Dominican monk named Tetzel.

## Prince Albert indulges the pope

Martin Luther was the pastor of a village church near the German region of Mainz. Albert was both the archbishop and the ruling prince of Mainz. Pope

*Saint Peter's Basilica*

Leo X needed cash to finish St. Peter's Basilica, so he made a deal with Prince Albert: The German prince could sell indulgences in Mainz if he turned over half of his profits to the pope.

One of Prince Albert's peddlers was Tetzel. "As soon as the coin in the coffer rings," Tetzel claimed, "the soul from purgatory springs." Tetzel's misuse of the church's power enraged Martin Luther. Martin decided to debate the indulgence peddler. One week in October, he angrily scribbled a list of 95 topics to debate ("theses").

All Martin wanted to do was challenge Tetzel's teachings about indulgences. What he did was shake the world.

AD 1500 – AD 1609

## A wild pig, a broiled bull, and a Diet of Worms

A few years ago, a Lutheran group rented the Roman Catholic cathedral in St. Louis, Missouri, for a meeting. The priest greeted them with this comment: "We are pleased to provide the cathedral. Please don't nail anything to the doors this time." The crowd roared.

On October 31, 1517, Martin Luther nailed his theses on the chapel door in Wittenberg. That time, no one laughed. At first, his theses upset only a few scholars. Pope Leo X muttered, "Luther is a drunk German. He'll recant when he's sober."

Three years later, Leo X realized that, if Luther was still drunk, his intoxicated condition must be permanent and that some response was needed. The pope published a bull entitled, "Arise, O Lord"—remember a "bull" had nothing to do with beef; it was a notice written in the pope's name.

"A wild pig," Leo's bull lamented, "has invaded the Lord's vineyard!" The "wild pig" was Luther; the "vineyard" was the church. Martin Luther responded by broiling Leo's bull in a bonfire.

Two months later, Luther received a letter from the Holy Roman Emperor. The letter read, "Come under safe conduct, to answer with regard to your books."

The Latin word for an imperial meeting is *diet*, and the meeting would occur in the German city of *Worms.* So the meeting became known as the Diet of Worms. (And no, I'm *not* making that up.)

*Lutherstube at Wartburg Castle where Luther translated the Bible*

Martin expected to die at the Diet of Worms— which is probably how I would feel about a diet of worms too, though for very different reasons. Martin had good reason to fear the Diet: Remember what had happened a century earlier when an emperor had promised safe conduct to Jan Hus? Hus was burned at the stake. How could Luther possibly escape the same fate?

AD **1500** – AD **1609**

### from the **ones** who were there

**Martin Luther**
"The pope has no power to remit guilt, except by confirming it has been remitted by God."
"Confidence in salvation through letters of indulgence is vain."
Theses, 6, 52

The diet began on April 15. A bishop pointed to a heap of books on the floor. He asked Martin, "Did you write these?" "They are all mine," Martin answered. "Do you defend them?" the bishop demanded. This time, Martin did not reply with his typical boldness. Instead, he whispered, "Give me time to think it over."

The next day, the bishop posed the same question.

As sweat flowed from Martin's face, he replied: "My conscience is captive to the Word of God. I cannot and I will not recant anything, for to go against conscience is neither right nor safe. God, help me."

Martin would have suffered the same fate as Hus, but the ruler of Saxony secretly sent soldiers to safeguard him. As Martin headed home, five men attacked his wagon. They blindfolded him and took him to an abandoned castle. Martin had been kidnaped to save his life.

**THINK** about **it**...

Don't ignore the Roman Catholic diet's response to Luther: "If anyone who contradicts councils and the church's common viewpoints must be overcome by Scripture, nothing will be certain!" In other words, "If all Christians follow their own understandings of every Scripture instead of the church's interpretation, chaos will result." The reformers tried to overcome this problem by using clear Scripture passages to interpret unclear passages. How can you apply this principle to your personal Bible study?

## "Other women have even worse faults"

Ten months later, Martin emerged from hiding. A dozen Cistercian nuns had recently embraced his ideas and wanted to leave their convent. Because it was a capital crime to remove a nun from her convent, one of Martin's friends spirited the nuns away in herring barrels. Eight nuns married; three returned to their homes. Only Katherine von Bora, a feisty, red-haired 26-year-old, remained.

In April, 1525, Katherine commented that she might marry Martin. She was probably joking. After all, Martin was 42 years old, and marriage did not seem to interest him. Yet Martin decided to marry "Kaetie" for three not-quite-romantic reasons: It would please his father, provoke the pope, and pass on his name. While preparing for his marriage, Martin wrote, "I would not exchange Kaetie for France ... because God gave her to me and other women have even worse faults."

Despite his doubtful reasons for marriage, Martin grew to love and enjoy his "lord Kaetie," as well as their six biological children and four adopted children. He nicknamed Galatians, his favorite book of the Bible, "my Katherine." When the neighbors saw the great reformer hanging diapers on the clothesline, Martin quipped, "Let them laugh. God and the angels smile."

## How is Christ among us? Or, is he?

Soon after Martin nailed his theses on the chapel door, the citizens of Zurich, Switzerland, also defied their church's teachings. During Lent, Ulrich Zwingli [ZWEEN-glee], their

*Statue of Martin Luther*

AD 1500 – AD 1609

priest, led them to go on a diet of sausages—which certainly sounds more palatable than Luther's Diet of Worms.

Now, two reformers were working to renew the church. One German Lutheran realized that, if Luther and Zwingli united their movements, their chances for survival would increase. So he asked them to meet in the German city of Marburg.

A single primary issue kept the Zwinglian and Lutheran movements apart: *How is Christ present in the Lord's Supper?* Luther and Zwingli agreed that transubstantiation missed the point, but what was the biblical alternative? (If you can't define transubstantiation, glance back at Chapter Five.)

According to Luther, the communion elements never change. Yet, in the bread and cup, Christ's body is present with the visible elements. Christ's bodily presence conveys grace to persons who are at peace with God. Nothing less could explain Jesus' words, "This is my body." (This belief became known as *consubstantiation*.) Zwingli, on the other hand, taught that Jesus' words merely meant, "This symbolizes my body."

When he faced Zwingli at Marburg, Luther pulled a chunk of chalk from his pocket. He scrawled his central thesis on the banquet table: "This is my body."

Five days later, neither side had budged. The rift remained. The last words of the Marburg Colloquy were, "We have been unable to agree on the issue as to whether the true vine and blood of Christ are corporally present in the bread and wine. Still, each party will prove toward the other its spirit of Christian love, insofar as conscience permits." In 1530 Luther's followers published their own statement of faith, the Augsburg Confession.

on the web

Want to dig deeper into Reformation history?

www.gty.org/~phil/rformers.htm

## All he wanted was a place to study

### The reforming refugee

In 1534 another lawyer traveled along another rutted road. His life had been shaken, but not by lightning. He was a Renaissance humanist fleeing the University of Paris. His name? John Calvin.

A few months earlier Calvin had helped a friend write a speech. They peppered the address with quotes from Luther and Erasmus. The speech angered the French

**What did Calvin believe?** Calvin did teach that salvation depends on God's choice. Yet, predestination was only one part of his theology. The center of Calvin's thinking was the knowledge of God—the awe-inspiring awareness that, by God's grace, God chooses to be revealed among sinful humanity.

government and forced Calvin to flee. Soon afterward, Calvin became a Protestant and a Christian.

Calvin fled first to Noyon, France, his home-town. From Noyon, Calvin turned toward Switzerland. There, he wrote the first systematic summary of Protestant theology, *Institutes of the Christian Religion*.

## The long detour home

After the *Institutes* were published, Calvin decided to move to the Protestant city of Strasbourg, France. On the way, a war forced him to veer east, through Geneva. He intended to stay in Geneva for one night, concealed by the alias "Charles d'Espeville." That night stretched into a lifetime.

A preacher named Farel had already promoted Protestant ideas in Geneva. One of Calvin's companions told Farel that d'Espeville was actually the well-known author of the *Institutes*. That evening, Farel confronted Calvin at the inn.

"Stay here!" Farel begged, "Geneva needs someone with your gifts."

"But I need a rest," Calvin countered.

Farel exploded, "May God curse your rest and the calm you seek for study, if you leave behind such a great need!"

Calvin chose to stay. Within a year, Geneva agreed to Calvin's vision for the Reformation.

**Missions deeply concerned Calvin.** He sent missionaries to Scotland, France, and Brazil. A dishonest guide forced the missionaries to Brazil to turn back.

Two years later, after a series of religious and political quarrels, the Geneva city council forced Calvin to leave the city. Calvin found refuge in Strasbourg, his original destination. There, Calvin cared for French Protestants ("Huguenots") who, like Calvin, had fled because of persecution. Finally, he found the life of study that he always wanted. In 1539 Geneva needed someone to debate a Roman Catholic thinker. The city council swallowed its pride and asked Calvin to return.

When Calvin returned to his pulpit, everyone in Geneva expected a severe rebuke. Calvin did not preach the expected sermon. Instead, he began to preach precisely where he had stopped three years earlier, without a trace of spite.

AD 1500 – AD 1609

John Calvin

# All they wanted was to be obedient

**THINK** about **it...**

Do you resent someone who has wronged you? How could Calvin's example when he returned to Geneva inspire you to forgive your enemy?

Calvin—as well as Luther and Zwingli—never escaped the idea that the church and the government ought to be linked with one another. The Genevan government enforced the Genevan church's beliefs. In 1553 the Genevan city council even burned Michael Servetus, a theologian who denied the Trinity.

It was in Zwingli's Zurich that a movement arose with the radical idea that no government should enforce theological truths. Priests in Zurich still conducted communion in Latin. Some of Zwingli's best students, including Felix Manz, urged them to lead the Lord's Supper in the people's language.

"When he introduced the Lord's Supper," one student argued, "Christ didn't speak nonsense! He used understandable words."

Zwingli referred the matter to the city government. For Felix and his friends, this was not a question for the government; this was a question of submission to Scripture. Felix Manz decided to start a weekly Bible study in his home. There, Felix and his "Swiss Brothers" came to an unexpected conclusion: *The New Testament never commanded infant baptism.* In 1524 the Swiss Brothers openly criticized infant baptism.

In January, 1525, one Swiss Brother asked one of his friends, "Baptize me with true Christian baptism, upon my faith." Water was poured over his head in the name of the threefold God. One by one, all of the Swiss Brothers, including Felix, received believers' baptism. Their revolutionary act earned them the name "Again-Baptizers," or "Anabaptists." That night, the city council of Zurich banished the Anabaptists.

Most Anabaptists fled to nearby villages. Still, they could not escape. Felix Manz was seized and sentenced to life in prison. After five months in a dungeon, he escaped. He was recaptured in October, 1526. The Zurich city council sentenced Manz to death. Their charge against him? "He wanted to gather those who wanted to accept Christ ... and unite with them through baptism."

**ON the web**

Learn more about the Anabaptists:

www.spurgeon.org/~phil/anabapt.htm

In a cruel mockery of his beliefs, it was by water that Felix Manz died. The executioner tied Manz's arms behind his back and shoved him into an icy river. Manz died singing, "Into your hands, Lord, I commit my spirit."

**THINK** about **it...**

Read Acts 16:30-33 and Colossians 2:11-12. Which does the Bible teach—believers' baptism or infant baptism? Give reasons for your conclusion. Support your reasons through careful study of Scripture.

Felix Manz was the first non-Catholic to be martyred by a Protestant, but he wasn't the last. The persecution of Anabaptist leaders spread rapidly. This loss of reliable teachers and leaders allowed a series of heresies to spread unchecked among the Anabaptists. These heresies led to a tragic twist in Anabaptist history.

## The Munster massacre

Imagine with me: A self-appointed biblical scholar preaches an apocalyptic message. He and his followers create a compound where they can follow their fanatical beliefs. An army cuts off the sect's food and communications. After a tense siege, troops swarm into the compound. The leaders are killed, and the movement wanes.

Sound familiar? Probably. Yet the date wasn't 1993. And the place wasn't Waco, Texas.

The year was 1535. The place was Munster, in the German province of Westphalia. The rebels were a heretical group of Anabaptists.

**IN CASE** you're **confused**

Sixteenth-century baptism was not simply a consequence of one's faith. Nor was it only an entrance into church membership. Through baptism, people became citizens of a (supposedly) Christian society. Anabaptists did the unthinkable: They separated the community of faith from the civil society.

After the Munster massacre, Protestant and Roman Catholic princes brutally oppressed all Anabaptists. Even Calvin urged rulers to destroy the Anabaptists. "It is far better that two or three burn now," Calvin wrote, "than to have thousands perish in Hell." Erasmus was one of the few leaders to defend the Anabaptists' right to follow their beliefs. By 1600 the Anabaptist death toll would reach 10,000. It was a Dutch preacher named Menno Simons who helped to save the Anabaptists.

*Menno Simons*

## Peace amid persecution

Menno Simons became a priest in 1524. He performed his duties and accepted his paychecks. Yet he spent most evenings at a local bar with a mug of beer in one hand and a deck of cards in the other.

Two years after his ordination, Menno wanted to impress other pastors. So, he began to study his Bible for the first time. Despite his mixed

AD **1500** – AD **1609**

motives, Menno couldn't escape the truths that he read. He became a believer in Jesus Christ. A few years afterward, he left his comfortable lifestyle and joined the Anabaptists, knowing that the name "Anabaptist" could be fatal.

"The Anabaptist minister's only payments," he later wrote, "are fire, sword, and death."

Menno salvaged two beliefs from the jumble of heresies that had marred Anabaptist thought after the Munster massacre: (1) *The church should baptize only believers.* And, (2) *no government should enforce religious beliefs.* In the process, Menno became the Anabaptists' most esteemed leader.

Menno Simons strictly observed New Testament patterns. During the Last Supper, Jesus had washed his disciples' feet; during communion, Menno washed his followers' feet. In literal obedience to the words of Jesus, Menno's followers refused to fight or to swear oaths (Matthew 5:33-39).

In 1542 Menno's radical ideas landed his name on the Empire's "most wanted criminals" list. Menno and his family escaped capture for 19 years, but the stress took a heavy toll. Menno's wife and two of their children preceded him in death. Menno himself became severely crippled.

Menno Simons died a natural death in 1561—a privilege that few sixteenth-century Anabaptists shared. So profound was Menno's influence on the Anabaptists that they soon became known as "Menno's people" or "Mennonites."

did **YOU know?**

In the 1700s, Jakob Ammann led a group of conservative Anabaptists to separate from their fellow Mennonites. These stricter Anabaptists were called "Amish," after their leader. When the German Amish migrated to the northeastern United States, they became known as the "Pennsylvania Deutsch" (or "Pennsylvania Germans").

## All he wanted was a Bible that everyone could read

College students frequently fall into—and out of—love, but few fall in love with their studies. At Cambridge University in England, however, one student fell in love with Greek and with Renaissance humanism. William Tyndale's two loves would cost him his life.

After he completed his studies, Tyndale became the chaplain of a wealthy family. At a banquet, Tyndale and a priest debated the meaning of a scripture.

**IN CASE** you're **confused**

Why did church leaders frown on private translations of the Bible? One translator might press personal prejudices into a translation. Church leaders felt that authorized groups of scholars could pool their knowledge to produce a more precise translation.

AD **1500** – AD **1609**

"It would be better to be without God's law than the pope's," the priest remarked.

"If God spares my life," Tyndale retorted, "I will cause the plow-boy to know more about Scripture than you do!"

So what was the problem with Tyndale's plan? Tyndale's bishop refused to let him translate the Greek New Testament into simple English. Tyndale fled to the German provinces to publish his New Testament without the bishop's interference. In 1526 a printer in Worms, Germany, published 6,000 copies of Tyndale's New Testament. Three months later, the testaments poured into England.

English bishops bought and burned thousands of Tyndale's testaments. Yet ecclesiastical arsonists didn't bother Tyndale. He used the money to finance a revision of his New Testament. The revised testaments were smuggled into England in flour sacks. It wasn't, however, just Bibles that would cost Tyndale his life.

*William Tyndale*

## All he wanted was a son

Before the Reformation, English monarchs usually supported the pope. In 1520 a tract that attacked Martin Luther sported King Henry VIII's name on the front cover, even though Henry's chancellor Thomas More probably wrote it. Pope Leo X rewarded Henry's zeal with the title "Defender of the Church." Little did Leo X know that the Defender of the Church would soon be damned by the church.

### "Henry the Eighth, I am, I am; the head of the church, I am"

The problems began with Henry's need for an heir. Henry's current queen, Catherine of Aragon, had not produced a son to succeed Henry as king. Catherine had been Henry's sister-in-law, and Henry was already enchanted with an attractive 25-year-old named Anne Boleyn. Henry claimed, based on a skewed interpretation of Leviticus 20:21, that God would never let Catherine have a son and his marriage should be annulled.

AD 1500 – AD 1609

In 1529 Henry asked Pope Clement VII to revoke his vows to "that Spanish cow." Typically, the pope would have granted this request. This time, there was a problem: The Holy Roman Emperor Charles V currently controlled the pope, and Emperor Charles V also happened to be Catherine's nephew. The pope could not afford to anger Charles V.

Thomas Cranmer, a professor at Cambridge, suggested a solution: Cranmer would ask the lawyers at Europe's universities to overturn the pope's decision. In 1533, newly ordained as England's archbishop, Cranmer repealed Henry's vows. Henry married Anne Boleyn and declared himself head of the English church. Chancellor Thomas More refused to recognize Henry's rule over the English church. After More's resignation, one of Henry's advisors, Thomas Cromwell, had him beheaded. And, in the words of one of Henry's jesters, "Chancellor More became chancellor no more."

## "Lord! Open the king of England's eyes!"

So, how did Henry's marriage problems affect William Tyndale? In 1530 one of Tyndale's tracts denounced Henry's attempt to dispose of Catherine. A supposed friend betrayed Tyndale to the king's soldiers. William Tyndale was captured, strangled, and burned. Tyndale's last words were, "Lord! Open the king of England's eyes!"

God answered Tyndale's prayer. In 1538 Henry approved the Matthew's Bible, a completed edition of Tyndale's work. The next year, the king placed a "Great Bible," a revised edition of Matthew's Bible, in every English church.

Still, the English Reformation was far from complete. In 1537 Jane Seymour, Henry's third queen, finally had a son. Under the reign of Henry's son, Thomas Cranmer edited a *Book of Common Prayer*. This common order of worship replaced elaborate Latin liturgies with simpler English versions. Cranmer's *Book of Common Prayer* led the English churches away from Roman Catholicism.

*Portrait of Henry VIII*
*Hans Holbein the Younger (1497-1543)*

AD 1500 – AD 1609

Henry's son died as a teen in 1553. Mary Tudor, Henry's daughter by Catherine, took the throne. She propelled England back toward Roman Catholicism. She earned the title "Bloody Mary" by executing more than 300 Protestants for their faith. Among those killed during her reign were Archbishop Thomas Cranmer and Bishop Hugh Latimer.

*The editor of the Matthew's Bible placed William Tyndale's initials on the last page of the Old Testament to honor Tyndale's contribution to the translation.*

**Tyndale's New Testaments ignited a Protestant movement in Scotland. John Knox led the Scottish Parliament to deny the pope's power in Scotland. Elders ("presbyters") directed Scottish Reformed churches. Scottish Protestants became known as Presbyterians.**

As soldiers prepared to burn Latimer, he declared, "We shall this day light such a candle by God's grace as I trust shall never be put out."

It was Queen Elizabeth, Henry's daughter by Anne Boleyn, who placed England on a middle route between Catholicism and Protestantism. She refused the title "Supreme Head of the Church," yet she also rejected the pope's power. Her revised *Book of Common Prayer* included Protestant and Catholic ideas. Today, it is still Elizabeth's middle way that shapes the Church of England, a church that's also known as the Anglican Church.

## All they wanted was a renewal

Martin Luther wasn't the only sixteenth century Roman Catholic who wanted to see the church reformed. Roman Catholic leaders had been envisioning reforms several years before Luther nailed his theses to the chapel door.

The Protestant Reformation forced the Roman Catholic reformers to rethink their original plans. At first, the Catholic reformers tried to reunite with the Protestants. In 1541 several Protestants—including Luther's aide, Philip Melanchthon [me-LANK-thawn]—met with Roman Catholic leaders in Ratisbon-Regensburg, Germany. Their goal was reunion.

on the web

Dig deeper into the English Reformation:

www.bbc.co.uk/history/british/tudors/english_reformation_01.shtml

For more about Thomas More:

www.luminarium.org/renlit/tmore.htm

Foxe's *Book of Martyrs* records the deaths of many English Protestants:

www.luminarium.org/renlit/foxe.htm

AD 1500 – AD 1609

It was not the issue of justification that prevented reunion. Both sides agreed that God's grace justifies the sinner by faith and that saving faith produces good works. But the Roman Catholic delegates demanded agreement on the pope's power and on the Lord's Supper. From that point, the Conference of Ratisbon-Regensburg quickly headed downhill. From that moment onward, Roman Catholics forged their own distinct road to reform.

S.FRACISCUSXAVERIVS SOCIE KTISV

*Francis Xavier, a Jesuit priest and missionary, took the message of Catholic faith to southeast Asia.*

A soldier named Ignatius Loyola [loy-OH-lah] represented one of the new faces of Catholic faith. Ignatius Loyola was wounded in a battle in 1521. While his wound healed, he read Thomas A'Kempis's *Imitation of Christ*. Kempis's emphasis on direct knowledge of Jesus Christ transformed Loyola's life. Loyola and six friends committed themselves to poverty, chastity, and obedience to the pope. In 1540, Pope Paul III approved Loyola's "Society of Jesus," forming the foundations of the Jesuit Order.

The Jesuits became the Roman Catholic Church's most effective missionary force. One Jesuit priest, Francis Xavier, preached in India and Japan 150 years before Protestants sent missionaries to either country.

## Being Catholic in a post-Reformation world

Pope Paul III called for a reforming council in 1538. The delegates met in Trent, near the border of the modern nations of Austria and Italy. Between 1545 and 1563 the Council of Trent reshaped the Roman Catholic Church. Widespread marketing of indulgences and church offices ended. Priestly celibacy was enforced again. The Council of Trent also made doctrinal decisions. Scripture and church tradition were given equivalent authority. Both faith and works were viewed as necessary for salvation. And, it became mandated that the Mass be said in Latin. These decisions defined for more than 400 years what it meant to be Roman Catholic.

# The aftermath

Medieval Europe had been, in the eyes of many citizens, a Christian society, united under the Roman bishop. The Reformation forced folk to ask themselves, "How can we remain unified if every person follows a different form of Christianity?"

In the German provinces, the Peace of Augsburg tried to help Protestants and Catholics to coexist peacefully. In the end, the prince of each province

AD **1500** – AD **1609**

chose his people's confession of faith. If a Protestant found oneself ruled by a Catholic prince, the Protestant could move unhindered to a Protestant prince's province and *vice versa*. Yet the Peace of Augsburg only allowed Lutheran Protestants. What about Calvinists and Zwinglians? And what about the Anabaptists? From a religious perspective, Europe was in fragments at the end of the sixteenth century. Could anyone pick up the pieces?

# Building something better

Were the divisions that shattered sixteenth-century Christianity desirable? Perhaps not. Were they necessary? Probably, yes. The divisions returned millions of people to a renewed awareness of God's sovereignty, of the Bible's authority, and of salvation by grace through faith. Even within the Roman Catholic Church, the divisions fostered many needed moral reforms.

> **KEY concept**
> Division is never desirable, but sometimes it is necessary.

Division is never desirable, but sometimes it is necessary. So, like a certain six-year-old ring-bearer at his sister's wedding, I accept the division. I believe that God preserves a people for God's own glory, despite the divisions that tear apart God's church. And I work to build something better on the foundation that remains.

*The council of Trent responded to many of the Reformers' criticisms of the Roman Catholic church.*

**3 EVENTS you should know**

**1. Persecution of Japanese Christians (1596-1643):** In 1597, the Japanese government crucified 26 native Christians for their faith. Persecution continued until 1643. In 1859 and 1890, the Japanese government issued agreements that legalized Christianity again.

**2. Chinese Rites Controversy (1704):** Dominican monks taught Chinese Christians neither to venerate their ancestors nor to partake in Confucian rites. Jesuit monks allowed both practices. The pope decided the Dominicans were correct. Severe oppression erupted against Catholics in China.

**3. Suppression of the Jesuits (1759-1767):** Theological and political disputes led to the removal of Jesuit priests from Portugal, Spain, and the Americas.

**8 NAMES you should know**

**1. John I of the Cross (1542-1591):** "Mystical Doctor" of the Roman Catholic Church.

**2. Matteo Ricci (1552-1610):** Jesuit missionary to China. Believed the Confucian Supreme One was also the threefold God of Christianity.

**3. Rene Descartes (1596-1650):** French philosopher. To find a firm basis for thought, he decided to doubt everything. He concluded that everything could be doubted except his own existence (hence his famous maxim, "I think, therefore I am"). He reasoned all other truths from that basis.

**4. Blaise Pascal (1623-1662):** French scientist and Catholic thinker. Supported Jansenism. Fragments of his defense of Christian faith were published after his death as *Pensees*.

**5. Johannes Amos Comenius (1592-1670):** Bohemian educator. For him, the final goal of education was not simply gaining information, but developing Christian character.

**6. John Milton (1608-1674):** English Christian poet. Argued for the separation of church and state. Wrote *Paradise Lost*.

**7. Sor Juana Ines de la Cruz (1651-1695):** Latina nun and Catholic theologian. Her bishop disallowed her studies, but she kept studying until a mystic experience fulfilled her longings.

**8. Antonio Vieyra (1608-1697):** Portuguese priest. Worked to convert and protect Native Americans. Clashed with Sor Juana over theological issues.

**3 TERMS you should know**

**1. Dissenters:** English church members who agreed with the link between church and state but who disagreed with the Anglican Church's theology. This group included Puritans and Catholics.

**2. Nonconformists:** English church members who disagreed with the entire concept of linking the church with the state. This title included Independents, Separatists, Congregationalists, English Presbyterians, Methodists, Quakers, and Baptists.

**3. Jansenism:** Jansen, a Catholic theologian, asserted that humans can do nothing good apart from God's grace. Jansen derived his teachings from Augustine of Hippo. Jansenism was condemned by the pope in 1653.

# CHAPTER 9

# Change Doesn't Always Do You Good

## IN THIS CHAPTER
## 1510 – 1767

Christopher Columbus
Jacob Arminius
Galileo Galilei • King James I
John Bunyan

**KEY concept**

Change doesn't solve everything.

When I wrote this book, my mind required two primary fuels—Diet Coke and constant change. That's why I didn't write this book at a library or in my office. These words were written at McDonald's.

One morning, two buses pulled into the parking lot at McDonald's, and a horde of uncouth creatures swarmed without warning into the lobby. The front-line crew looked as if they wanted to don steel helmets. The manager began to hyperventilate. Innocent customers reviewed their life insurance policies. It was—horror of horrors!—a sixth grade field trip!

Soon, three food fights were threatening my notebook computer's survival. (I never knew a Chicken McNugget could fly *that* far!) I questioned the sanity of the person who put noisemakers in Happy Meals. (Don't sixth-graders make enough noise without help from their Happy Meals?) That morning, I wanted change, but I got more change than I wanted.

Reformation Christians wanted change—and they got it. Yet some of the changes brought conflict, disunion, and chaos. In some cases, people received more change than they wanted. More than a few church members seem to have wondered whether reform was really what they needed after all.

## Paris, predestination, and a Polish scientist: conflicts in post-Reformation Europe

Post-Reformation Europe encompassed an untidy blend of Lutherans, Calvinists, Anglicans, Roman Catholics, and Anabaptists. But people could follow their own consciences. So, peace would soon settle across the continent—right?

Wrong.

### "We'll always have Paris"—whether we want it or not

One example of the types of religious conflicts that shattered post-Reformation Europe: In 1572 the queen of France convinced her husband that the "Huguenots"—a term for French Protestants—were plotting to rebel against him. On the evening of St. Bartholemew's Day, the king's soldiers swept through Paris, slaughtering the Parisian Protestants in the streets. The next day, Protestant blood still

**WORDS from the ones who were there**

De Thou Describing the St. Bartholomew's Day Massacre: "One Huguenot woman was about to deliver a baby.... They ripped her open and threw her infant against the wall.... Old men were thrown into the river. A pack of boys dragged the infant child of a Protestant family through the streets with a rope around its neck."

— Histoire des choses arrivees de son temps

trickled down the steps of the Louvre. Ten thousand Protestants died in the St. Bartholemew's Day massacre. Not until the Edict of Nantes in 1598 did Protestantism become legal in France.

Internal battles afflicted the Protestant movements, too. The Lutherans argued for 20 years about whether humans are fully or partly depraved. (Their own inability to get along should have given them a hint.) In 1577 the Formula of Concord reunited the Lutherans, at least for a few years.

## Predestination—on what does it depend?

You'd think that Calvin's followers would have been predestined to fare better than the Lutherans. Evidently, they weren't.

Jacob Arminius [arr-MIH-nee-uss] was a popular Dutch pastor. In the late 1500s, another pastor argued that Calvin had been wrong about the issue of predestination. Arminius agreed to defend Calvin's views. Arminius lost the debate before it began. As he studied both sides, he became convinced that his opponent was correct.

Arminius' conclusions split the Calvinist movement. Arminius died in 1609, but the conflict about predestination didn't. The next year, the followers of Arminius published the *Remonstrance*, a statement that outlined five Arminian beliefs about salvation:

1. *On their own, humans can do nothing good.*

2. *Before the foundation of the world, God chose to save everyone who would freely choose to trust Christ.*

3. *Jesus died for everyone, but his death only redeems believers.*

4. *People can choose to reject God's attempts to save them.*

5. *Scripture doesn't clearly state whether Christians can forfeit their salvation.*

"These Articles," the Arminians' *Remonstrance* concluded, "set out what is ... sufficient for salvation. It is unnecessary to look higher or lower."

**ON the web**

Read the proceedings of the Synod of Dort:

www.spurgeon.org/~phil// creeds/dort.htm

A Dutch prince tried to end the conflict in 1618. The prince despised the Arminians for political and religious reasons. So he invited Calvinist pastors throughout Europe to gather at the city of Dort. Their task? Denounce the Arminians.

AD 1510 – AD 1767

Despite the council's political overtones, the Synod of Dort attempted to draft a balanced declaration of Calvinist beliefs. The Calvinists responded to each of the Arminians' five statements with their own declarations. From the Calvinists' responses, we get the five points of Calvinism:

1. **Total Depravity**: *Human beings are by nature spiritually dead. No one naturally desires to seek Christ (Romans 3:10-12; Ephesians 2:1-3).*

2. **Unconditional Election**: *If someone trusts Christ, it is because God chose to regenerate that person. God's choice is unconditional; it isn't based on any human decision (John 6:44; Romans 9:10-16).*

3. **Limited Atonement**: *Christ's death atoned only for those who would trust in him. Jesus laid down his life only for his followers, not for all humanity (John 10:14-15, 28).*

4. **Irresistible Grace**: *When God regenerates someone, that person will neither resist nor reject God's grace (John 6:37, 44).*

5. **Perseverance of the Saints**: *Every authentic believer will persevere in faith and in good works until the end (John 10:27-28; Romans 8:29-39).*

**THINK** about **it**...

Study the Scriptures listed with the five points of Calvinism. Do you agree with the Synod of Dort? Why or why not?

Predestination had been only one part of Calvin's theology. Its purpose was to assure Christians of God's love and to understand why some persons reject the gospel. After the Synod of Dort, predestination became the centerpoint of Calvinist theology in the minds of many people.

## How many Poles does it take to change the world?

When sixteenth-century Europeans looked at the stars, they knew humanity was special. After all, didn't everything—sun, moon, stars—spin in perfect circles around humanity?

did **YOU know?**

A flower can help you recall the five points of Calvinism. The points are TULIP:

1) Total depravity of mankind (absence of desire for Christ)

2) Unconditional election (unconditional choice by God)

3) Limited atonement

4) Irresistible grace

5) Perseverance of the saints (Christians will never forfeit their salvation)

In the mid-1500s Nicolas Copernicus [ko-PER-ni-kuss] of Poland challenged the common worldview. It's important to note that his ideas were *not* new: Several ancient Greeks had already suggested that the earth rotated around the sun. Copernicus realized that, mathematically, a sun-centered universe made more sense than an earth-centered universe.

*Nicolaus Copernicus memorial situated in Warsaw, Poland*

The Pole knew his ideas would turn the galaxy inside out, literally. He refused to release his manuscript until he was close to death. A Protestant pastor's preface presented Copernicus's ideas as speculations to simplify math, not as scientific theories. Copernicus was dying, and few people were interested in a book about math anyway. As such, his views remained virtually unchallenged.

Another scientist, Galileo [GAH-lee-LAY-oh], didn't wait until he was on his deathbed to publish his papers. His impatience almost sent him to his death. Galileo carried the ideas of Copernicus from speculation to science. One year after Galileo published his ideas, the Inquisition condemned his assertion that the earth moved around the sun. After all, didn't Scripture clearly teach that the sun, not the earth, moves? (See Joshua 10:12-13.)

*Galileo Galilei*
*Justus Sustermans (1597-1681)*

Under the threat of death, Galileo reduced his ideas from theories to speculations. He spent the rest of his life under house arrest in a luxuriant villa. Yet he had started a revolution that no wall could confine. (In 1992, the Roman Catholic Church closed the case in Galileo's favor. I'm sure Galileo felt much better afterward.)

Once, the world had been a vast puzzle. The church explained the puzzle, and people trusted the church's explanation. After Galileo, the world was still puzzling, but the established church was losing its grip on how people viewed the physical world.

# Changing perspectives

## Well, that's one way to adjourn a business meeting

Not only did the churches begin to lose their voice in matters of science; the Roman Catholic Church also began to lose its place in politics. Here's one example of how that happened: In 1618 several Bohemian Protestants met their Catholic king's envoys in the city of Prague. The Catholic envoys refused to listen to the Protestants' complaints. So, a mob adjourned the meeting with a violent motion—a motion that no one seconded.

They threw the envoys through a second-story window.

As he plunged out the window, one envoy screamed, "Mary, mother of Jesus! Help me!" A Protestant yelled through the window, "Let's see if your Mary helps you now!" When he saw movement below, the Protestant murmured, "By God, his Mary has helped him."

AD 1510 – AD 1767

King James I

Fortunately, the envoys survived. Unfortunately, they survived because they landed in a heap of horse manure. The Holy Roman Emperor immediately declared war on the Protestants. Historians have named this foul-smelling event the "Defenestration of Prague." The resulting conflict would become known as the "Thirty Years' War," although they didn't call it that then because they didn't know how long it was going to last.

At first, the conflict was a war for religious toleration. The Thirty Years' War quickly faded into a series of political skirmishes and senseless pillaging. Before the conflict ended, it had enmeshed France, Denmark, and the entire Holy Roman Empire. In the Empire alone, soldiers slaughtered 10 million citizens. In 1648 the Peace of Westphalia ended the Thirty Years' War.

Prior to the Peace of Westphalia, Roman Catholic leaders had presided over international treaties. Yet the pope didn't even appear at Westphalia in 1648. Sickened by religious conflict, Europeans began to search for something beyond faith to cement their societies together.

## Puritans—they weren't what you may think

England wasn't directly involved in the Thirty Years' War, but England did endure religious struggle during those three decades. In 1604, a few years before the Thirty Years' War began, a band of English reformers had met with King James I at Hampton Court. Unlike the Bohemians in Prague, these reformers didn't throw anyone through the window. Their desire was simply to purify the Church of England. So they became known as "Puritans."

Who *were* these "Puritans?" A social critic once commented, "Puritanism is the haunting fear that someone, somewhere, may be happy." His perception was dead wrong. When Puritans worshiped, they did wear dull-colored clothing—but not to be gloomy. They wanted to turn their thoughts away from one another and toward God. Otherwise, they wore both vivid and plain colors.

Memorial to Separatist puritans at Fishtoft, Lincolnshire, England, close to the spot where they were arrested in 1607

Explore Puritan theology:
www.puritansermons.com

Puritans enjoyed beer and complained bitterly when it ran out. They expected spouses to sustain mutually satisfying sexual relations. They swam and skated, hunted and bowled. They expressed their faith through lively relationships with one another and with God.

For Puritans, the Bible was vital. Why? They wanted to purify the church of all practices not required by Scripture. "The Church ought not," the Puritans wrote to King James, "to be governed by ... any human invention, but by the laws and rules which Christ hath appointed in his Testament." Their preferred translation was the Geneva Bible.

King James disliked the Geneva Bible because it included study notes that were quite Calvinistic. So when one Puritan at the 1604 Hampton Court Conference suggested a new translation of the Scriptures, James quickly agreed. Forty-seven scholars worked for 33 months on King James' version. In 1611 the first King James Version of the Bible rolled off the presses. Though unpopular for many years, the King James or "Authorized Version" of the Bible eventually became the most popular English translation of the Scriptures and remained popular until the closing decades of the twentieth century.

It would, however, take more than a new Bible to solve the problems in the Anglican Church. After the Hampton Court Conference, some Puritans separated from the Anglican church. In 1607, persecution drove the so-called "Separatist" churches to flee to Holland. For safety's sake, one of those Separatist churches reorganized into two smaller congregations.

*Page from the Geneva Bible*

Each half would, in its own way, change the world.

One group would sail west, to a New World. They would settle on the coast of Massachusetts. American Christians know these people as the Pilgrims.

In Holland, the other group's understanding of the church would change radically. Their heirs would include John Bunyan, Charles Spurgeon, Martin Luther King, Jr., and Billy Graham. The world knows them as Baptists.

*Page from the King James Bible*

AD **1510** – AD **1767**

## The first English Baptists

The leader of the second group was an uncommon man with a very common name, John Smyth. In Amsterdam, very likely influenced by a group of Anabaptists, Smyth embraced the radical idea that only believers' baptism was valid.

Smyth and his followers wanted to receive believers' baptism. But there was a problem: If infant baptisms were invalid, no one in Smyth's church had been rightly baptized. Could an unbaptized person baptize anyone? Smyth wasn't sure. In 1609 John Smyth took a chance. He "cast water on himself." Smyth's self-baptism spawned a new congregation—the "Brothers of the Separation of the Second English Church in Amsterdam." Later, they became known by a name that can fit a bit more easily on a church sign—the Baptists.

**THINK about it...**
With whom should Christians share the Lord's Supper? Only members of their church? Only members of their denomination? All believers?

The Brothers of the Separation embraced Arminian theology, emphasizing the *universal* or *general* extent of Christ's atonement. For this reason, they became known as "General Baptists."

**did YOU know?**

In 1610 Smyth questioned whether self-baptism had been valid. He tried to join a group of Mennonite Anabaptists, but he died before they accepted him. The next year, Smyth's closest friend, Thomas Helwys, led the congregation home. Near London, they founded England's first Baptist church.

In 1643, Parliament invited English Puritan pastors to form a new church. They gathered at Westminster Abbey. The Westminster Catechism's opening words express the essence of Puritan faith: "What is the chief end of man? The chief end of man is to glorify God and enjoy him forever."

## The Bunyan who wasn't a lumberjack

One of the most famous English Baptists was John Bunyan. When John was nine, King James' son, Charles, commanded every church in Britain to follow the Anglican church's rituals. This church dispute quickly turned into a political dispute, and chaos spilled across England.

Oliver Cromwell, a member of Parliament, formed a pro-Puritan army. Within five years, Cromwell controlled Britain. His troops beheaded King Charles and his archbishop. Cromwell's army drafted a man named John Bunyan on Bunyan's sixteenth birthday. After two uneventful years, Bunyan's military unit disbanded. At this time, the "Lord Protector" Cromwell was already growing unpopular.

AD 1510 – AD 1767

**John Bunyan**

Around 1648—at about the time that the Thirty Years' War was ending in central Europe—Bunyan married. He built his bride a thatched hut. Unfortunately, he had nothing to put in his hut. The entire dowry of his wife, Mary, consisted of two Puritan books! "We had not so much household stuff," Bunyan later remarked, "as a dish or spoon."

Whether the Bunyans ever bought any flatware, no one knows. What *is* certain is that Bunyan read Mary's Puritan books, as well as John Foxe's *Book of Martyrs.* (Without a bed or dishes, what else was there to do?) Those books changed Bunyan's life. As he read, Bunyan realized that he had never truly trusted Christ. After an intense struggle, he surrendered his life to the living Lord. "Down fell I," he wrote, "as a bird shot from a tree."

In 1653 Bunyan received believers' baptism by immersion at a Baptist church in Bedford, England. The Bedford Baptist Church seems to have been one of the earliest Baptist churches to baptize by immersion instead of pouring. Bunyan soon recognized that God was calling him to preach; he quickly became one of the Baptists' most popular traveling preachers.

Unlike other Baptists, Bunyan shared the Lord's Supper with all faithful believers in Jesus Christ, regardless of their denomination. "The Church," Bunyan argued, "hath not warrant to keep out of their communion [any] Christian."

In 1660 Cromwell's Commonwealth ended, and King Charles's son suppressed all non-Anglican churches. A few months later John Bunyan was jailed in Bedford for preaching without the permission of the Church of England. In prison, Bunyan penned his most famous work; it was an allegory entitled *Pilgrim's Progress.* John Bunyan died in 1688, only a few months before a new ruler returned religious toleration to England.

In 1688 William of Orange and Mary—the daughter of King James— became the rulers of England. Their "Glorious Revolution" returned England to Queen Elizabeth's "middle way." The Toleration Act allowed anyone who agreed to a list of thirty-nine doctrines—known as *The Thirty-Nine Articles*—to worship without fear.

The Puritan movement in England was over, but some aspects of the Puritan ideal would persist for centuries among Presbyterians, Separatists, and Baptists. And, for a few years, in an unruly band of American colonies, the Puritan dream would thrive.

AD 1510 – AD 1767

*Columbus claiming possession of the New World in a chromolithograph made by the Prang Education Company in 1893.*

# Changing cultures

While religious wars transformed Europe, another conflict was changing another hemisphere. The clash began in 1492 when Christopher Columbus sailed the ocean blue. Christopher Columbus wasn't only looking for a passage to the Indies when he collided with Central America. He was looking for gold. Why? He wanted Spain to finance a crusade that would crush the Muslims. Columbus lacked one thing to make his journey across the ocean—money. Columbus used the Bible to convince kings to finance his quest. He claimed that his journey would fulfill Isaiah 11:11-12.

In 1492 Columbus' boats landed in the Bahamas. Eventually, he also landed on the coast of Honduras. When Columbus died, he still believed that he had found an eastern route to India. What he had actually found was more marvelous than India. He had, at least from the perspective of Europeans, discovered a new world.

*Replica of the Santa Maria*

## The trust-Jesus-or-else campaign

Spain and Portugal were quick to send soldiers to subdue the Americas. The Spanish and Portuguese were not—they claimed—conquering the Native Americans. They were evangelizing them.

Before each battle, soldiers read aloud—in Spanish!—a summary of Christian beliefs. If no one responded to their evangelistic invitation they slaughtered the natives—giving new meaning to "Evangelism Explosion." In the settlers' minds, the natives were going to hell anyway. Why did it matter whether they went sooner or later? The settlers even found a scripture to excuse their violence: Didn't Jesus command his people to "compel them to come in"? (Luke 14:23, *King James Version*).

## Pour some sugar on me

Until the 1500s only honey could indulge Europe's sweet tooth. In the Americas, Europeans found a whole new way to gain weight—sugar. The problem was that they didn't have sufficient laborers to harvest the sugar cane. Spain and Portugal could make vast profits if they overcame one problem: It was illegal to enslave a native.

**THINK** about **it...**

How did Christopher Columbus misapply Isaiah 11:11-12? What about the Spanish soldiers' misuse of Luke 14:23? How can contemporary Christians avoid similar misinterpretations of Scripture?

AD **1510** – AD **1767**

The Spanish solved their problem with the *encomienda* [en-KOM-ee EN-dah] system. This system "entrusted" natives to Spanish settlers. The settlers were supposed to teach their natives about Christ, but the actual results were worse than slavery. Because the settlers received natives without making any financial investment in them, the native workers were often treated worse than slaves.

One seventeenth-century Aztec claimed that he saw a vision of a Native American Virgin Mary. Eventually, a bishop was compelled to build a shrine at the site of the vision. Since then, the Virgin of Guadalupe has been a symbol of Mexican self-rule.

## Bartolome's barren battle

In 1510 Bartolome de Las Casas became the first priest to perform his first Mass in the New World. To enhance his income, the Spanish priest acquired an *encomienda* in Haiti. For four years, his plantation produced a healthy profit. Then, on Pentecost Sunday, 1514, something happened to Las Casas. He became deeply convicted that his treatment of the natives was wrong. He released his natives, closed his *encomienda,* and declared that no true Christian could exploit the natives.

Las Casas returned to Spain to campaign for natives' rights. Five years later, the Holy Roman Emperor actually did something holy. He approved Las Casas' *New Laws of the Indies*—a law-code that limited Spain's power over the natives. Most settlers ignored the *New Laws,* and Las Casas quickly became unpopular. The Spanish Inquisition even listed his writings in their *Index of Forbidden Books.* Still, Las Casas persisted. Until the day he died, Bartolome de Las Casas tried to curb his country's cruelty with no success.

## A new source of slaves, a new curse on the Americas

The natives might have survived European brutality. What they couldn't survive were European diseases. In Mexico alone, European diseases likely killed 17 million of the 18 million natives.

The Spanish and Portguese settlers were troubled—but not because they had destroyed entire cultures and communities. They were upset because workers were dying and their plantations could not make a profit without workers. The settlers' solution would lead to difficulties and wars beyond anything they could have imagined: They decided to enslave and import Africans into the Americas.

One ancient philosopher had suggested that some races were intended for slavery. Settlers claimed that African people fit the philosopher's suggestion. Some even used Scripture to defend their actions. They connected the Africans with Canaan in Genesis 9:25 to justify their treatment of African natives.

from the **ones who** were there
*Bartolome de Las Casas*
"The Indians are our brothers; Christ has given his life for them. Why do we treat them with such inhuman savagery?... They aren't stupid or savage!... I do not know of any other people more ready to receive the gospel."
*Defense Against the Persecutors and Slanderers*

AD **1510** – AD **1767**

## The slave of the slaves

Imagine yourself as a seventeenth-century African. Light-skinned men with tremendous weapons have ripped you from your native land. They cram you and hundreds of others into the dank belly of a ship. You receive little food, little water, no light. You are naked. Several of your fellow-slaves die. The living and the dead lay together on a solid sheet of human waste. With the stench comes sickness. Day after day, you vomit bile. Bitter gall congeals on your chin and chest.

*The Slave Trade*
*Auguste-Francois Biard, 1840*

Your captors' destination is Colombia. A furlong from the beach, light-skinned men drag you from the ship's hold. Flies swarm around you as you collapse at the dock.

You glimpse a man running toward you. He wears a robe. He pours water into your mouth. He is not like other light-skinned men. Several Africans surround him. They speak to you ... in your language. You do not quite understand the words that the Africans speak to you. You do recognize one phrase, though ... "living water." The light-skinned man points to himself. His name feels strange on your swollen tongue. "Pedro ... Claver."

When Pedro Claver took his priestly vows, he committed himself to helping slaves. He even added a phrase to his name, "always a slave of Africans." In other words, "always a slave of the slaves." In 1622 Pedro became a Jesuit missionary in Colombia. He didn't know any African languages, so he convinced his monastery to buy some Africans so that the monks could communicate with slaves. Pedro demanded that the African translators be treated as brothers—not as slaves.

When a slave ship neared the coast, Pedro ran to meet the ship. He gave each slave a drink of water. He grouped the Africans according to their native languages. In each group, he shared the good news about Jesus Christ, the "living water." Pedro showed each slave a snake's skin. Just as a snake leaves behind its skin, Pedro said, so a person who receives baptism must leave behind one's old life. Pedro baptized anyone who wanted to trust Christ.

After decades of service, Pedro became paralyzed. His fellow priests refused to nurse him. Instead, they hired an African slave to care for the priest. Years of abuse had taught the slave to hate white men. He treated Pedro

**on the web**

**Does Pedro Claver's story inspire you?**

www.cin.org/petclavr.html

Claver like his owners had treated him. Pedro lay in the same cot for months, until his own waste seeped into his bedsores.

Nearly everyone despised Pedro Claver. Several slave-owners realized that Claver might be declared a saint, though. If this happened, his possessions could become priceless relics. They invaded his cell and stole everything he owned—even his clothing and a cross that he had carried most of his life. In 1654 Pedro Claver died, naked and alone, "always a slave of the slaves." Two hundred years later, he was officially listed as a saint.

Pedro Claver wasn't the only Jesuit to defend the oppressed. In Paraguay, Jesuit priests built settlements for the Native Americans who had survived slavery and disease. In 1628 Portuguese and Spanish plantation owners attacked these Jesuit missions and enslaved their natives. The Jesuits moved their missions farther inland, but the slave traders pursued them. In 1640 the Jesuits armed the missions and allowed the natives to defend themselves. At first, the experiment worked. By 1731 nearly 150,000 Native Americans were living safely within Jesuit missions. Still, in the end, the slave owners' greed and superior weapons won. In 1767 Spain forced the Jesuits to leave the New World. By 1800 slavery, disease, and greed had destroyed the missions that had once provided safe havens for tens of thousands of Native Americans.

## It takes more than change

Christians put a lot of faith in change. Is Sunday school faltering? "We need different literature." Is the church's income plunging? "We need a new pastor." Do the people fail to catch the pastor's vision? "I think I'll look for another place to serve."

Change isn't necessarily bad, but change alone doesn't solve our problems.

Remember New Coke? The Edsel? Certain aspects of post-Reformation Christianity?

Before Christians try to change something, perhaps we should ask ourselves, "What is God doing here that we may be missing?" Maybe God is preparing the church for a new spurt of growth. Maybe the pastor's vision isn't the Holy Spirit's vision. Maybe people's hearts simply are not open to what Scripture has to say. Maybe post-Reformation Christians were still looking for earthly power when God's power was all that they needed. And maybe contemporary Christians sometimes follow the same path. "Savior, like a shepherd lead us; much we need thy tender care."

AD 1510
AD 1767

**KEY concept**
Change alone doesn't solve every problem.

## 5 EVENTS you should know

**1. Cyril Lucar Befriended Protestants (1623-1637):** Lucar, the Orthodox patriarch of Constantinople, embraced Calvinism and gave the king of England one of the earliest known copies of the New Testament, the Alexandrian Codex. Four Orthodox synods denounced Lucar's Calvinist views.

**2. Czar Peter Placed the Russian Orthodox Church Under the Government's Control (1721).**

**3. The Great Awakening (1720s-1750s):** This religious revival began in the Congregational and Reformed churches of Massachusetts and New Jersey, emphasizing outward signs of conversion.

**4. Methodist Conference Formed Within the Anglican Church (1784).** The formation of the Methodist Conference paved the way for the Methodists to become a separate denomination.

**5. Pope Pius VII Restored the Jesuit Order (1814).**

## 6 NAMES you should know

**1. Roger Williams (1603-1683):** Upheld religious liberty in his booklet *The Bloody Tenent of Persecution.* Founded Providence, Rhode Island, after being expelled from Massachusetts.

**2 . George Fox (1624-1691):** Founder of Friends Society. Fox removed all human elements, including baptism and communion, from worship, because he believed God guides Christians through an "inner light." The Friends were harshly persecuted for their beliefs. One Friend told a judge he should "quake" before God's wrath. So, the Friends also became known as "Quakers."

**3. Margaret Fell (1614-1702):** Leader of the Friends Society. In 1666, wrote *Women's Speaking Justified by the Scriptures,* a defense of women preaching.

**4. Nikolaus Zinzendorf (1700-1760):** Wealthy Pietist leader. Sheltered the Moravian Brethren and founded Herrnhut, a Moravian community.

**5. John Wesley (1703-1791):** Founder of the Methodist movement. Emphasized the pursuit of holiness and the achievement of "Christian perfection."

**6. Francis Asbury (1745-1816):** Methodist circuit-riding preacher. He and Thomas Coke were the first Methodist superintendents in America.

## 5 TERMS you should know

**1. Separatists:** English church members who separated from the Anglican Church over several issues, including the degree of adornment in the church's worship. (Separatists preferred simple worship; Anglican worship tended to be ornate.) Most Separatists became Congregationalists.

**2. Moravian Brethren:** Pietist descendants of the Bohemian Protestants, who derived from Jan Hus' followers. Today, they are known as the United Brethren.

**3. Pietists.** Eighteenth-century Christians who emphasized experiencing God's presence through intense, personal prayer and Bible study.

**4. The Enlightenment:** An intellectual movement in the eighteenth and nineteenth centuries that focused on human reason, words, science, natural law, and the created order.

**5. Deism:** From the Latin *deus* ("deity"). A movement that searched for a universal foundation on which all religions could agree. Most deists believed that a divine being had created the universe and natural laws. However, they also believed that this divine being was revealed to humanity primarily through the created order.

# CHAPTER 10

# You Say You Want a Revolution?

# IN THIS CHAPTER
## 1620 – 1814

Anne Hutchinson
Salem Witch Trials
Jonathan Edwards
George Whitefield
American War for Independence

KEY concept

When former forms of faith fail to inspire them, folk forge fresh—and, sometimes, false—forms of faith.

When I tell people that I'm a writer, one question always seems to surface: "How do you get your ideas?" I dread that question. It's not that I don't have an answer. It's just that the answer sounds so ... undignified.

I call my method "creative scenery changes." (Warning! To the uninitiated, my methodology looks suspiciously like loafing.) I sit for awhile in one spot. If that spot does not inspire me, I go somewhere else. I keep moving until I'm inspired. After inspiration strikes, a revolution begins within my brain. That's how I get my ideas. (Nothing, I might add, is more inspiring than an editorial deadline.)

In the 1600s and 1700s, many people found that their parents' faith no longer inspired them. So they performed a series of creative scenery changes. Puritans and patriots found their inspiration in new societies. Pietists searched for religious revival. Rationalists created a new vision of the divine. The result was a series of revolutions that still shape our world today.

## You say you want a revolution in the social order?

In 1620 one hundred English Separatists left their native land, accompanied by a military escort. Every American knows the rest of the story: These "pilgrims" founded a colony where everyone could worship freely.

Right?
Wrong.

In the first place, the Mayflower excursion turned out to be a little bit like the first episode of *Gilligan's Island.* The Pilgrims had intended to land in Virginia—not Massachusetts. Storms and faulty steering sent them far north of their goal. Their goal wasn't religious freedom for all people; what they wanted was the freedom to form a society based on their own beliefs.

The Pilgrims named their landing point "Plymouth." A few years later, the Puritans' Massachusetts Bay Colony absorbed the Plymouth settlement. The Pilgrims and Puritans worked toward a society based on their beliefs, and it worked—for a few years. To become voting citizens, residents had to confirm that Christ had saved them;

*Replica of the Mayflower in Plymouth, Massachusetts*

AD 1620 – AD 1814

as such, their church and their society remained firmly linked. The arrangement didn't last.

## Roger Williams' providential experiment

It was a Separatist named Roger Williams who first challenged the colony's alliance with the church. When Roger arrived in Massachusetts, the Puritans' Congregationalist Church offered him the position of pastor-teacher. Roger, unlike the Puritans, contended that civil judges should not enforce religious beliefs. So he refused the position; he preached among the Native Americans instead. Few people cared about Roger's beliefs until he made a political claim that the colony's leaders couldn't allow. And what was this claim? Roger Williams declared, "The Natives are the true owners" of the colonists' land.

In 1635, a court in Massachusetts banished Roger Williams. His daughter was two years old. His wife was pregnant. Winter was approaching quickly. Roger had no horse. Still, he had to leave. He trekked alone through the icy eastern landscape for 14 weeks. Finally, a Native American tribe gave him shelter.

did **YOU** know**?**

Roger Williams wasn't the only person who instructed Native Americans in the Christian faith. In the late 1600s Jacques Marquette and other French priests preached the Roman Catholic faith to natives along the Mississippi River. In 1614 John Rolfe, a Puritan settler, married a native princess named Pocahontas. "I will never cease," Rolfe wrote about his efforts to convert Pocahontas, "until I have brought to perfection so holy a worke, in which I will daily pray God to blesse me." Pocahontas eventually became a Christian and moved with her husband to Europe.

The next year, Roger Williams paid a Native American tribe a fair price for a small bay to the south of Massachusetts. His wife, children, and several friends joined him there. Roger named his patch of earth "Providence." Every faith was welcome in Providence. Roger's charter declared, "No person within said colony shall be called in question for any opinion in matters of religion. Persons may enjoy their own judgments in matters of religious concernment."

Three years after he founded Providence, Roger became the first Baptist in the New World. He even founded the first Baptist church in the colonies. Eight months later, he questioned his new beliefs and became the first former Baptist in the colonies.

One of the first folk to flee to Providence was Anne Hutchinson. On Wednesday nights, the 44-year-old midwife and six other women discussed their pastor's Sunday sermon in Anne's Boston home. Soon, sixty church members regularly attended Anne's classes.

did **YOU** know**?**

In 1681, a member of the Friends' Society, William Penn, received a tract of land from King Charles II. Like Roger Williams, Penn refused to link his colony to any belief beyond monotheism. He embraced everyone who believed in one God. His colony became known as "Penn's Forest" (or "Pennsylvania").

AD 1620 – AD 1814

Such meetings were common in the Massachusetts Bay Colony. What was uncommon was that Anne was "a woman of ready wit and bold spirit."

Anne Hutchinson

Anne's boldness led her to make a risky claim: Christians aren't bound to obey any human laws. Maybe Anne was trying to echo Paul's emphasis on grace rather than law (Romans 3:24-28). In the process, Anne clearly neglected another truth—real faith leads to good works, including obedience to civil authorities (Romans 13:1-7; James 2:14). The leaders of the Massachusetts Bay Colony accused Anne Hutchinson of promoting treasonous ideas.

During the trial, it became clear that Anne knew as much about the Bible as her judges. When the governor denounced the idea of a woman teaching, Anne quoted Acts 18:26 ("Priscilla ... explained to [Apollos] the way of God") and Titus 2:3-5 ("older women ... [should] admonish the younger women"). "But neither of them will suit your practice," a judge replied. "Must I," Anne countered, "show my name written therein?"

Then, Anne made a mortal mistake: She appealed to a personal experience in which she believed that God had spoken directly and authoritatively to her.

The governor challenged her: "How did [you] know that it was God that did reveal these things?"

"How," Anne retorted, "did Abraham know that it was God that did bid him offer his son?"

"By an immediate voice!"

"So to me," Anne said, "by immediate revelation."

This was too much. The court banished Anne Hutchinson. She and her family fled to Providence, Roger Williams' refuge in the region known today as Rhode Island. Rhode Island would remain America's smallest colony. Yet, in that bay, a radical idea was birthed—a civil government that refused to favor any religious faith. That idea transformed our world.

## Reclaiming the colony

A generation after their arrival, a perennial problem confronted the Puritans: Christian parents don't always produce Christian children. Most of the first-generation settlers had professed a personal

from the **ones** who were there

John Cotton, Puritan Pastor
"[Anne] did much good in our Town.... She was not only skillful [as a midwife] ... but readily fell into good discourse with the women about their spiritual estates.... Many of the women and their husbands were ... brought to inquire more seriously after the Lord."

**THINK** about **it...**

"Many men are in a deep sleep and flatter themselves," one Puritan pastor preached, "that God will not deal so harshly with them as to damn them." Read 2 Corinthians 13:5-6. Meditate on Paul's words. Are you, like some people in the Puritan churches, in a spiritual sleep? If you are relying on anything you have done for your salvation, you are under God's wrath. Only a living faith-relationship with Jesus can save you.

relationship with Christ. Yet about half of their children showed no outward signs of a conversion experience. If some persons in the colony had never trusted Christ, could Christian principles still govern their society?

The first answer was a "Halfway Covenant." For years, pastors had baptized only the children of Christians. Under the terms of the Halfway Covenant, hoping to retain a bond between the children and the church, pastors began to baptize the children of parents who had never produced a "conversion narrative." Still, the fervent faith that had marked the early Puritan communities seemed to have faded.

It seems as if a spiritual uneasiness may have settled in the Puritan communities. In Salem, Massachusetts, in 1692, uneasiness erupted into open fury. Someone caught a 12-year-old girl practicing magic. The girl and her friends falsely charged several older women with witchcraft. At some point, righteous anger seems to have turned into mass hysteria. Fifty citizens admitted, under pressure from the colony's leaders, that they had practiced magic. All 50 were freed. Nineteen citizens refused to confess. All 19 were hanged. One man was tortured to death because he refused to testify against his wife.

This event became known as "the Salem witch hunt." It lasted less than a year. In Europe, witch hunts were longer, bloodier, and far more frequent. One Puritan judge later confessed "the blame and shame" of the Salem trials. Still, a blot would blacken the Puritan experiment, at least in the popular mind, for centuries.

After the witch hunt, the Massachusetts Bay Colony endured several political conflicts with England. By the early 1700s a "deep sleep" had replaced the early Puritans' fiery faith. "There hath been a vital Decay," one pastor wrote. "There is already a great Death upon Religion, little more than a name left to live."

## You say you want a revolution in human reason?

If you attend Sunday school, you have probably asked yourself at least once, "How can two people read the same Scripture and arrive at two different conclusions?" Here's a key to the answer: Throughout your life, you collect certain experiences and assumptions, some true, some false. You

AD 1620 – AD 1814

read the Bible through the lens of these assumptions. Different experiences and assumptions lead to different understandings of the same text. Of course, every biblical text *does* have an objective, historical meaning—and every Christian is responsible to seek the objective, historical intent that the original author intended. At the same time, our assumptions influence how we understand and apply these objective, historical intentions. And sometimes, these assumptions make it difficult to see the original intent of the text clearly.

Before the Reformation, Christians tended to look at their world through the lens or the assumptions of church tradition. In their eagerness to return to Scripture alone, sixteenth-century Protestants discarded many church traditions.

**THINK about it...**
Look up "[the] Enlightenment" in an encyclopedia. Define the Enlightenment in your own words.

Here's what seems to have happened in the seventeenth and eighteenth centuries: What replaced church tradition as the primary way to understand the world was an internal power shared, at least in theory, by all humans: *Reason.*

This emphasis on human reason was a chief feature of the eighteenth-century movement that became known as "the Enlightenment." Before the Enlightenment, people had tended to look toward past traditions for guidance. The Enlightenment turned people's attention away from past traditions, toward human reason, and ultimately toward themselves.

## The Universe—from cosmic puzzle to reasonable machine

This emphasis on reason fed the early stages of the scientific revolution. The astronomer Copernicus had realized that the planets moved around the sun. Yet he couldn't explain why. Perhaps angels pushed them in their places. Or maybe the universe itself was alive. Isaac Newton, a professor from England, shattered these earlier assumptions. Through scientific reasoning, Newton proved that gravity could explain the mystery of the planets' movements.

*Isaac Newton*

When Newton published his ideas, people throughout the world gasped. It seemed that one man had applied his reason and solved an infinite mystery! And the explanation was so simple! One Enlightenment poet exulted, "Nature and Nature's Law lay hidden in Night;/God said, Let Newton be: and all was light."

AD **1620** – AD **1814**

## God—from personal Savior to distant Creator

Newton's discoveries provided the foundation that Enlightenment thinkers would employ to construct a new way of thinking. The old world of unseen spirits and unruly fate was fading. In its place, Enlightenment thinkers began to mold a new vision: The universe was a self-maintaining machine, endowed by a Divine Creator with forces that forever followed the unvarying laws of nature.

**THINK** about **it...**

"The results of [Deism were] not all of the best. If God is first and last a Maker, then what happened after? Certainly nothing much which involved God. He might have gone off to a retirement cottage once his contract was completed, and for some Christians he did just that."
*Gavin White, How the Churches Got to Be the Way They Are (London: S.C.M. Press, 1990) 1.*

Skeptics soon asked, "If human reason can grasp nature's inner workings, why does humanity need the Bible? or religious creeds? or redemption?" Perhaps reason and nature were sufficient! In this context, a new vision of God arose; this vision became known as "Deism."

**IN CASE** you're **confused**

Freemasonry arose in the 1100s to guard the secrets of building stone structures. After the Renaissance, the "Masonic brotherhoods" became clubs dedicated to charity, peace, and education. Their focus on education and peace led them to support Deism in the 1700s.

In many cases, Deists rejected every belief that reason could not confirm. Miracles? Impossible. The Trinity? Absurd. Jesus? A human Messiah. God's mystery? Gone. For such Deists, to be Christian was simply to live according to Christ's ethics. Creation was the first and last meaningful act for the Deists' so-called "God."

Deist ideas spread in Europe through Masonic brotherhoods. In 1738 Pope Clement XII denounced Deism and forbade Catholics from becoming Masons. Still, Deism remained popular. Influenced by Deism, many churches embraced "Unitarianism," the belief that God is not a Trinity.

In the 1600s narrow religious views had brought bloodshed, especially in the Thirty Years' War. "Maybe," people seem to have reasoned, "all religions can unite beneath the banner of Deism and end religious war." In this way, the false religion of Deism wove its way into the fabric of European and American religious life.

AD 1620 – AD 1814

*Jonathan Edwards preached the most famous sermon of the Great Awakening, "Sinners in the hands of an Angry God."*

# You say you want a revolution in religion?

## Revival in the colonies—the Northampton Awakening

When he was 18, an American colonist named Jonathan Edwards wrote in his diary, "Resolved: That all men should live to the glory of God. Resolved, secondly: That whether or not anyone else does, I will." And he did.

Yet Jonathan Edwards wasn't the type who could naturally move people's souls. In his day it was stylish to be short. Edwards was tall. Early in his ministry, he read his messages in a squeaky monotone. His sermons sometimes lasted two hours. He served as the pastor of Northampton Congregational Church for five years with few visible results.

Nevertheless, in 1734, flashes of revival began to pierce the Northampton church's spiritual darkness. The Holy Spirit convicted and converted 300 church members. What they once believed in their heads became embedded in their hearts. "The Town," Jonathan Edwards wrote, "was never so full of Love, nor of Joy, and yet so full of distress, as it was then." This first wave of revival lasted only three years. Had it not been for a new movement in Europe, the Northampton revival might never have developed into a "Great Awakening."

**from the ones who were there**

WORDS

**Jonathan Edwards**

"God seems now to be hastily gathering in his elect in all parts of the land.... Everyone that is out of Christ, awake and fly from the wrath to come. The wrath of Almighty God is now undoubtedly hanging over a great part of this congregation."

—*Sermons, "Sinners in the Hands of an Angry God"*

Read Jonathan Edwards's famous sermon: www.reformedsermonarchives. com/ed5.htm

## Revival in Europe—Pietism

In the late 1600s European Christianity wasn't in any better shape than American Christianity. God used a European movement known as Pietism [PI-eh-TIZM] to bring about a spiritual awakening that would reach around the world. Pietism began with a booklet entitled *Pious Desires* by a man named Jacob Spener. The book urged Christians to pursue a personal relationship with Christ through intense meditation on the Scriptures.

AD **1620** – AD **1814**

Count Nikolaus Zinzendorf was a wealthy noble who lived on a spacious estate near Dresden, Germany. Most importantly, he was an ardent Pietist.

Several nearby Catholic princes were still persecuting the Moravian Brethren, a small group of Bohemian Protestants. One rainy evening in 1722 a Moravian refugee knocked on Zinzendorf's front door. He asked if Nikolaus Zinzendorf might shelter the flourishing Moravian movement. Nikolaus agreed.

**Count Nikolaus Zinzendorf**

**Before Pietism, most churches sang only psalms. Nikolaus Zinzendorf, Charles Wesley, and Isaac Watts wrote Pietist hymns that remain popular today. Their hymns—like their theology—focused on the individual's relationship with Christ. In your church's hymnal, locate several songs written by Zinzendorf, Wesley, or Watts. Find one phrase in each song that reflects its Pietist origin.**

He helped the Moravians found a Christian community on his lands. They called their community "the Lord's watch" (or "Herrnhut"). By 1725, nearly one hundred Moravians had made Herrnhut their home.

Count Zinzendorf joined the Moravians in 1727. His Pietism infused the Moravians with a passion for prayer. Under Zinzendorf's guidance, the Moravians began round-the-clock prayer meetings. "The sacred fire was never permitted to go out on the altar (Lev. 6:13)," the community declared, "so the intercession of the saints should incessantly rise up to God." The Moravians at Herrnhut continued to meet for 24-hour prayer meetings for more than a century.

In 1731 Count Zinzendorf traveled to Denmark for an imperial meeting. There he met an African slave and a group of Christian Eskimos. Hans Egede, a Lutheran missionary, had led the Eskimos to Christ. God used the African and the Eskimos to infuse Zinzendorf with a passion for missions. In less than a century, the Pietist Moravians would send 300 missionaries throughout the world and baptize more than 3,000 converts.

**THINK** about **it**...
A few years after Herrnhut's prayer meetings began, the Great Awakening began in the American colonies. Coincidence or Providence? You decide.

So how did Pietism affect the Great Awakening? In 1736 an Anglican priest was sailing to the colony of Georgia to witness to Native Americans. Suddenly, a storm struck the ship. Most passengers screamed in terror. Yet a band of Moravian Pietists calmly sang psalms. The English priest was amazed. "This was," he wrote, "the most glorious day which I have hitherto seen." The priest's name? John Wesley.

AD 1620 – AD 1814

*Statue of John Wesley outside Wesley Church in Melbourne, Australia*

A Moravian later asked John, "Do you know Jesus Christ?"

"I know he is the Savior of the world," John answered.

"But do you know he has saved *you?*"

John stammered, "I ... I hope he has saved me."

"I went to America to convert the Indians," John wept that evening, "but, oh, who shall convert me?" After two fruitless years in the American colonies, John Wesley returned to England.

When John Wesley was a child, his mother, Susanna, had shared "awakening messages" in the Wesleys' home. "One Sunday," Susanna remarked, "we had above 200. Many went away, for want of room." Yet neither John nor his brother Charles had trusted Christ alone for salvation.

In 1738 Charles Wesley finally turned to Jesus. Three days later, his brother John visited Aldersgate Street in London. He heard someone teaching from Martin Luther's commentary on Romans and began to listen intently.

"About a quarter before nine," John wrote, "I felt my heart strangely warmed. I felt I did trust in Christ alone for salvation: And an assurance was given me, that he had taken away my sins, even mine, and saved me." This wasn't a case of heartburn. This was an awakening of the soul. This was conversion.

John and Charles Wesley had already organized Pietist societies, which they dubbed "Holy Clubs," within the Church of England. John urged members to seek God's presence through intense meditation on Scripture, fasting, and frequent participation in the Lord's Supper. John's well-ordered methods earned him the nickname "Methodist." The name stuck. After John's conversion, his "Methodist" followers encouraged outdoor preaching crusades. One Methodist preacher was Sarah Crosby. Sarah crisscrossed England, preaching the gospel, for 20 years.

*George Whitefield's preaching set the colonies ablaze with revival.*

The most popular Methodist preacher was George Whitefield [WHITT-feeld]. Whitefield had been a servant at Oxford University, working to pay his tuition. When Charles Wesley recruited the cross-eyed young servant, Whitefield showed little promise.

When Whitefield the former servant arrived in America, though, no one could ignore him. By the time his preaching tours throughout the colonies ended, eight out of every ten American colonists had heard a message from George Whitefield. Thousands of people responded positively to Whitefield's emotional pleas to accept Christ.

Whitefield preached in Northampton soon after the initial spiritual awakening in Jonathan Edwards' congregation. When Edwards heard Whitefield's message, Jonathan Edwards wept for joy. The response to Whitefield's messages was so amazing that people dubbed it the "Great Awakening."

For a few years, Whitefield and the Wesleys split over the doctrine of predestination. Whitefield was a Calvinist. The Wesleys' theology was closer to Arminianism than Calvinism. (If you can't define "Arminian" and "Calvinist," glance back at Chapter Nine.) Around 1749, Whitefield and the Wesleys agreed to disagree. Charles—always the poet—wrote, "Come, my Whitefield! (the strife is past)/ And friends at first are friends at last."

George Whitefield—unlike John Wesley—refused to condemn slavery. Whitefield did, however, preach to the African slaves. When Whitefield died, Phyllis Wheatley, an African-American poet, recalled: "He freely offer'd to the num'rous throng,/ That on his lips with list'ning pleasure hung. . . . 'Take [Christ], ye Africans, he longs for you,/ Impartial Savior is his title due.'"

Spiritual awakening continued in the colonies until the 1750s. In frontier areas and among the lower classes, Baptist and Methodist

**words from the ones who were there**

*George Whitefield*

"There are certainly Christians among all sects... I do not mean that there are Christians among ... those that deny the divinity of Jesus Christ ... I mean that there are Christians among other sects that may differ from us in the outward worship of God. Therefore, my friends, learn to be more catholic.... if you place the kingdom of God merely in a sect, you place it in that in which it doth not consist."
—*Sermons, "The Kingdom of God"*

*Some Methodist church leaders refused to ordain African-Americans as bishops. In 1816, Richard Allen formed the African Methodist Episcopal Church to give African-Americans freedom to serve as bishops.*

*(Courtesy of the Billy Graham Center Archives)*

AD 1620 – AD 1814

congregations blossomed. Then the colonies began their struggle for independence, and decline pierced the churches again.

## So you say you want a revolution in politics?

### Revolution in the churches, churches in the Revolution

*Firing a volley—Revolutionary War reenactment*

Religious rhetoric pervaded every stage of the colonial struggle for independence. If you don't believe me, pull a dollar bill from your purse or pocket. Assuming that three of your nation's initials are "U.S.A.," I can predict some of the words that appear on the back of your bill: *"Annuit Coeptis—Novus Ordo Seclorum."* Or "He has favored our enterprise—a new order now begins." This rhetoric didn't come only from the colonies' side, though. Both sides of the revolution claimed religious language in their attempts to defend their perspectives.

John Wesley strongly opposed the independence movement. Here's what Wesley had to say to patriots who wanted to rebel against the British: "I have no representation in Parliament, I am taxed, yet I am no slave.... Who then is a slave?... See the Negro, fainting under the load.... You and I, and the English in general, go where we will and enjoy the fruit of our labors: this is liberty. The Negro does not: this is slavery." Anglicans, Mennonites, and Quakers also refused to support the war. Many of them suffered dearly for their resistance. Patriots "tarred and feathered" Americans who objected to the war. Many objectors lost their property. Some lost their lives.

*The Quaker's Meeting House in Newport, Rhode Island, built in 1699*

In the end, most American churches supported the revolution. Many American pastors deserted their emphasis on revival and focused on defending the revolution instead. They turned biblical texts that described Israel's biblical battles into calls to fight the British. One pastor even proclaimed, "The cause of America is the cause of Christ."

Interestingly, despite the patriotism in many pulpits, the dominant religion of the founders of the United States was Deism, not Christianity. Thomas Jefferson referred to Jesus' miracles as "Vulgar ignorance ... and fabrications." Benjamin Franklin remarked, "I have some doubts as to

AD 1620 – AD 1814

**THINK** about **it**...
Many early Jews and Christians wanted to resist the Roman Empire—a pagan dictatorship in which they were taxed without representation. Read Matthew 22:17-21 and Romans 13:1-7. In light of these words from Jesus and Paul, should Christians revolt against their government? Why or why not?

[Jesus'] divinity … and think it needless to busy myself with it." The Declaration of Independence speaks of "Nature's God," a clearly Deist title.

Deists and Christians could agree on one issue, though: *Religious faith is not an issue that the state should dictate.* As such, when the new nation molded a Bill of Rights, the third article declared, "Congress shall make no law respecting an establishment of religion, or prohibiting the free exercise thereof." Roger Williams' dream had finally been realized. A government had refused to tie itself to any specific religious faith.

## What is truth?

A Roman ruler once muttered, "What is truth?" (John 18:38). It's still a popular question. One of today's most popular answers is, "The truth is whatever works for me." If something doesn't work for me, it must not be true. Or, at least, it must not be relevant.

did **you know?**

After the War for Independence, the Anglican Church in America became known as the Episcopal— or "Bishop-Guided" —Church.

That's what a lot of eighteenth-century people seemed to have believed. Ancient truths did not seem to be working. So many people forged a new faith—and a false vision of God. They placed their trust in human reason and called themselves "Deists."

A few people, however, tried to let God's Word stand above every human idea and institution. Roger Williams refused to tie the Christian faith to any human society. The Moravians begged for God's guidance, even when God seemed silent. Edwards and Whitefield continued to proclaim God's Word, even when it seemed uninspiring and irrelevant. When God's Word reigned supreme, people no longer needed to look for truth. "The way, the truth, and the life" revealed himself to them and revived their searching souls (John 14:6, 17).

AD 1620 – AD 1814

## 4 EVENTS you should know

**1. Publication of *Critique of Pure Reason* (1781):** According to Immanuel Kant's *Critique*, human reason can neither prove nor deny any spiritual reality, including the being of God.

**2. Formation of African Methodist Episcopal Church (1816).** Richard Allen, a free Black, formed the AME because some American Methodists refused to ordain African-American bishops.

**3. Five Fundamentals Declared (1895):** At a conference in Niagara the Evangelical Alliance, an association of conservative Christians, set forth five beliefs that they viewed as fundamental to their faith—the inerrancy of Scripture, and Jesus Christ's unique deity, virgin birth, substitutionary atonement, and future return.

**4. Boxer Rebellion (1901):** A Chinese political party reacted violently against foreign interference in China's national and cultural affairs. Many missionaries were murdered.

## 7 NAMES you should know

**1. G.W.F. Hegel (1770-1831):** German thinker. Taught that all ideas (theses), opposing opinions (antitheses), and debates (dialectics) are part of an upward process of intellectual evolution.

**2. Soren Kierkegaard (1813-1855):** Danish thinker. Emphasized subjectively experiencing God's revelation. Criticized coupling Christianity with any nation or culture.

**3. J. Nelson Darby (1800-1882):** Leader of the Plymouth Brethren, a Christian sect that stressed piety and simplicity. Taught a dispensational view of Scripture.

**4. Ralph Waldo Emerson (1803-1882):** Liberal philosopher and poet. Taught that "the highest revelation is that God is in every man."

**5. George Mueller (1805-1898):** Plymouth Brethren pastor and English social reformer. Founded orphanages that relied on Christians' gifts for support.

**6. Walter Rauschenbusch (1861-1918):** As a Baptist pastor in a New York slum, Rauschenbusch struggled to deal with social evils. He became the foremost proponent of the Social Gospel.

**7. Cyrus I. Scofield (1843-1921):** American lawyer. Wrote the study notes in the Scofield Reference Bible, which popularized dispensationalism among conservative Christians.

## 4 TERMS you should know

**1. Dispensationalism:** The belief that God's work can be divided into distinct eras (dispensations). Dispensationalism treats nearly all biblical references to "Israel" as references to the earthly nation. Most dispensationalists also believe that Christians will be removed from the world ("raptured") before God judges the world. J.N. Darby and C.I. Scofield popularized this view.

**2. Covenantalism:** The belief that God's covenants with Israel are fulfilled in the church. Covenantalism treats most New Testament references to "Israel" as references to the church (see Romans 9:6-7; Galatians 6:16). B.B. Warfield and J. Gresham Machen defended this view.

**3. Social Gospel:** A Protestant movement that stressed social reforms more than personal salvation.

**4. Holiness Movement:** A movement within Methodism that stressed a spiritual experience (a "second blessing") that leads to "entire sanctification" and "Christian perfection." Charles Finney spread Holiness ideas in America. A convention in Keswick, England, popularized the movement in Europe. In 1908 several Holiness groups merged to form the Nazarene Church. Modern Pentecostalism arose among Holiness Christians.

# CHAPTER 11

# Optimism
# Has Its Limits

## IN THIS CHAPTER
## 1780 – 1914

William Carey
Hudson Taylor • Barton W. Stone
Charles G. Finney
Charles H. Spurgeon • Dwight L. Moody

Every human heart longs for eternal satisfaction. The author of Ecclesiastes put it like this, "God has put eternity in their hearts" (Ecclesiastes 3:11). Fallen humanity tries to satisfy this eternal longing with more possessions, more pleasure, more knowledge, more power—with everything except the living God. All the heart finds is more restlessness, for only God can satisfy this longing. "O Lord, you have made us for yourself," Augustine of Hippo wrote, "and our heart is restless until it finds its rest in you."

**IN CASE you're confused**

The Modern Age lasted from the end of the Enlightenment in the late 1700s until the mid-1900s. In the Modern Age, people emphasized human potential, progress, and the material world.

In the nineteenth century, humanity's restless longings drove society to new heights of progress. With the progress came optimism. In some ways, the optimism of the Modern Age made sense. After all, Europe didn't suffer any major wars from the early 1800s until the beginning of the twentieth century. Mass production enabled people to purchase more possessions more cheaply. The train and the steamship conquered distance in ways that previous generations couldn't have imagined. Advances in farming diminished hunger. Medical discoveries reduced disease.

Yet the progress did not come cheaply. "It was," Charles Dickens observed, "the best of times, it was the worst of times." In many cases, people became commodities, consumed in the name of modern progress. European and American settlers transported "the white man's burden" into every corner of the globe. The dismal working conditions of the Industrial Revolution drove many people to despair. And still, the optimism about humanity's capacities persisted.

## Modern optimism and the modern missions movement

### The movement that began in a snuff box

Some Christians allowed the optimism of the Modern Age to produce a passion for missions. One of these mission-minded believers was an Englishman named William Carey. When William was seven, a skin disease forced him to find indoor employment; so he became a shoemaker.

**IN CASE you're confused**

Because of their emphasis on the limited—or "particular"—extent of Christ's redemption, Calvinist Baptists were known as "Particular Baptists." In the 1700s many Particular Baptists decided if God had predestined who would be saved, evangelism was unnecessary. Particular Baptist churches declined sharply until Carey helped them recover their passion for missions.

*William Carey*
(Courtesy of Billy Graham Center Archives)

William's cobbling skills were second-rate, but he was able to learn five languages while he waited for people to bring him shoes. Hoping that his language skills could lead to a better income than his cobbling skills, he opened a language school. Unfortunately, his skills as a teacher were even poorer than his skills with shoes.

Then God called him to be a Particular Baptist pastor. His preaching skills were worse than his teaching skills. Two years passed before his sermons even reached the minimum acceptable level for ordination.

When he was 26, Carey chose an unthinkable challenge—changing the Particular Baptists' perspective on missions. At this time, most Particular Baptists had concluded that it wasn't necessary to send people around the world to share the Gospel.

When Carey attempted to change his fellow pastors' minds, he was abiding by words he would later preach: "Expect great things from God! Attempt great things for God!" Again, failure flagged Carey's footsteps. A fellow pastor bellowed, "When God pleases to convert the heathen, he'll do it without consulting you or me!" Carey's written reply argued that Calvinism and evangelism go hand-in-hand.

Finally, Carey succeeded. A dozen Particular Baptist ministers formed a cross-cultural missions society "according to [Carey's] recommendations." Each one made a pledge to support the missions society financially. They dropped their initial pledges in a pastor's snuff box.

## "I can plod"

William Carey and a doctor volunteered to go to India. William's wife, Dorothy, and their children arrived in India the next year. Again, failure dogged William. The missionary doctor stole their funds. Two of the Careys' children died. While William focused on missions, depression seized his wife. After seven years, William had baptized only one person in India.

**THINK** about **it**...
Read 1 Samuel 3:11-14 and 1 Timothy 3:1-5. Is God pleased when ministers neglect their spouses or families for the church's sake? Does your church provide enough money and time for your missionaries' family lives? How about your ministers' needs?

AD 1780 – AD 1914

*Damien, a Roman Catholic priest in Molokai in the Hawaiian Islands, ministered to the spiritual and physical needs of 600 lepers and eventually contracted leprosy (Hansen's Disease) himself.*

Nevertheless, the cobbler's vision eventually engulfed the world. And what was his secret? "I can plod," he said. "I can persevere in any definite pursuit." Eventually, William Carey did translate and publish New Testaments in twenty-four of India's native languages. His work laid the foundation for thousands of future missionaries.

After William's death in 1834, Christian missionaries began to be sent into every corner of the world. Ann and Adoniram Judson continued William's work in India. John Veniaminou, an Orthodox priest, preached in Alaska. Damien, a Roman Catholic priest, cared for lepers in Hawaii and died of leprosy there. Another priest, Allemand Lavigerie, campaigned against slavery in Africa.

In 1860 Hudson and Maria Taylor founded the China Inland Mission. Both of them "became Chinese" to reach the Chinese. Hudson donned a black pigtail and baggy pantaloons. He also allowed single women to be missionaries. Hudson's fresh outlook opened doors for women like Lottie Moon and Amy Carmichael to spread the gospel in China and India.

Seventy-six years after William Carey's death, more than 1,200 missionaries from 160 mission boards met in Edinburgh, England. By that time, the number of Christian ministers living outside Europe and the Americas had increased more than one thousand percent.

Not bad for a movement that started in a snuff box.

## Modern optimism and the American frontier

Many people on the American frontier also embraced the optimism of the Modern Age. In fact, some folk were so optimistic that they embraced *universalism*—the belief that God would never condemn anyone. The result of such unbiblical theology was spiritual darkness.

Around 1800 many American Christians began to seek a renewed vision of the true God. The Presbyterians set aside days for prayer. They begged God to redeem their nation from darkness. In 1801 in Kentucky, an answer seemed to arrive in an unexpected way.

### The Cane Ridge Revival

Last weekend, I risked my life for Christ's sake. I spent three days at a youth retreat. The singers and speakers at Young Christians' Weekend in

Branson, Missouri, were completely contemporary. The retreat was, however, rooted firmly in the "camp meetings" of the 1800s.

When nineteenth-century families gathered for a camp meeting, they might set up tents near a church on Thursday or Friday. For two days, they sang and listened to speakers. On Sunday, anyone with a "communion token"— granted by one's local church—could share the Lord's Supper. The camp meetings were intended to provide Christian fellowship and spiritual renewal for frontier church members.

In 1801 all heaven broke loose at a camp meeting in Cane Ridge, Kentucky. Rev. Barton W. Stone expected ten thousand campers at most; more than twenty thousand Presbyterians, Baptists, and Methodists arrived.

On Saturday someone fell to the ground during a sermon and began to beg for God's grace. Other campers lurched and laughed hysterically. (Critics claimed that they "barked.") Hundreds of pioneers dropped

*Interior of the original meeting house at Cane Ridge, Kentucky*

to their knees and asked for God's mercy. The Second Great Awakening had begun. For 30 years, revival fires glimmered across America.

So, what actually happened at Cane Ridge, Kentucky? Critics called it a mass emotional outburst. "As many souls were conceived at the camp meetings," one person quipped, "as were saved." Were some antics bogus? Maybe. Yet what would cause hundreds of hardened pioneers to fall on their faces, weeping in repentance? What ... besides that Spirit who bursts into human self-satisfaction to convey God's word of judgment and grace?

## Do we really need denominations?

After the Cane Ridge camp meeting, Barton W. Stone took nineteenth-century optimism to a new level. He became convinced that if Christians forsook everything but the Bible, they could restore New Testament Christianity. Stone joined a band of former Baptists, led by Alexander Campbell. The Stone-Campbell Restorationist Movement urged believers to call themselves only "Christians" or "Disciples." "Where the Scriptures speak," they claimed, "we speak. Where the Scriptures are silent, we are silent."

The Restorationists' goal was to fulfill Jesus' prayer that all believers would be brought to complete unity (John 17:23). They urged

**Intrigued by the Restoration Movement?**

www.bible.acu.edu/crs/sites.asp

AD 1780 – AD 1914

did **YOU know?**

Christians to forsake all denominational loyalties and to unite on the basis of Scripture alone. Despite their desire for unity, the Restorationists soon dissolved into dozens of sects. Still, the movement left a lasting mark in at least one area: It weakened the grasp of older denominations and religious traditions on American Christians. The Restorationist legacy lingers today in the Churches of Christ, Disciples of Christ, and Christian churches.

## God's lawyer

One key figure in the Second Great Awakening was an aspiring lawyer named Charles Grandison Finney. A teenaged girl named Lydia Andrews met Charles in 1820. She quickly saw that he wasn't a Christian. So she began to pray for his salvation. A year later, God answered Lydia's request. Finney decided one morning that he would find God's grace that very day or die trying. Amid the autumn leaves of a New York forest, Charles G. Finney professed faith in Jesus. Little did Lydia know that the reply to her prayers would revolutionize American religion.

The day after he accepted Christ, Charles became a preacher. As he left his law practice, he remarked to a potential client, "I have a retainer from the Lord Jesus Christ to plead his cause, and I cannot plead yours." Charles' high-pressure preaching performances soon erupted across America.

Three years later, Lydia Andrews married Charles Finney. Lydia was shy. She struggled throughout her life with a poor self-image. Still, she traveled with Charles and led prayer vigils during his revivals.

Reason-centered optimism ruled Charles' theology. For Finney, revival was not a miracle. "Revival," he contended, "consists entirely in the right exercise of the powers of nature." Finney's so-called "New Measures" included pressuring people not to leave his meetings until they were sure of their salvation. Seekers walked the aisles and sought salvation on "anxious benches," areas near the platform set aside for prayer and counseling. So optimistic were Finney's beliefs that he even claimed that Christians could become morally perfect in this life.

Many of Finney's beliefs contradicted historic Christian theology. Still, some of his

**THINK** about it...
Do people in your church pray simply and spontaneously? Sponsor week-long revivals? Urge new converts to "walk the aisle?" If so, Finney's "New Measures" affect your church. What do you think of his "New Measures"? Is revival a human act or a divine act? Can Christians become perfect in this life?

Learn more about
Finney's theology:

www.spurgeon.org/~phil//
articles/finney.htm

practices can be respected. For example, Finney never divorced evangelism from social reform. Many churches charged "pew rent," yearly fees for attending church. Finney openly embraced all people, rich and poor. When Finney was president of Oberlin College, African-Americans and women attended the same classes as white males. The college later became a station on the Underground Railroad.

# Modern optimism and the rise of modern theology

**THINK** about **it...**

Are religious emotions wrong? No, not as long as Christians balance their emotional experiences with solid, biblical theology.

## A boring book and a new theology

Do you suffer from insomnia? I possess the perfect panacea—*Critique of Pure Reason* by Immanuel Kant.

Try to read the German philosopher's *Critique* and you will sleep—guaranteed. For contemporary readers, the book seems hopelessly boring. And yet, this text represents nothing less than a revolution in human thinking.

If you aren't an insomniac, let me attempt to summarize Kant's *Critique* in a couple of sentences: *Reason can comprehend anything within the phenomenal realm, or the realm of space and time. Beyond space and time—in the noumenal realm—reason is useless.*

What's wrong with Kant's ideas?

For starters, God surpasses space and time. So, if Kant was correct, reason would be unrelated to faith. Christianity would affect primarily what we do and feel, not what we think. In some sense, Christianity could cease to function as a commitment of one's whole being—including one's intellect—and could become perceived as nothing more than a system of ethics.

A few years after the *Critique* was published, another thinker built on the worldview for which Kant had laid the foundations. Friedrich Schleiermacher [SHLI-err-MAW-kerr] argued that the core of Christian faith is not any historical event, such as Jesus' resurrection. It is, instead, *a feeling of one's absolute dependence on a reality beyond oneself;* such awareness could (according to Schleiermacher) lead a person to imitate Jesus' good deeds.

"The true nature of religion is," Schleiermacher claimed, "immediate consciousness of the Deity as found in ourselves and in the world."

AD **1780** – AD **1914**

In truth, the resulting vision of God stood closer to the Force of *Star Wars* than to the God of Holy Scripture. Schleiermacher's new focus earned him the title "the father of modern theology" or even "the father of theological liberalism."

Christians still live with hints of the worldview that Kant and Schleiermacher developed—and not simply in the form of theological liberalism. Hints of their worldview can be found in the architecture and worship practices that surround us even now.

A 19th-Century Christian Church

## A field trip into the present

Let's take a trip to a small conservative, evangelical congregation in central Missouri. The name of the church is Elm Spring Baptist Church; the building is set alongside Interstate 44, on the way to Kansas City.

First, take a careful look at the windows. The sides curve inward to form points at the top. These windows are known as Gothic windows. Gothic designs first appeared in medieval cathedrals in the 1100s. In the 1800s, Gothic motifs became popular again, especially in church buildings, replacing the "classical" architectural styles of the Renaissance era. When the people at Elm, Missouri, designed their church building in the late 1800s, they followed a popular trend.

did **YOU know?**

> "A.W. Pugin claimed that you could not convert England to Christianity with pagan, by which he meant classical, architecture. For the Houses of Parliament he designed Gothic inkwells, thus encouraging parliamentarians to write their letters in a Christian frame of mind, or at least a Christian frame of ink. There were Gothic railway stations, Gothic prisons, Gothic bakeries and Gothic horse troughs, though no Gothic horses."
>
> *From Gavin White, How the Churches Got to Be the Way They Are (Philadelphia: Trinity Press, 1990) 13-14*

**IN CASE you're confused**

The barbarian Goths migrated into the Roman Empire in the early Middle Ages. Late medieval cathedrals were called "Gothic" because they blended barbarian ideals with classical Roman designs. The nineteenth-century "Gothic Revival" (also known as "Romanticism") popularized Gothic designs again.

Why did medieval designs become popular in the 1800s? Nineteenth-century folk wanted feelings to fuel their Christian faith. Many people viewed the Middle Ages as a romantic era of pure feelings. So, they revived designs and motifs from the Middle Ages.

Follow me through the front doors of Elm Spring Baptist Church. Do you hear the congregation singing a nineteenth century hymn?

"The great Physician now is near, the sympathizing Jesus;/He speaks the drooping heart to cheer, Oh! hear the voice of Jesus." Do you hear the emphasis on feeling God? Even though the theology of such churches in the 1800s and early 1900s was far from Schleiermacher's, these sorts of emotional lyrics are rooted in the "romantic" feeling-centered worldview of the nineteenth century. And still today, we sing many of these nineteenth century hymns.

## Modern optimism and the quest for the historical Jesus

*Friedrich Schleiermacher, the father of modern theology*

Schleiermacher's new focus also encouraged a process that became known as "higher criticism." Higher critics tried to reconstruct the various sources that biblical authors might have used. In the process, many higher critics began to question the Bible's accuracy. After all, if faith was—as Kant and Schleiermacher implied—a matter for people's emotions and ethics, couldn't the Bible be merely a record of ancient people's feelings about God?

Some higher critics became convinced that the Gospel writers didn't write about the real, historical, flesh-and-blood Jesus Christ. Instead, the Gospel writers described how the stories of Jesus transformed the early Christians' lives. According to these critics, Jesus' miracles were legends, not historical events. Jesus' death was an example, not a sacrifice. What was revived on Easter was the disciples' love for Jesus, not Jesus himself.

For these critics, all that mattered were Jesus' teachings about divine love and social reform. The essence of Christianity was, one liberal theologian claimed, "the universal fatherhood of God, the brotherhood of man, and the infinite worth of the human soul." The higher critics' search for the supposed "real Jesus" became known as "the quest for the historical Jesus."

## Modern optimism and social reform

### The era of reform

A very contemporary world usually surrounds my writing—McDonald's, when I first wrote this text. Today, however, I am surrounded by a 1562 edition of Calvin's *Institutes,* an original Geneva Bible and an 1856 printing of

ON the web

Take a virtual tour of Spurgeon's library:

www.spurgeon.org/fsl.htm

AD 1780 – AD 1914

*Pilgrim's Progress.* What encompasses me is the library of a nineteenth-century English pastor named Charles H. Spurgeon.

It was in Spurgeon's era that Christians—many of whom took a postmillennial view of the end of time—began to ask, "How can Christ's kingdom come while orphans roam the streets?" Those questions, asked in the midst of the Industrial Revolution, turned the 1800s into an era of social reform.

In the late 1700s Robert Raikes had started "Sunday schools" to educate urban children in Britain. In the 1800s the concept of Sunday schools spread to the United States. In this same

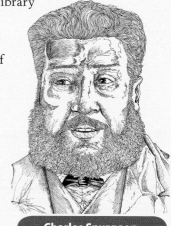

**Charles Spurgeon**

era, Charles Sheldon's book *In His Steps* urged Christians to express their faith through social action. Angelina and Sarah Grimke crusaded for women's rights. William Wilberforce, an evangelical Anglican and a member of Parliament, worked to outlaw slavery in Britain. Catherine and William Booth organized the Salvation Army. Wealthy British evangelicals founded the YMCA.

## IN CASE you're confused

In the 1800s many Christians were postmillennialists; they believed Jesus would return after (post-) God's people initiated God's reign on earth. Premillennialists believe Jesus will return before (pre-) this reign begins. Dispensational premillennialists typically believe God will "rapture" Christians out of the world before a time of tribulation. Historic premillennialists believe Christians will endure tribulation. Amillennialists place the kingdom here and now, among God's people.

In the process of such social reforms, some church members allowed their emphasis on social reforms to overwhelm their concern for evangelism. This tendency became known as the "Social Gospel."

Charles H. Spurgeon, pastor of the Metropolitan Tabernacle in London, was one preacher who balanced social reforms with an emphasis on evangelism. He denounced American slavery. He founded schools, orphanages, and nursing homes. During a strike, Spurgeon took the side of the poor laborers.

At the same time, Spurgeon never believed that social reforms were enough. For Spurgeon, social reform was meaningless without sound theology and a personal relationship with Christ. Every Sunday, more than 6,000 people packed the London Metropolitan Tabernacle to hear Spurgeon's homespun metaphors and his passionate pleas for people to accept Christ.

AD 1780 – AD 1914

## The scratch of slavery

In the United States, an African-American Christian named Isabella became a resounding voice for social reform. Isabella had been a slave in the southern United States. She gained her freedom around 1843. Afterward, she became convinced that Christ was calling her to "travel up and down the land, showing the people their sins." She even changed her name to fit her mission.

*Sojourner Truth albumen silver print c. 1864 National Portrait Gallery*

Throughout the northern United States, "Sojourner Truth" preached about slavery and salvation.

In one city, a man snarled at Sojourner, "I don't care any more for your talk than I do for the bite of a flea."

"Perhaps not," she replied, "but, Lord willing, I'll keep you scratching."

Sojourner's messages were so well-crafted that some people denied she was a woman. Others doubted that she had ever been a slave. Still, she kept Americans "scratching"—chafing at the sin of slavery.

# Modern optimism and the coming kingdom

## Miller's mixed-up mathematics

While Sojourner kept America scratching, other preachers kept America unstrung. William Miller, a self-proclaimed biblical scholar from Vermont, claimed Christ would return by March 21, 1844. Spring 1844 passed without a peep from Gabriel's trumpet. Miller decided he had made a mathematical mistake. Christ would return, Miller claimed, on October 22, 1844. Again, nothing happened. (A New York farmer did later claim that he saw a *vision* of the Second Coming on October 22.)

Even after this double disappointment, a few people remained convinced by Miller's math. One of them was a nineteen-year-old woman named Ellen G. H. White. Ellen prophesied that one reason Christ hadn't returned was because Christians were not obeying God's Old Testament laws. Her Sabbath-keeping followers became known as "Seventh-Day Adventists."

did **YOU** know**?**

William Miller wasn't the only person to express his optimism through failed prophecies. Charles Taze Russell claimed that Jesus returned spiritually in 1872. Russell's followers—known today as "Jehovah's Witnesses"—revived the Arian heresy. Mary Baker Eddy claimed that Christ returned around 1875, through her Gnostic-flavored writings. She founded the Christian Scientists.

AD 1780 – AD 1914

*Americans on both sides of the Civil War assumed that God supported their cause. (Civil War reenactment)*

## The American Civil War

After a stock-market crash in 1857, a Third Great Awakening began in Canada and swept England and America. Prayer revivals, led by a Methodist laywoman named Phoebe Palmer, became popular in the northeastern United States. Yet nothing could divert the coming conflict over American slavery. On the eve of the war, Methodists, Presbyterians, and Baptists all suffered internal splits over the slavery issue.

did **YOU** **know?**

In 1847 Missouri outlawed African-American schools inside the state's borders. John Berry Meachum, a Black Baptist, conducted Sunday school on a steamboat in the Mississippi River near St. Louis. For nearly 20 years, Black children learned to read on Meachum's "Steamboat Sunday School."

Throughout the Civil War, Americans on both sides assumed that God supported their cause. A Southern pastor claimed, "The Confederacy will be the Lord's peculiar people." A Union victory, a Northern writer contended, would unleash the "millennial glory."

Only a few Americans realized that God's reign does not depend on human triumphs or defeats. One of them was an unbaptized politician who never joined a church. "Each party claims to act in accordance with the will of God," he noted. "Both may be, and one must be, wrong.... It is quite possible that God's purpose is something different from the purpose of either party." The politician's name? Abraham Lincoln.

After the Civil War southern farmers freed four million slaves. This newfound freedom could not, however, erase centuries of racism. Slavery lingered for over a century under new names—names like "sharecropper" and "Jim Crow laws."

## The optimism unravels

did **YOU** **know?**

In the late 1800s the optimism that had marked the Modern Age began to unravel. Liberal churches had reduced the Christian faith to a "Social Gospel." Conservative church members saw that social reforms were not enough. Yet they couldn't agree on an alternative. Some religious leaders, like D.L. Moody and Pope Pius IX, tried to resist and reject the modern world. Others, like B.B. Warfield, tried to express their faith in ways that a modern world could understand. Let's look at Moody, Warfield, and Pius

Lyman Beecher, a Congregational pastor, sent rifles to anti-slavery forces in the Midwestern United States. The weapons were shipped in crates marked "Bibles;" so, the rifles became known as "Beecher's Bibles." Beecher's daughter wrote the book *Uncle Tom's Cabin.*

AD **1780** – AD **1914**

IX, to understand how different religious leaders responded to this new, modern world.

## Resisting the modern age—Pope Pius IX

By the middle of the nineteenth century, modern people's mistrust of traditional powers had sapped the pope's religious and political powers. Pope Pius IX was slow to accept such changes. He denounced the idea that "the Roman pontiff should harmonize himself ... with recent civilization."

In 1854 Pope Pius IX defied attempts to limit his authority in doctrinal matters. He personally decreed the doctrine of the Immaculate Conception—the tradition that Mary was free from original sin. Many Catholics questioned the new dogma. What they were protesting was not so much the doctrine itself, though. What they questioned was whether a pope could define a doctrine without the consent of a church council. In other words, was the pope infallible when he alone defined a doctrine? Or could only a council make such claims?

The pope convened a council to answer the question. In 1869 more than 500 bishops gathered at the Vatican. This council, known as the First Vatican Council, lasted nearly a year. Near the end, Pope Pius IX joked, "If the council lasts much longer, I shall doubtless be infallible, but I shall also be bankrupt!"

did **YOU** know**?**

Only once has any pope used the infallibility ascribed by the First Vatican Council. In 1950 Pope Pius XII declared, "When the course of [Mary's] life was finished, she was taken up body and soul into glory."

In the end, the doctrine of the Immaculate Conception was confirmed, and the bishop of Rome was declared infallible—but only when he "defines a doctrine ... by the Divine assistance promised to him in the blessed Peter." Even with the power of infallibility, a pope can only redefine the outward expressions of the Catholic Church's faith. No pope or council has the power to change any essential doctrine of the Church.

## Rejecting the modern age—Dwight L. Moody

Dwight L. Moody arrived in Chicago as a teenaged shoe salesman with a very modern goal—making money. He was a backwoods bumpkin with a fifth-grade education and lots of energy. He had been a Christian less than a year. In only five years, he saved $7,000. Then, a financial panic rocked his plans. Moody went from selling shoe soles to winning people's souls. He began to witness full-time.

In 1871 a fire destroyed large portions of Chicago, including Moody's home. Instead of lamenting his loss, D.L. Moody headed across the Atlantic

AD 1780 – AD 1914

*Dwight L. Moody*

Ocean to preach in Britain. There another preacher remarked, "The world has yet to see what God can do with a man fully consecrated to him." Those words lit a blaze in Moody's soul.

The next year, Ira Sankey, a singer and composer, joined Moody for a revival tour. Moody aimed his simple sermons at the middle class—a class that also enjoyed Sankey's singing. In Great Britain alone, four million people flocked to the Moody-Sankey revivals.

D.L. Moody ignored modern scholarship and rejected theological studies. "Except to go in one door and out the other," he once boasted, "I've never been to seminary." For Moody, the Bible was a source of simple quotes, often treated without reference to their contexts. He traded the optimistic postmillennialism of previous generations for a dispensational premillennialist view of the endtimes. His sole focus was soul-winning. "The world [is] a wrecked vessel," he once said, "God has given me a lifeboat and said, 'Moody, save all you can.'" And that's precisely the goal on which Moody focused his life.

## Redeeming the modern age—The Fundamentals

Perhaps one of the wisest and most balanced responses to the Modern Age arose at a Bible conference in Niagara, New York. There, several conservative believers in Jesus Christ listed five truths that are basic (or, "fundamental") to Christian faith. These five truths were:

1. Jesus was uniquely divine,

2. He was born of a virgin,

3. He died as a sacrifice for sin, and

4. He will come again.

5. The Scriptures contain no errors; the Bible is "inerrant."

After the conference, a Christian entrepreneur financed a series of pamphlets that defended these five basic, biblical beliefs. The pamphlets contained articles written by prominent Christian scholars. The pamphlets were called *The Fundamentals.* Persons who accepted the five basic beliefs became known as "fundamentalists."

Like Moody, the authors of these pamphlets believed in the absolute authority and inerrancy of Scripture. Unlike Moody, they believed that faith in the accuracy of Scripture could go hand-in-hand with serious theological scholarship that wrestled intelligently with the claims of the modern world.

*Some members of the Women's Christian Temperance Union, including Carrie Nation, were known to burst into saloons with hatchets, attempting to rid their communities of alcoholism.*

The pamphlets did not try to fight against every aspect of the Modern Age. Some of the writers were postmillennialists; others were premillennialists. Three authors in the first volume of *The Fundamentals* believed that God may have used evolution in his creation of the earth and that God's creation occurred over a long period of time. B.B. Warfield—a major contributor to the pamphlets, a staunch inerrantist, and the principal of Princeton University—declared, "I do not think that there is any general statement in the Bible or any part of the account of creation, either as given in Genesis 1 and 2 or elsewhere alluded to, that need be opposed to evolution."

Most of the authors of these pamphlets even embraced the modern world's optimistic confidence in human reason and progress. It would take an economic depression and two world wars to shatter that confidence.

**did YOU know?**

In the 1800s women couldn't vote. In some areas, a husband could beat his wife, as long as he used a stick no bigger around than his thumb. After the Civil War, women's rights movements arose. Some women—like Lucretia Mott and Susan B. Anthony—focused on voting rights. Others— like Frances Willard and Carrie Nation—worked to outlaw liquor.

*Frances Willard served as president of the Women's Christian Temperance Union from 1879 until her death in 1898.*

Special thanks to the Partee Center for Baptist Historical Studies and the Spurgeon Library at William Jewell College for providing lodging, research facilities, and access to Spurgeon's archives while I completed this chapter.

AD 1780 – AD 1914

**4 EVENTS you should know**

**1. Azusa Street Revival (1906):** William Seymour, a Black Holiness preacher, founded a mission on Azusa Street in Los Angeles. There, many people began to speak in "unknown tongues." The Pentecostal movement is still growing today.

**2. Edinburgh Conference (1910):** More than 1,200 delegates gathered for this missions conference. The gathering helped to trigger the modern ecumenical movement.

**3. Wycliffe Bible Translators Organized (1934):** Cam Townsend founded this organization to translate the Bible into other languages. By 1980, the Bible was translated into more than 1,600 languages. Translation continues today.

**4. Dead Sea Scrolls Discovered (1947):** A shepherd-boy found the earliest known copies of the Jewish Scriptures at Qumran, near the Dead Sea. The scrolls verified that modern copies of the Hebrew Bible were nearly identical to ancient copies.

**7 NAMES you should know**

**1. Charles Fox Parham (1873-1929):** Holiness preacher. Taught that speaking in "unknown tongues" was the sign of the "second blessing." One of his students was William Seymour.

**2. Teilhard de Chardin (1881-1955):** Controversial Catholic theologian and scientist. Taught that all life is a process that will eventually be drawn into God's being. For Teilhard, God is both the goal of this process and the power within the process. Teilhard influenced the beliefs that became known as "process theology."

**3. Albert Schweitzer (1875-1965):** Theologian, musician, and missionary doctor. Schweitzer criticized the "quest for the historical Jesus." At the same time, he argued that Jesus mistakenly expected the immediate end of the world.

**4. Paul Tillich (1886-1965):** Liberal Lutheran theologian. Tried to bridge the gap between modern culture and Christianity by adapting the Christian faith to modern people's questions.

**5. Harry Emerson Fosdick (1878-1969):** Liberal Baptist pastor. His sermon "Shall the Fundamentalists Win?" questioned the inerrancy of Scripture and the Virgin Birth.

**6. Bob Pierce (1914-1978):** Evangelical leader. Founder of World Vision and Samaritan's Purse.

**7. Hans Kung (1928- ):** Controversial Catholic theologian. In the late 1960s he questioned the extent of the pope's power. His license to teach as a Catholic theologian was withdrawn in 1979.

**4 TERMS you should know**

**1. Fundamentalists:** Originally referred to people who accepted the five fundamental beliefs (see Chapter Eleven). By the 1950s the term referred to conservative Christians who focused on precise personal standards and on separation from every hint of liberalism.

**2. Theological Liberals:** Persons who altered Christian theology to fit the outlook of the Modern Age by separating Christian theology from traditional doctrines and biblical texts.

**3. Evangelicals:** Originally synonymous with "fundamentalists." During the 1950s the term "evangelical" replaced "new [or neo-] evangelical" as a description of believers who emphasized Christian unity, the truthfulness and unique authority of Scripture, salvation by grace through exclusive faith in Jesus Christ, and the need for evangelism.

**4. Postmodernity:** The worldview that arose at the end of the Modern Age. The Modern Age lasted from the late 1700s until the mid-1900s. Modernity stressed words, reason, and the material world. Postmodernity has tended to emphasize personal experiences and the spiritual realm.

# CHAPTER 12

# Modern, Postmodern, and Beyond

IN THIS CHAPTER
1906 – 2009

Karl Barth • C.S. Lewis
Charles Fox Parham
Dietrich Bonhoeffer
Second Vatican Council
Mother Teresa • Billy Graham

D o you wear glasses? If so, chances are that you're either hyperopic or myopic. If you have bifocals, you have the dubious distinction of living with dual deficiencies. To be myopic means that the farther an object gets from you, the fuzzier it seems to your eyes. If you're hyperopic, distant objects seem clear, but nearby objects look blurry.

Doing history is unavoidably hyperopic.

Here's what I mean by that: Events that happened long ago seem clearer than events that are near. That's what people are hinting at when they mutter the cliché, "Hindsight is twenty-twenty." The further an event has passed into the past, the easier it becomes to glimpse its real meaning.

Which is why it's difficult—and maybe even a bit dangerous—to say much about Christianity in the twentieth and twenty-first centuries.

Truth be told, neither I nor any other human being knows how terms such as "postmodern," "liberal," or even "evangelical" will strike people's ears in the future. Such terms could remain highly significant. Or they may seem about as trendy as the mauve sanctuaries of the early 1990s, the stone-washed jeans and poufy hair that seemed so stylish in the 1980s, or the avocado shag carpeting that was all the rage in the 1970s.

With that in mind, it's my hope that you see a strand of humility woven through the fabric of these pages. At the core of this hoped-for humility is a simple recognition: God alone possesses exhaustive knowledge of past, present, and future. As such, I don't know whether the importance that I ascribe to trends, people, and events of the twentieth and twenty-first centuries rightly reflects their significance in God's design. Yet, simply because our historical knowledge is hyperopic doesn't release us from a responsibility to grapple with what we do know, striving to see how and where God is working in our world.

In this chapter, we'll look at four trends that seem to be shaping Christianity's third millennium:
(1) First, we'll consider in detail the rise of evangelicalism, followed by a look at (2) the rise of Pentecostalism and (3) postmodernity. (4) Last, we'll examine how the principal percentage of the world's Christian population is shifting from Europe and North America to Africa and Asia, as well as what that means for the future of Christianity.

AD 1906 – AD 2009

# The rise of evangelicalism

## "Nineteenth-century theology no longer held any future for me"

At the end of the twentieth century, at least one trend was clear: Active membership in theologically liberal churches was declining. Between the 1960s and the early 2000s, more than two million members left one theologically liberal denomination; another has lost just over one million. Between 1990 and 2000 alone, liberal denominations lost between five percent and fifteen percent of their membership. According to a sociological study entitled *Vanishing Boundaries*, the

from the **ones** who were there

**H. Richard Niebuhr,** American theologian describing nineteenth-century liberal theology: "A God without wrath brought men without sin into a kingdom without judgment through ... a Christ without a cross." —*The Kingdom of God in America*, 193

*Karl Barth*

pattern of decline looks something like this: Pastors, then laypeople, embrace the idea that faith in Jesus isn't the sole pathway to salvation; within a few decades, church membership declines because the line between belief and unbelief has vanished. Simply put, if it isn't absolutely necessary to believe in Christ, why be active in the fellowship of people that claims his name? If the stories of Jesus are mere mythic fiction, why are they any better than the mythic fictions of the culture and of other religions? Some might disagree, but I think that a theologian named Karl Barth glimpsed these problems with theological liberalism long before the declines began.

When World War I erupted in 1914, Karl Barth [pronounced BART] was pastoring a small church in Switzerland. Karl Barth's professors, well-schooled in the nineteenth-century theological liberalism of Schleiermacher, had trained Barth how to dissect biblical texts and to discover the supposed human sources behind them. Yet, for most of Barth's teachers, the power behind the biblical text was not its witness to God's decisive actions in human history; the text was only meaningful because of how it could help people to become aware of their dependence on a power

from the **ones** who were there

**Karl Barth** criticizing the "God" of nineteenth-century theology: "[This deity] isn't even righteous. He cannot prevent his worshippers ... from falling upon one another with fire and sword.... It is time for us to confess openly and gladly that this god, to whom we have built the tower of Babel, is not God. He is an idol. He is dead." —*Das Wort Gottes und die Theologie*, 22

AD 1906 – AD 2009

greater than themselves. Theological liberalism consisted "of a God without wrath [bringing] men without sin into a kingdom without judgment through the ministrations of a Christ without a cross." The lines between definite belief and unbelief had eroded. What mattered most, from the perspective of theological liberalism, was helping society to progress in knowledge and ethics—and often, European culture was viewed as the pinnacle of this "progress."

What Barth soon realized as a church leader was that such perspectives offered little hope to the people in his congregation. The young pastor found himself ill-equipped "to undertake activity in the pulpit or at the sick-bed."

Soon after German soldiers invaded Luxembourg and Belgium, a statement supporting Germany's war policy surfaced in Switzerland. Nearly all of Barth's professors had signed the statement. His professors had tightly tied their theology to their ideals of modern progress. So tightly had they linked these ideals together that they were willing to connect Christ's name to Germany's military campaign. German theologians weren't alone in this perspective. During World War I, every German soldier marched into battle with the same words engraved on his belt buckle: "Gott mit uns" ("God is with us").

After he read the statement supporting Germany's war policy, Karl Barth later recalled, "Nineteenth-century theology no longer held any future for me."

In his despair, Barth turned to the Bible. In the past, he had read the Bible as a human religious record. Now he began to read the Bible as a testimony to God's decisive actions in human history. In 1919 Barth published a commentary on Paul's letter to the Romans that introduced his radical perspective to pastors throughout Europe. Among pastors who were willing to question theological liberalism, the result was a renewed focus on God's transcendence, above and beyond every human effort or institution.

In his zeal to abandon theological liberalism, Barth argued that nothing within fallen creation can reveal truth about God. To understand why Barth made this argument, remember where nineteenth-century liberal theologians had focused their attentions: Theological liberalism had focused on finding the presence of the divine in the created order and in human feelings of absolute dependence on this greater power. And what was the result? Theological liberals did not view definite, essential beliefs about God and about the Bible as vital. Adolph von Harnack, one of Karl

*In the trenches: Infantry with gas masks, Ypres, 1917*

Barth's professors, had defined the essential truths of Christianity as "the universal fatherhood of God, the universal brotherhood of man, and the infinite value of the soul"—nothing more.

Karl Barth reacted against such perspectives by placing the Word of God at the center of his theology. Here's where Barth's theology gets a little confusing, though: For Barth, no human object or entity can be identified with the Word of God; alone, not even Scripture ought to be considered God's Word, according to Barth. For Barth, there is only one Word of God, and this Word is not an object but an event—the living event of God's self-revelation, expressed supremely in Jesus Christ. As such, the Bible couldn't be God's Word; instead, the Bible *became* God's Word whenever the Holy Spirit revealed Jesus through the Scriptures. Similarly, preaching could become God's Word whenever the Holy Spirit used a preacher's words to point to Jesus. This doesn't mean that Barth downplayed the value of the Bible, though. For Barth, faithful exposition of Scripture was essential for people to experience any authentic awareness of God. According to Barth, "The presence … of Jesus Christ both in His congregation and in the world has its visible form, in the time between His resurrection and His return, in the witness of His chosen and appointed prophets and apostles.… [The biblical authors] bear witness to Jesus Christ, and thus to the work of the gracious God, as the beginning, middle, and end of all things."

Some portions of Barth's theology echoed the theology of the sixteenth-century reformers, especially of John Calvin. At the same time, much of Barth's thinking differed radically from historic Christian theology. That's why Barth's approach became known as "neo-Reformation" or "neo-orthodox" theology.

did **YOU** know?

Fragments of modern optimism persisted in the United States until the Great Depression began in 1929. During the Depression, an American pastor named Reinhold Niebuhr employed Barth's theology to find a halfway point between liberalism and fundamentalism. Niebuhr also wrote the famous Serenity Prayer: "Lord, give us the serenity to accept what cannot be changed, courage to change what should be changed, and wisdom to distinguish the one from the other."

## The problem with progress

Liberal theologians of the late 1800s and early 1900s, intoxicated by the optimism of the Modern Age, had stressed humanity's capacity to create a perfect world. During World War I, the progress that had promised to produce a perfect world led not only to modern medicines and motor-cars but also to mustard gas and machine guns. Ten million soldiers died on the battlefields of Europe. Europe's modern optimism began to die there too—and yet, old theological habits die hard. Despite Barth's challenge to theological liberalism, much European theological thinking after Karl Barth maintained the same skepticism about Scripture that had tarnished theological liberalism.

AD 1906 – AD 2009

Even some theologians who were identified as "neo-orthodox" at first, such as Reinhold Niebuhr and Rudolf Bultmann, treated the Gospels as fictional myths—as myths that tell us much about the feelings of first-century church members but nothing about the historical Jesus. Rudolf Bultmann treated the historical and miraculous claims of the New Testament as "husks" that could be discarded to experience a "kernel" of ethical truth. In an essay entitled "The Impossible Ethical Ideal," Reinhold Niebuhr echoed nineteenth-century liberalism by suggesting that the "Jesus of history" was not the same person as the "Christ of faith" in whom Christians placed their trust.

> **IN CASE** you're **confused...**
>
> "Fundamentalist" originally referred to anyone who accepted the five fundamental beliefs (see p. 162). After World War I, many conservative Christians added other beliefs, such as premillennialism and a rejection of evolution to the five fundamentals.

## John Barleycorn, voting women, and the rise of American fundamentalism

Christians on the other side of the Atlantic Ocean also glimpsed inadequacies in theological liberalism—but the North American response followed a different path from Barth's.

Even after World War I, the idealistic optimism of the Modern Age remained strong in the United States. This optimism impelled moral crusades that called for the recognition of women's right to vote and for the prohibition of alcoholic beverages. The United States prohibited the manufacture and sale of beverage alcohol in 1919; one year later, women received the right to vote. When Congress mandated Prohibition, a popular baseball-player-turned-evangelist named Billy Sunday preached a public funeral for "John Barleycorn," the evangelist's epithet for alcohol abuse.

*Detroit police inspecting equipment found in a clandestine underground brewery during the prohibition era.*

Yet Prohibition couldn't keep John Barleycorn in the grave. And, in 1920, women and men alike chose one of America's most corrupt leaders as president. Even worse, increasing numbers of people were living out the freewheeling optimism of the Modern Age in ways far removed from moral crusades—primarily, the pursuit of personal pleasure. This became the era of jazz and flappers, of short skirts and speakeasies. In the minds of many people, something seemed seriously wrong in America.

## Shall the Fundamentalists win?

If something is wrong, people naturally look for the problem. Usually, it's easier to locate one problem than to admit there might be several problems.

In this context, conservative church leaders became convinced that liberalism was the primary problem, while theologically liberal church leaders began to view conservatives as the problem. Harry Emerson Fosdick, pastor of First Presbyterian Church in New York City, even preached a message in 1922 entitled, "Shall the Fundamentalists Win?" According to Fosdick,

*Harry Emerson Fosdick*

conservative Christians should make space for liberal beliefs. In the process of making his case, Fosdick reinterpreted the inerrancy of Scripture, the virgin conception of Jesus, and the second coming of Jesus in ways that denied any miraculous elements. The American industrialist John D. Rockefeller funded the nationwide distribution of this call for the acceptance of liberal theology. Two years later, Fosdick felt compelled to resign from his congregation.

"These are the things we have stood for," Fosdick declared in his farewell message, "tolerance, an inclusive Church, the right to think religion through in Modern terms, the social applications of the principles of Jesus, the abiding verities and experiences of the gospel.... They call me a heretic. I am proud of it." Following Fosdick's resignation, Rockefeller had Riverside Church built in Manhattan for the purpose of providing Fosdick a place to preach.

In the 1920s, many conservative Christians increasingly reacted against theological liberalism by rejecting every notion that might be associated with liberalism. Even though their beliefs grew far narrower than the five fundamentals that had been declared at the Niagara Bible Conference in the late 1800s, these conservatives became known as "fundamentalists." Liberalism had sometimes been linked with a postmillennial view of the end of time; so fundamentalists fled to dispensational premillennialism. Because theological liberalism dominated so many seminaries, fundamentalists often rejected academic training in theology. Billy Sunday was known to boast, "I don't know any more about theology than a jackrabbit knows about ping-pong!" The evolutionary theories of Charles Darwin were crucial to the thinking of many liberals; so fundamentalists rejected every form of evolution. In 1925, fundamentalists in Tennessee even convinced their state legislature to pass the Butler Act "prohibiting the teaching of the Evolution Theory in all public schools of Tennessee." The American Civil Liberties Union (ACLU) placed advertisements in newspapers, offering to provide legal defense for anyone willing to defy the Butler Act. That summer, the debate over evolution metamorphosed into a nationwide media melee.

AD 1906 – AD 2009

John Scopes in 1925

## The Scopes Trial

John Scopes coached football in Dayton, Tennessee. Scopes also taught freshman biology. After the Butler Act passed, a few citizens in Dayton wanted to make their town famous. A local businessman convinced Scopes to say that he had claimed apes and people sprang from a common ancestor.

Scopes' case went to trial in July 1925. The trial should have been open-and-shut. After all, Scopes himself said that he had violated the Butler Act! But one lawyer who volunteered to provide a defense was Clarence Darrow, a well-known agnostic. Three-time presidential candidate and former Secretary of State William Jennings Bryan was asked to prosecute Scopes. With these lawyers in place, the case quickly became perceived as a face-off between liberalism and fundamentalism. Throughout the trial, more than one thousand spectators tried to squeeze into a small, sweltering courtroom to witness this historic showdown.

It was a made-for-television event.

Unfortunately for such an event, television hadn't been invented yet, so most Americans settled for a radio broadcast instead. On the fifth day of the trial, Darrow placed Bryan on the witness stand.

"Do you claim that everything in the Bible should be literally interpreted?" Darrow demanded.

Bryan replied, "I believe everything in the Bible should be interpreted as given there. Some of the Bible is given illustratively."

Darrow began to prod Bryan about the earth's age, "Does the statement 'The morning and the evening were the first day' mean anything to you?"

"I do not," Bryan admitted, "think it necessarily means a 24-hour day.... My impression is that they were periods." Darrow tried to force Bryan to state the length of these "periods" until Bryan bellowed, "The only purpose Mr. Darrow has is to slur the Bible!"

from the **ones** who were there

"At the best, Mr. Darrow's agnostic views completely disqualify him to represent any but the most extreme antagonists of the Bible.... There is a convincing argument for the conservative position, but Mr. Bryan ... has neither the mind nor the temper for the task."
*The Christian Century, Editorial on the Scopes trial, 1925*

"I object!" Darrow retorted, "I am examining you on your fool ideas that no intelligent Christian on earth believes."

In the end, Clarence Darrow himself asked that Scopes be found guilty so that Bryan wouldn't be able to deliver a closing statement. Eight minutes later, the trial was over. John Scopes was convicted of violating the Butler Act. William Jennings Bryan offered to pay the football coach's fine. Despite Scopes' conviction, neither side emerged triumphant; the tensions between fundamentalists and moderates only intensified.

## Getting together, falling apart

In the opening years of the twentieth century, organizational unity among churches had seemed like a real possibility. A 1910 missions conference in Edinburgh, Great Britain, had led to the formation of a "Faith and Order Conference" that claimed to achieve eighty-five percent agreement on doctrinal issues. By the 1920s, it became clear that organizational unity would not be so easy to achieve.

In the 1920s, modernist-fundamentalist tensions split both the Northern Baptist Convention and the Northern Presbyterian Church. Fundamentalists and liberals alike formed their own denominations and organizations, separated from one another. In 1925, the "Life and Work Conference" downplayed doctrinal distinctives and brought together ninety-one groups that had aligned themselves with theological liberalism.

Then everything seemed to fall apart.

In 1929, the United States stock market crashed. By the early 1930s, economic depression had reached around the world. The depression became so severe in Europe that the Germans were allowed to postpone the payments that had been required as punishment for their actions during World War I.

Near the end of the 1930s, it seemed to some as if the Great Depression might be drawing to a close. In 1938, the Life and Work Conference and the Faith and Order Conference merged to form the foundations of the "ecumenical movement"—a movement that hoped to draw all churches together as one. Participants referred to this new organization as a "World Council of Churches." Plans for a permanent World Council of Churches were suspended the next year when global conflict tore the world apart.

## Bonhoeffer's search for the gospel

A conservative politician campaigned for family values in Europe in the 1930s. He condemned

**ON the web**

Read about the World Council of Church's contribution to the ecumenical movement:

www.oikoumene.org/en/who-are-we/background/history.html

AD 1906 – AD 2009

homosexuality, pornography, and Communism. Baptist World Alliance delegates declared, "He gives to the temperance movement the prestige of his personal example since he neither uses intoxicants nor smokes." German Protestants even formed a Christian coalition to support him.

The politician's name?

Adolf Hitler.

Hitler planned to transform Europe into an invincible empire, ruled by a race of physically flawless "Aryans." In the process, he helped to trigger a world war. At the time, few Christians resisted Hitler. One Christian who did resist was a young Lutheran named Dietrich Bonhoeffer [BONN-hoh-ferr].

Karl Barth was now a theology professor in Germany; as a seminary student, Bonhoeffer had been deeply influenced by Barth's thinking. In 1928 Bonhoeffer moved to New York to attend Union Theological Seminary. At first, American preaching disgusted Bonhoeffer.

"One may," Bonhoeffer wrote, "hear sermons [in America] on almost any subject; only one is never handled: ... the gospel of Jesus Christ."

Then Bonhoeffer went to an African-American church in Harlem. Amid people depressed by poverty and prejudice, he heard the gospel that he hadn't heard from upper-class pulpits. He also realized that to be like Jesus was to identify with the oppressed. A year later he wrote, "I became a Christian."

## The confessing church

While Bonhoeffer attended Union Theological Seminary, Hitler attempted to merge all German Protestants into a single pro-Nazi denomination. In 1934, five thousand Christians—including Karl Barth—gathered in Barmen, Germany, to protest. Their Barmen Confession pledged absolute obedience to God's Word, regardless of the cost. The signers of this document became known as the "Confessing Church." Karl Barth personally mailed a copy of the Barmen Confession to Hitler. Seeing what was happening in his native land, Dietrich Bonhoeffer returned to Germany to found a seminary for the Confessing Church.

By the mid-1930s Hitler's claws had begun to clench the Confessing Church. The state commanded all professors to pledge allegiance to Hitler. Karl Barth balked; Hitler had him deported. Next, the state required pastors to pledge allegiance to Hitler. Despite objections from Bonhoeffer and Barth, even the Confessing Church failed to protest this requirement.

In 1938 a 17-year-old Jewish boy was accused of shooting a minor German official. It was the excuse that Hitler was awaiting. In one night, the Nazis killed or imprisoned more than 30,000 Jews.

on the web

Learn more about Bonhoeffer's life and beliefs:

www.dbonhoeffer.org

from the **ones** who were there

*Dietrich Bonhoeffer*

"Cheap grace is our church's deadly enemy.... Costly grace is the gospel which must be sought again and again.... Such grace is costly because it costs one's life; it is grace because it cost God his Son's life.... Above all, it is grace because God did not reckon his Son to be too dear a price to pay for our life."

*Nachfolge*

Hundreds of homes and synagogues were destroyed on the night that became known as "Kristelnacht" or "the Night of Breaking Glass."

Bonhoeffer was the sole Christian who publicly protested the pogrom. Bonhoeffer declared, "Only the one who protests on the Jews' behalf has a right to sing [Christian songs]!" Some Christians—including Magda and Andre Trocme and Corrie ten Boom's family—risked their lives to rescue Jews during World War II. Pope Pius XI's letter "With Burning Sorrow" protested a few of Hitler's crimes. A Roman Catholic document entitled "The Ten Commandments as Laws of Life" indirectly criticized the Holocaust. Pope Pius XII sheltered some Jewish refugees in the Vatican. And yet most church members, Protestant and Catholic alike, did little to stop Hitler's atrocities.

## The cost of being a disciple

Recognizing that Bonhoeffer was in danger in Germany, the American theologian Reinhold Niebuhr secured a teaching post for him in the United States. Bonhoeffer accepted the position at first, but he couldn't escape what he had learned in Harlem: To follow Jesus Christ was to identify with the oppressed. Bonhoeffer wrote to Niebuhr, "I shall have no right to participate in the reconstruction of Christian life in Germany after the war if I do not share the trials of this time with my people"—and he returned to his native land.

In 1939, Bonhoeffer became involved in a plot to assassinate Adolf Hitler. Four years later, the Gestapo jailed Bonhoeffer for helping to smuggle Jews out of Germany. When the assassination plot failed, Gestapo agents found Bonhoeffer's name in the plans to kill Hitler. Bonhoeffer was placed in the Flossenberg concentration camp. On April 5, 1945, Hitler decreed his death. Three days later, Bonhoeffer

*Dietrich Bonhoeffer (1932)*

preached a short sermon to his fellow prisoners. Gestapo agents burst through the doors before the service ended.

"Bonhoeffer!" they barked. "Come with us!"

"This is," Bonhoeffer whispered, "the end—for me, the beginning—of life."

AD 1906 – AD 2009

The next morning, Dietrich Bonhoeffer knelt and prayed beside the gallows. He was hanged using piano-wire. The wire was suspended from a meat-hook and tightened slowly to prolong his torment. This method of execution caused such anguish that even hardened soldiers were known to walk away from the gallows, unable to watch. And yet, the camp physician later commented, "I have hardly ever seen a man die so entirely submissive to God's will."

Four weeks later, the Allied forces secured victory in Europe. Three months after Hitler's defeat, the atomic bomb ended the war and hurled humanity into the nuclear age.

## The birth of evangelicalism

In the middle of the twentieth century, it had seemed to some that there were only three theological options for churches: Theological liberalism, neo-orthodoxy, and fundamentalism.

The theological liberalism of Friedrich Schleiermacher and his heirs wasn't really an option for anyone who understood the Bible to be truthful and authoritative. Neo-orthodoxy seemed like an alternative to some Christians. Yet it had become clear that—even though neo-orthodox theology correctly critiqued many shortcomings of liberalism—neo-orthodoxy slipped easily into liberal perspectives on the biblical text. It was primarily liberal and neo-orthodox churches that gathered after World War II to form the World Council of Churches (WCC). At first, the sole affirmation required by the WCC was acceptance of Jesus as "God and Savior." This basis eventually expanded to confess "the Lord Jesus Christ as God and Savior according to the scriptures" and to affirm the Trinity. Yet even this confession may be reinterpreted or ignored as each denomination chooses; the WCC has refused to make any determination about "the sincerity or firmness with which member churches accept the basis." Because of this emphasis on unity at the potential expense of theological integrity, many theologically conservative denominations have refused to join the World Council of Churches.

The other option was fundamentalism. Yet by the early 1940s more than a few Bible-believing Christians had begun to question the fundamentalist focus on total separation from everything modern. These believers joyfully embraced fundamentalists' emphasis on the truthfulness and authority of Scripture. Unlike many twentieth-century fundamentalists, they also saw value in understanding others' perspectives, and they recognized that even conservative Christians could agree to disagree on some issues.

In October 1941, several of these conservative Christians gathered at Moody Bible Institute to lay the foundations for the National Association of Evangelicals (NAE). "We will not be," the chairperson declared, "negative or destructive." Fundamentalism had focused on separation and precise external standards. The NAE was willing to listen to anyone who recognized the truthfulness of Scripture and salvation by grace through faith in Jesus.

**THINK** about **it...**
To learn more about C.S. Lewis, check out www.cslewis.org/resources/cslewis.html

A few years later, Harold Ockenga—president of the newly-founded Fuller Seminary—coined the term "neo-evangelical" or "new evangelical" to describe this perspective on life and faith. Eventually, the "neo-" was dropped, and these believers became known simply as "evangelicals." Throughout the second half of the twentieth century, the writings of a British Christian named C.S. Lewis encouraged many evangelicals to think more deeply about their common faith.

**C.S. Lewis**

## Two men from wheaton

In the second half of the twentieth century, two Baptists—each with a very different calling—deeply influenced the form and the future of evangelicalism. The two men first met each other while they were students at Wheaton College in Illinois. After graduation, one would pursue advanced degrees in theology while the other became a world-famous evangelist.

Their names?

Carl F.H. Henry and Billy Graham.

## An evangelist with a passion for unity

It was a series of evangelistic tent meetings in Los Angeles in 1949 that catapulted a thirty-one-year-old named William F. Graham into the national spotlight. At first, few non-Christians attended the meetings. Then a popular radio host interviewed Graham. By the campaign's final night eight weeks later, eleven thousand people had packed the tent. Billy Graham was a celebrity.

Billy Graham's approach was to work with anyone who was willing to support his simple message of

*Billy Graham*
*April 11, 1966*

AD 1906 – AD 2009

**from the ONES who were there**

**Billy Graham** reflecting in 1998 on his early ministry: "I preached Americanism too much ... I began to realize we are not the kingdom of God.... The real kingdom is the kingdom of believers."

"People were ready for a message that pointed them to stability and lasting values. In the providence of God, we were able to take advantage of the spiritual hunger."

*"Withholding Judgement,"* *USA Today (2/5/1998): D-1; Just As I Am, 729*

salvation by grace through faith in Jesus alone. New parachurch organizations—such as Young Life, Youth for Christ, Campus Crusade for Christ, and InterVarsity Christian Fellowship—were following similar patterns of open cooperation for the sake of evangelism. Some fundamentalists, such as Bob Jones and John R. Rice, sharply criticized this approach, claiming that the new evangelicals were forsaking biblical separation. Still, Billy Graham persisted in his single-minded focus on evangelism, pleading with millions of people to place their faith in Jesus. When Graham chaired the International Congress on World Evangelism in Lausanne, Switzerland, the central message was that "evangelism ... summons us to unity."

## A scholar with an uneasy conscience

While not downplaying the importance of evangelism, Carl F.H. Henry focused his life's work in a very different direction. Henry's contributions formed the theological foundations for the growing evangelical movement.

Henry's introduction to the idea of a living God came when he was a teenager, proofreading newspaper articles alongside a middle-aged woman. Whenever Henry turned the Lord's name into a curse, the woman commented, "Carl, I'd rather you slap my face than take the name of my best Friend in vain." A few years later, her best Friend also became Henry's Friend, when Carl F.H. Henry recognized Jesus Christ as his Savior and Lord.

After completing his doctorate in theology at Northern Baptist Theological Seminary, Carl F.H. Henry published the book that set forth the theological case for evangelicalism. This tiny text—fewer than one hundred pages long—was entitled *The Uneasy Conscience of Modern Fundamentalism*. From Henry's perspective, fundamentalism had retreated from any meaningful communication with the modern world. Fundamentalists had focused so completely on external, personal standards— standards that were "secondary and ... even

*Carl F.H. Henry*

**ON the web**

For more on the life of Carl F.H. Henry go to:

www.wheaton.edu/bgc/ archives/memorial/carlhenry/ carlhenry.html

obscure"—that fundamentalists seemed to have nothing intelligent to say to secular society. Fundamentalism had, according to Henry, divorced social reformation from personal transformation, leaving social reforms in the hands of liberalism. And what was Henry's solution? Henry called evangelicals to speak intelligently to the modern world without compromising their commitment to core Christian beliefs.

"It is needful," Carl F.H. Henry wrote, "that we come to a clear distinction, as evangelicals, between those basic doctrines on which we unite ... and the area of differences on which we are not in agreement while yet standing true to the essence of biblical Christianity."

## Christianity yesterday or Christianity today?

Around 2:00 a.m. one morning in 1953, Billy Graham had a great idea. His idea would help draw together English-speaking evangelicals throughout the world. "I wish we could," he commented, "start a magazine ... from an evangelical viewpoint ... [that would] avoid extremes." Two years later, Graham described his vision in a letter to Carl F.H. Henry. In his letter, Graham urged Henry to become the first editor of this new magazine. In 1956, the first issue of *Christianity Today* rolled off the presses, with Carl F.H. Henry as the editor.

One of Henry's goals in editing the magazine was to "win a hearing for evangelical orthodoxy from non-evangelical scholars." And that's precisely what Carl F.H. Henry worked to do throughout his life—to stand for evangelical theology while interacting intelligently with non-evangelicals. While attending a luncheon in honor of neo-orthodox theologian Karl Barth, Henry introduced himself as the editor of *Christianity Today* and asked Barth a pointed question about how he viewed the historical fact of Jesus' resurrection.

"Did you say you were the editor of 'Christianity today' or 'Christianity yesterday'?" Barth gibed.

The audience had a good laugh at Henry's expense—until Carl F.H. Henry gently but firmly countered, "Yesterday ... today ... and forever."

In 1978, Henry was instrumental in formulating The *Chicago Statement on Inerrancy*, a vital document that clearly outlined what evangelicals mean when they say that the Bible is "without error." According to this statement, "Scripture is inerrant, not in the sense of being absolutely precise by modern standards, but in the sense of making good its claims and achieving that measure of focused truth at which its authors aimed."

I met Carl F.H. Henry briefly in the spring of 1996, seven years before he died. At that time, my theological thinking was far closer to liberalism and neo-orthodoxy than to the thoughtful conservatism that Henry represented. I am sorry to say that I did not consider the degree to which the hand I shook was a

AD 1906 – AD 2009

hand that had laid the foundations for serious evangelical scholarship. Even then I was struck by an awareness that, in this man's thinking, there was a depth that stood far beyond anything I had yet imagined. Someday, I plan to shake his hand again; then, I will know.

Two twentieth-century Catholics inspired the world with their passion for the poor. Dorothy Day founded the Catholic Worker farm communes. Mother Teresa, an Albanian nun, devoted her life to the poor of India.

## Evangelicalism expands

As evangelicalism grew, so did the gap between fundamentalists and evangelicals. Some fundamentalists focused their efforts on fighting everything from new versions of the Bible to rock music and contemporary fashions. Evangelicals became increasingly open—perhaps too open, in some cases—to interacting with non-evangelical churches and to using the tools of the culture in attempting to change the culture.

The results of this openness have included a wide range of trends, including seeker-sensitive churches, political lobbying for laws that reflect a Christian worldview, a booming industry for evangelical books and music, popular parachurch movements such as Promise Keepers, and—in the final decades of the twentieth century—a readiness to dialogue with Roman Catholics.

## Roman Catholics and Evangelicals at the end of the twentieth century

To understand the relationship between evangelicals and Roman Catholics at the end of the twentieth century, let's take a look back to the middle of the century. In 1958 John XXIII—that's "John the Twenty-Third," for those of you who don't do so well in Roman numerals—became pope. Most people did not expect the 76-year-old Italian to live long or do much. Pope John XXIII didn't live long, but he did a lot.

**Mother Teresa**

Previous popes had condemned all Protestants; John XXIII called Protestants "separated brothers." He seemed responsive to how the world had changed in the past century. As a result, the pope's linguists received requests that no previous pope had even imagined. Once, the pope asked his linguists to come up with a Latin word that means "rotor-blade."

Pope John XXIII had decided to bless a helicopter.

Many Catholics assumed that, because the First Vatican Council had ascribed infallibility to the pope, no church council would ever gather again. Pope John XXIII disagreed. In 1962 he gathered more than 2,500 church leaders for the Second Vatican Council.

The key word at Vatican II was *aggiornamento*—"updating the outward forms." John XXIII died after the first session. The next pope, Paul VI, continued the council. Between 1962 and 1965 the council gathered four times, issuing statements allowing for Mass in native languages and encouraging Catholics to study the Bible. The council's final declaration was a joint statement from Pope Paul VI and the leader of the Orthodox Church. The Roman Catholic Church and the Orthodox Church forgave each other for the schism of AD 1054, when each church had condemned the other. The two leaders declared that they "regret the offensive words [that] … accompanied the sad events of this period. They likewise … remove … the sentences of excommunication."

In 1978, John Paul II became the first non-Italian pope in 456 years. He was from Poland. John Paul II described himself as a "universal pastor," traveling throughout the world. John Paul II even apologized for his church's "lack of moral leadership" during the Holocaust.

## Evangelicals and Catholics together— or maybe not

did **YOU** know**?**

Here are some key results of Vatican II:

**Session One:** Allowed translation of Mass into native languages. Urged laypeople to study Scripture. Stated that Scripture is the primary source of divine truth. Declared that all Christians —not just priests, monks, and nuns—are called by God to be God's people.

**Session Two:** Created a college of bishops to assist the pope.

**Session Three:** Non-Catholics "are not deprived of significance … in the mystery of salvation." Mary must "never take away from … Christ the One Mediator." Discouraged praying to saints.

**Session Four:** "In matters religious no one is to be forced [by ones' government] to act in a manner contrary to one's beliefs."

It was during the papacy of John Paul II, in 1994, that forty Roman Catholic and evangelical leaders signed a statement entitled, "Evangelicals and Catholics Together: The Christian Mission in the Third Millennium" (ECT). The ECT statement called for Catholics and evangelicals to cooperate on social issues. The statement also emphasized the beliefs that evangelicals and Catholics share, such as the Apostles' Creed and "justification by grace through faith because of Christ."

**ON the web**

To understand the "Evangelicals and Catholics Together" controversy, browse:

www.leaderu.com/ect/

Supporters of the ECT statement included Charles Colson, Bill Bright, J.I. Packer, Elizabeth Achtemeier, and Richard John Neuhaus. Several respected evangelicals—including R.C. Sproul, John MacArthur and D. James Kennedy—criticized the statement,

AD 1906 – AD 2009

however. Critics of the ECT statement pointed out that the statement ignored the Protestant belief in "justification by grace alone through faith alone."

Three years later, ECT supporters issued a second statement, "The Gift of Salvation." This statement dealt directly with the issue of justification. In "The Gift of Salvation," a group of evangelical and Roman Catholic theologians agreed that "justification is not earned by any good works or merits of our own; it is entirely God's gift…. The gift of justification is received through faith." Yet, as theologian Albert Mohler has pointed out, "Justification by faith alone, if genuinely affirmed by Catholics and evangelicals, would require repudiation of baptismal regeneration, purgatory, indulgences, and many other issues presently affirmed by Roman Catholic doctrine." In the end, the statement "The Gift of Salvation" was only an agreement between certain evangelical and Roman Catholic theologians— not an affirmation from the Roman Catholic Church itself. And so the rift between the Roman Catholic Church and evangelical Protestants remains.

WORDS from the **ones** who were there
*Timothy George, Evangelical leader* supporting the statement *The Gift of Salvation*:
"We sense the urgency in our Lord's high-priestly prayer for all his disciples— 'that they may all be one … so that the world may believe that Thou has sent me' (John 17:21). True Christian unity, we believe, is not so much a goal to be achieved as a gift to be received."
*"Evangelicals and Catholics Together: A New Initiative."* Christianity Today (12/8/1997): 34-35

Pope John Paul II passed from this life in 2005. Pope Benedict the Sixteenth— that's XVI in Roman parlance—succeeded him and reaffirmed that the Roman Catholic Church is the sole true church. According to Benedict XVI, organized groups of believers outside the Roman Catholic Church are merely "ecclesial communities" that should "not be called churches in the proper sense."

## Defining "evangelical"

In the opening years of the twenty-first century, evangelicalism seemed to have grown so broad that it was necessary to consider anew the question, "What is an evangelical?" In 2008, a statement entitled "An Evangelical Manifesto," composed by Os Guinness and Timothy George and signed by seventy-five evangelical leaders, attempted to provide the emerging generation with a lasting definition for "evangelical."

The manifesto denotes evangelicals as "Christians who define themselves, their faith, and their lives according to the Good News of Jesus of Nazareth," then points out the core theological beliefs implied in this definition. Recognizing that some evangelicals have been perceived as a political group standing only against certain cultural trends, the statement wisely points out that "evangelicals are for Someone and for something rather than against anyone or anything."

Yet many of the theological affirmations in the manifesto remained hazy, possibly opening the door marked "evangelical" a little too wide. And thus, evangelical Christians continue the decades-old struggle from which their movement was born, still striving to secure a spot between liberalism on the one hand and fundamentalism on the other.

**did YOU know?**

Several women, including Aimee Semple McPherson and Kathryn Kuhlman, earned prominent places in Pentecostal pulpits. McPherson popularized the "Foursquare Gospel": Jesus is the Savior, Healer, Baptizer and Bridegroom.

# The rise of pentecostalism

Evangelicalism wasn't the only Christian movement to emerge in the twentieth century. In the 1800s, the "Holiness" movement had grown out of Methodist churches; in the 1900s, many Holiness Christians embraced a perspective that would become known as "Pentecostalism."

*Charles Fox Parham*
*(Courtesy of Mrs. Les Hromas)*

## From Topeka to Azusa Street

In 1900 Charles Fox Parham, a Holiness evangelist, founded a Bible college in Topeka, Kansas. Parham taught his students that "speaking with other tongues" should accompany "the second blessing"—an act of the Spirit that, according to Holiness believers, results in "Christian perfection."

After searching the scriptures, forty students concluded they had been missing the complete power of the Holy Spirit. On January 1, 1901, one of Parham's students began to speak in a language unknown to them. A linguistics expert later said that the language sounded similar to Mandarin Chinese, though this was not confirmed. Nearly all the students went as missionaries to other countries, believing that they had miraculously received the capacity to speak in languages unknown to them.

Five years later, Parham's perspective was—much like Dorothy and Toto in *The Wizard of Oz*—"not in Kansas anymore." Well, at least, it wasn't *just* in Kansas; it had reached California. William Seymour, a Black Holiness preacher, preached the Pentecostal message at the Apostolic Faith Gospel Mission on Azusa Street in Los Angeles.

AD 1906 – AD 2009

**on the web**

Learn more about Pentecostal history:

www.oru.edu/library/special_
collections/holy_spirit_research_
center/pentecostal_history.php

Many of Seymour's hearers seemed to speak in languages unknown to them. Soon, hundreds of Holiness Christians were flocking to Azusa Street to

experience "baptism with the Holy Ghost." Many returned to their churches with the message that speaking in tongues should accompany the second blessing. In 1914 the Assemblies of God, the first Pentecostal denomination, merged several Pentecostal groups.

And how did other Christians respond to the Pentecostals?

*The modern Pentecostal movement began at the Apostolic Faith Gospel Mission on Azusa Street in Los Angeles.*

In the 1910s and 1920s, many non-Pentecostal Christians called Pentecostal worship "hell-hatched free lovism." They ridiculed Pentecostals because Pentecostals tended to be poor and uneducated. Some Pentecostals seemed to think that their "Holy Ghost baptism" placed them at a higher spiritual level than other believers. Such attitudes led to much mutual mistrust between many Pentecostals and non-Pentecostals.

did **YOU know?**

Many twentieth-century Christians who introduced Pentecostal ideas in non-Pentecostal churches called themselves "Charismatics," from the Greek word for spiritual gifts. In the 1970s the "Jesus Movement" spread Charismatic ideas among youth.

## From Azusa Street to the ends of the earth

Still, Pentecostal churches grew. The greatest expansion didn't occur near the movement's birthplace, though. Pentecostalism has expanded most rapidly in Africa, Asia, and Latin America. By the end of the twentieth century, the two largest Latino congregations in the world were both Pentecostal.

In Africa in 1921, Simon Kimbangu was a popular healer and preacher who proclaimed a native form of Christianity. Six months after his ministry began in Zaire, Kimbangu was imprisoned on false charges of treason. Though Kimbangu died in prison, his African Independent Church became one of the world's fastest growing Christian denominations.

In India, the ministry of Sundar Singh began in 1903 with a dazzling vision, after which Singh's wealthy father disowned him. Singh became a sadhu—a poor, wandering preacher—in southern Asia. Although Singh did not specifically mention speaking in tongues, he claimed other miraculous powers. In China, "Watchman" Nee Duosheng similarly emphasized miraculous healings, beginning in 1922 and lasting until 1952 when he was imprisoned. Today, the world's largest church is a Pentecostal congregation in southeast Asia. Each Sunday, more than a quarter-million people attend Yoido Full Gospel Church in Seoul, South Korea.

AD 1906 – AD 2009

# Whatever happened to modernity?

Ever heard the term "postmodern"? How about "Generation X" or even "Generation Y"? Do you completely understand what they mean? Well, don't feel bad—neither do the people who are tossing these terms around. Toss in the terms "emerging" or "emergent" and things can get even more confusing. Still, there are a few common ideas that may be helpful as you try to understand twenty-first-century Christianity.

## What does it mean to be "postmodern"?

After the Second World War, one might say that the rising generation of "Baby Boomers" became dissatisfied with the previous generations' obsession with human progress. (Remember, the Modern Age had emphasized human progress and the power of science and reason to explain life in meaningful ways.) In the first place, African-Americans and other minorities had been cut out of the American dreams of progress. African-American soldiers received equal pay and suffered equal pain during the war. Yet

upon their triumphant return, they continued to be treated as second-class citizens. In the 1950s and 1960s, leaders such as Baptist minister Martin Luther King, Jr., called Americans to resist such inequality.

Yet the dissatisfaction with previous perspectives ran deeper than racial concerns. What seems to have emerged by the mid-1960s was widespread discontent with the entire modern fixation on reason and progress. "Generation X" or "the Busters"—the children born between the mid-1960s and the early-1980s—were the first generation to be identified as "post-modern," which is to say "born after the Modern Age."

By the end of the twentieth century, at least a few unique features of postmodernity seemed clear: Modern people had emphasized reason and words. Postmoderns see the limitations of human language and logic; as a result, they seem to focus more on shared experiences and images. Moderns, because of their fixation on progress, felt satisfied in large, efficient organizations. Postmoderns aren't so concerned with massive, countable growth; postmoderns seem to place a higher value on personal connections and relationships.

AD 1906 – AD 2009

## When Orthodoxy becomes too generous: Postmodernity and the Emerging Church

In the opening decade of the twenty-first century, a movement known as "emergent church" came to epitomize some aspects of postmodern Christianity. This movement is too young to know what its long-term legacy will look like.

In some cases, emergent church leaders have simply called evangelicals to refuse identification with any particular political party and to take broader perspectives on social issues. These perspectives have included not only standing against issues such as abortion but also working toward ending poverty and caring for the environment.

There are, however, other aspects of the emergent church—aspects that trouble many conservative evangelical Christians. Some emergent church leaders have called for "a generous orthodoxy." (Remember, "orthodoxy" with a small initial "o" refers to "right belief," which is to say, that which has been believed and preserved by Christians throughout the church's history.) According to one emergent leader, this "generous orthodoxy" means that "it may be advisable in many circumstances to help people become followers of Jesus and remain within their Buddhist, Hindu, or Jewish contexts." This same leader views the Bible not as inerrant or infallible but merely as "a unique collection of literary artifacts that together support the telling of an amazing and essential story."

From the perspective of many evangelicals, such "orthodoxy" is not orthodox at all; this "generous orthodoxy" is, from their perspective, so generous that it amounts to little more than repackaged nineteenth-century theological liberalism. Theologian Russell Moore has picturesquely described it as "Schleiermacher with a soul-patch."

## Christianity goes south

At the beginning of the twenty-first century, Christianity is headed south, but not in the sense of declining or going downhill. For nearly two thousand years, the bulk of the Christian population lived north of the equator—but that clustering is about to change.

There are about two billion persons in the world who would call themselves "Christian." Around 530 million live in Europe, 510 million are Latin American, 390 million live in Africa, while around 300 million are Asian. Less than 250 million live in North America. If current trends continue, the majority of the world's Christian population will live in Africa or Latin America no later than the year 2025.

Why is Christianity turning south? It's partly because of the amazing explosion of Christianity in Africa and Latin America. It's also due to declining birthrates among Christian families in Europe and North America. Other reasons for slower growth north of the equator include the oppression that churches in Eastern Europe endured during the heyday of Communism. Even when Christians were not directly persecuted, Communist officials often forced Christians to live in inferior housing. Children of Christians—whether evangelical or Eastern Orthodox—found themselves placed in low-quality schools. To survive the Communist onslaught, the Russian Orthodox Church appointed leaders who were willing to work with the Communist government. Even after the fall of Communism in the early 1990s, government leaders attempted to limit the expansion of Christian faith in Russia, especially among believers who weren't part of the Russian Orthodox Church. Even as Christianity grows exponentially in the southern hemisphere, churches in the northern half of the globe are growing more slowly. In many areas of the northern hemisphere, the expansion of Islam is far outpacing the growth of Christianity.

Here's one way to envision the southward movement of the global church: Imagine that you placed a dot on a world map to represent Christianity's center of population. In 1800 you would have placed that dot somewhere in Italy; by 1900 that dot would have moved west, into Spain. By 1970, the dot would have dropped  southward, to the northwestern coast of Africa. At the beginning of the twenty-first century, the dot would have settled around Timbuktu, in the African nation of Mali—still north of the equator, but steadily shifting south. By the quarter-point of the twenty-first century, that dot is likely to find its spot south of the equator, somewhere between the African Congo and the Mid-Atlantic Ridge in the Atlantic Ocean.

For hundreds of years, churches in North America and Europe sent missionaries around the world. In a few decades, it seems that the European and North American continents may be the ones receiving Christian missionaries.

AD **1906** – AD **2009**

# Epilogue

## Final Reflections

"After supper she got out her book and learned me about Moses and the Bulrushers," Huckleberry Finn recalled after his time with Widow Douglas, "and I was in a sweat to find out all about him; but by and by she let it out that Moses had been dead a considerable long time; so then I didn't care no more about him, because I don't take no stock in dead people."[1] Neither do most Christians. Yet "dead people" form the heart of Christian history.

"We are," the author of Hebrews remarked, "surrounded by such a great cloud of witnesses" (Hebrews 12:1). The Apostles' Creed echoes, "I believe ... in the communion of the saints." When Christians gather, it isn't only the living who are present. By some means that transcends human understanding, the saints of the past—Huck Finn's "dead people"—are present too. Like a cloud, Blandina and Athanasius, Francis of Assisi and Catherine of Sienna, Kaetie Luther and D.L. Moody surround us. Their presence points us toward Jesus Christ, "the author and perfecter of our faith" (Hebrews 12:2).

Together, the saints of the past and present form a living house for the living God (Hebrews 3:6). Christ is its unchanging cornerstone (1 Peter 2:5-7). Through their testimony about Jesus, the apostles supplied a foundation (Revelation 21:14). Yet the walls are still growing, and what Christians do today decides the shape of tomorrow's walls (1 Corinthians 3:9-17).

"In the history of the church the old may suddenly become new," Gavin White has noted, "and the new may suddenly become old. What seemed to be permanent often fades away, and what seems to have faded is there after all. The church is pushed this way and that by waves and by winds, and yet it never quite goes on the rocks. Henry Scott Holland described it in 1914 when the Bishop of Zanzibar wrote a pamphlet asking where the church stood. Scott Holland said it did not stand at all, but 'moves and pushes and slides and staggers and falls and gets up again, and stumbles on and presses forward and falls into the right position after all'. That is church history."[2]

1. Mark Twain, *The Adventures of Huckleberry Finn* (New York:Grosset and Dunlap, [n.d.]) 2.

2. Gavin White, *How the Churches Got to Be the Way They Are* (Philadelphia: Trinity Press, 1990) 120.

# Rose Bible Basics: Christian History Made Easy

## STUDY GUIDE

A FREE downloadable version of this study guide is available at rose-publishing.com. Click on "News & Info," then on "Downloads."

Group sessions are approximately 40–60 minutes (60–90 minutes if you lecture or show a video). Suggested times are for an 8–12 person group. When you use a video, show only a 15–30 minute portion that clearly portrays a central point of the chapter.

## INTRODUCTORY SESSION

### Session Goals
This session will help students:
• Understand why Christians should study church history.
• Recognize that this study will be taught on their level.
• Recognize that this study will be applicable to their lives.

### Supplies
One large piece of poster-board or shelf paper for a sign
OPTIONAL: PowerPoint® slideshow for this session, available from Rose Publishing

### 1. Preparation
• Ask God to guide you throughout the session.
• Obtain a *Christian History Made Easy* book and a *Christian History Time Line* pamphlet for each student.
• Carefully read "Why Does Church History Matter?" in the book.
• Study Introductory Learning Activity.
• Make a sign that reads: *CHURCH HISTORY IS YOUR FAMILY HISTORY.* Hang it wherever your group will meet.
• Select songs for the session. Consider choosing a theme song for the entire study, such as, "O God, Our Help in Ages Past," "Word of God, Across the Ages," "Faith of Our Fathers," "For All the Saints," "God of Grace and God of Glory," or "The Church of God, in Every Age."

### 2. Before the Session
• As students enter, hand out the books and pamphlets.
• Ask students to complete Introductory Learning Activity as other students arrive.

### 3. Worship—*4–6 minutes*
• After everyone arrives, sing the theme song. Or, sing another appropriate song, such as, "The Church's One Foundation."

### 4. Learning Activity—*12 or 30–40 minutes*
• Have students locate Introductory Learning Activity. Tell them the answers to the questions. Discuss the answers. Never let them feel ignorant, even if their answers are incorrect.

**ANSWERS: 1**–Peter, **2**–Houses, **3**–Constantine, **4**–Chrysostom, **5**–Hildegard, **6**–Wycliffe, **7**–Luther, **8**–Calvin, **9**–Simons, **10**–Las Casas, **11**–Wesley, **12**–Spurgeon, **13**–Barth, **14**–Bonhoeffer, **15**–Graham

• [If you want to lecture or show a video, do so here.]

### 5. Small Group Discussion—*10 minutes*
Organize the class into several groups of 3–5 people. Ask each group to select a discussion leader. Each group should discuss these questions:
1. What is the "church"?
2. Some Christians don't care about church history. Why?
3. Why should we study church history?

### 6. Large Group Discussion—*12 minutes*
Ask each group's discussion leader to respond to the questions. The following answers are suggestions. Use them as you interact with the groups.
1. What is the "church"?
• Have someone read Colossians 1:18 and 1 Timothy 3:14–15.
• The church is both a local, visible fellowship of baptized believers and the invisible fellowship of all God's people, living and dead.
2. Some Christians don't care about church history. Why?

• Sometimes, church history isn't easy to understand.
• Church history is often difficult to apply to our lives.
3. Why should we study church history?
• Church history deeply affects every Christian. It affects how we read Scripture. It affects how we view God. It affects our worship. If we are church members, the church's story is our family history.
• Point to the poster and, drawing from "Why Does Church History Matter?" in the book, talk about what it means to say that church history is "family history."

### 7. Upcoming Assignment—*1 minute*
• Say: "Read the preface and first chapter of *Christian History Made Easy* and complete the Chapter One Learning Activity before our next group session. Be sure to bring a Bible to every group session!"

### 8. Prayer—*9 minutes*
• End the session by asking each group to spend some time praying.
• Encourage them to let this study draw them into a deeper relationship with God and into a deeper understanding of God's work.

### Digging Deeper
*Christian History Time Line* pamphlet (413X) (Rose Publishing)
*How We Got the Bible.* Pamphlet (407X) (Rose Publishing)
*God's Peoples* by Spickard, P. and K. Cragg, eds. (Grand Rapids: Baker, 1994)

## CHAPTER ONE  (AD 64–177)
## DISCUSSION AND REVIEW SESSION

### Session Goals
This session will help students:
• Reinforce the knowledge they have gained by reading Chapter One.
• Understand how God uses human factors and human failures to bring glory to himself.

### Supplies
• Six 3x5 cards
• One large piece of poster-board or shelf paper
OPTIONAL: PowerPoint® slideshow for this session, available from Rose Publishing

### 1. Preparation
• Ask God to guide you throughout the session.
• Read Chapter One in the book and complete the Chapter One Learning Activity.
• Post a sign: *GOD USES HUMAN FACTORS TO PRODUCE SPIRITUAL RESULTS.*
• On each 3x5 card, write one of the following references: Acts 18:12–15; 1 Corinthians 10:23–25; 1 Timothy 2:5; 2 Timothy 4:16–18; Jude 1:12.
• Select songs for the session. "God Moves in a Mysterious Way," "For All the Saints," or "Must Jesus Bear the Cross Alone" might be appropriate, as well as the theme song for the study if you have chosen one.

### 2. Before the Session
• As students enter, select five people who can read well and ask them if they would be willing to read a biblical text. Give each willing participant one of the cards.

### 3. Worship—5–7 *minutes*
• Sing a few songs.

### 4. Learning Activity—*12 or 30–40 minutes*
Ask the students to locate the Chapter One Learning Activity. Share the answers to questions 1–11. State that you will discuss question 12 later.
**ANSWERS: 1**–TRUE; **2**–FALSE: The fire probably began by accident in an oil warehouse; **3**–TRUE; **4**–FALSE: Romans preferred proven products; **5**–FALSE: Christians wouldn't let unbelievers observe the Lord's Supper; **6**–TRUE; **7**–FALSE: Domitian demanded the title "Lord and God"; **8**–FALSE: The temple burned in AD 70; **9**–FALSE: After AD 70, it was difficult for Christians to return to the Jewish religion; **10**–FALSE: Domitian persecuted Christians because they wouldn't worship him; **11**–Possible answers include: Christianity excluded other gods; Christianity challenged the social order. Ask: *"What lessons did you learn as you studied the early churches?"* Allow two or three responses. Don't let the discussion wander away from the question.

• [If you choose to lecture or to show a video, do so here.]

## 5. Large Group Discussion—*12–15 minutes*

• Ask students who received cards to find the verses indicated on the cards.

• Have someone read Acts 18:12–15. Ask the group: *"According to this passage, how did Roman rulers view the early church?"* (They treated Christianity as a Jewish sect.)

• Have someone read 2 Timothy 4:16–18. Ask: *"When was Paul probably arrested the second time? What was the outcome of Paul's trial?"* (Paul was probably arrested again during Nero's reign, after the fire in Rome. Paul was likely beheaded.)

• Have someone read 1 Timothy 2:5. Say: *"This verse would have offended many Romans. Why?"* (This verse denies the presence of any god besides the God of the Bible, as revealed in Jesus Christ.)

• Have someone read 1 Corinthians 11:23–25 and Jude 1:12. Ask: *"How did the Romans understand the church's references to "flesh," 'blood,' 'brothers,' 'sisters,' and 'love–feasts'?"* (Many Romans believed that Christians committed incest and cannibalism.)

## 6. Life Application—*15 minutes*

• Review Question 12. Possible answers include: Because of the tragedy in Jerusalem, Christianity became distinct; Pagan religions were no longer perceived as adequate; People wanted moral guidance. Ask: *"Do you think that early Christians saw clearly how God would use these factors?"* Allow persons to respond briefly. Say: *"Sometimes, the early church may have noticed how God was using social and political factors. At other times, it was probably unclear where and how God was working. Yet human factors and even human failures became opportunities for God's work. What do people long for in your community? in your school? at your job? How might God use these human factors to bring glory to himself?"* Discuss three practical responses to these questions.

## 7. Upcoming Assignment—*1 minute*

Remind students that at the next meeting they should be ready to discuss Chapter Two.

## 8. Prayer—*5 minutes*

Close with a benediction. This prayer, from the account of Polycarp's death, would be fitting: *"Good-bye, brothers and sisters. May the word of Jesus Christ give you life through God's good news. May we give glory, with Jesus Christ, to God the Father and to the Holy Spirit, until the salvation of God's chosen people. Amen."*

## Digging Deeper

*Backgrounds of Early Christianity* 2nd ed. by E. Ferguson (Grand Rapids: Eerdmans, 1993) 70–74; 556–564.

*A History of the Christian Church* 4th ed. by W. Walker, et al. (New York: Scribner's) 50–53.

*Wars of the Jews*, Book 2 by Josephus

*Antiquities*, Books 19–20 by Josephus

*The Gospel of John* by F.F. Bruce (Grand Rapids: Eerdmans, 1983) 215.

*Romans* rev. ed. by F.F. Bruce (Grand Rapids: Eerdmans, 1985) 252–259.

## CHAPTER TWO (AD 90–250) DISCUSSION AND REVIEW SESSION

### Session Goals

This session will help students:

• Reinforce the knowledge they have gained by reading Chapter Two.

• Consider how to view the events of the present in light of God's past revelation of himself in Holy Scripture.

### Supplies

• A piece of paper and a pencil for each student

• One large piece of poster-board or shelf paper

• A copy of Albert Mohler's article "A Call for Theological Triage and Theological Maturity" for every student. The article is available for free download at www.albertmohler.com

OPTIONAL: PowerPoint® slideshow for this session, available from Rose Publishing

### 1. Preparation

• Ask God to guide you throughout the session.

• Study Chapter Two and the Chapter Two Learning Activity.

• Use the poster-board to post a sign that reads: *WHAT IS ESSENTIAL?*

• Have a piece of paper and pencil for each student.

• Select appropriate songs, such as, "The Great Creator of the Worlds" (from the "Words from the Ones Who Were There" found in Chapter

Two), "We Are God's People," and "The Church of Christ, in Every Age."

## 2. Before the Session
• As students enter, gently remind them to complete the Chapter Two Learning Activity.
• Give each person a piece of paper, pencil, and copy of the article from Albert Mohler.

## 3. Worship—*4–6 minutes*
• Sing the theme song and one or two other songs.

## 4. Learning Activity—*8 minutes*
• Work as a class through the Chapter Two Learning Activity. **ANSWERS:** 1–A; 2–B; 3–C; 4–A; 5–C; 6–A; 7–C; 8–B; 9–A; 10–B

## 5. Large Group Discussion and Review—*20 or 40–45 minutes*
After finishing the learning activity, ask the following questions, guiding participants toward the correct answer: *"Why did persecution decrease during the late second century?"* (The Roman government was in turmoil. So, most rulers ignored the churches.) *"What did Gnostics deny about Jesus Christ?"* (According to Gnostics, Jesus was not fully God and fully human.) *"How did Christians decide which New Testament books were authoritative?"* (The first and primary standard was whether the book could be clearly connected to an eyewitness or close associate of an eyewitness.)

• [If you want to lecture or to show a video, do so here.]

• Say: *"One of the church's responses to the Gnostic heresy was the Rule of Faith. The Rule listed several teachings that must never be compromised. These teachings were essential doctrines—teachings on which a Christian's salvation depends. The Bible lists many teachings that we can't compromise. Paul wrote:* [Read **1 Corinthians 12:3**]. *Yet the Bible also lets us disagree peaceably about nonessential teachings:* [Read **Romans 14:1–5**] *Take a few minutes to read the article "A Call for Theological Triage and Christian Maturity." Then, at the top of your paper, write: FIRST-LEVEL (ESSENTIAL FOR SALVATION);*

*SECOND-LEVEL (IMPORTANT FOR FELLOWSHIP); THIRD-LEVEL (AGREE TO DISAGREE). As we discuss different beliefs, list them on your papers, beneath the appropriate heading."*

## 6. Individual Life Application—*12–15 minutes*
• If you have a chalkboard or whiteboard, write FIRST LEVEL, SECOND LEVEL, and THIRD LEVEL at the top of the board. Discuss as a group what doctrines might belong in each list. *Christianity, Cults, & Religions* (see Digging Deeper) outlines several essential beliefs and may be helpful.
• Discuss as a class what beliefs belong in each list.
• Discuss the ancient Rule of Faith, pointing out that the beliefs found in the Rule of Faith belong in the FIRST-LEVEL list.
• Ask: *"How can we embrace Christians who hold different second-level and third-level beliefs?"* Try to come up with four practical responses to the question.

## 7. Upcoming Assignment—*1 minute*
Remind the students that, before the next meeting, they should study Chapter Three.

## 8. Benediction—*5 minutes*
Close the session by singing a chorus that emphasizes Christian unity.

## Digging Deeper
"Creed." *A Liturgy, A Legacy, and a Ragamuffin Band* by R. Mullins (Word Records)
*Christianity, Cults & Religions* pamphlet (404X) (Rose Publishing)
*Early Christianity* by R. Bainton (New York: Van Nostrand, 1960) 35–46.
*A History of the Christian Church* 4th ed., by W. Walker, et. al. (Prentice: 1985) 45–50, 72–77
*To the Philippians* by Polycarp, 3:2–3; 9:1.
*Against Heresies* by Irenaeus, 3:2–2.

## CHAPTER THREE (AD 247–420) DISCUSSION AND REVIEW SESSION

### Session Goals
This session will help students:

- Reinforce the knowledge they have gained by reading Chapter Three.
- Consider how churches can avoid seeking growth in unhealthy ways.

## Supplies
- Four 3x5 cards
- Copy of "Of the Father's Love Begotten" and "Glory Be to the Father" for each student
- One large piece of poster-board or shelf paper
OPTIONAL: PowerPoint® slideshow for this session, available from Rose Publishing

## 1. Preparation
- Ask God to guide you throughout the session.
- Study Chapter Three and Chapter Three Learning Activity.
- Post a sign: *GROWTH! HOW SHOULD THE CHURCH RESPOND?*
- On each 3x5 card, write one of the following song titles: "Of the Father's Love Begotten," verse 1; "Of the Father's Love Begotten," verse 2; "Of the Father's Love Begotten," verse 3; "Glory Be to the Father."
- Copy "Glory Be to the Father" and "Of the Father's Love Begotten" for every student.
- Select songs to sing during the session.

## 2. Before the Session
- As students enter, remind them to complete Chapter Three Learning Activity.

## 3. Worship—*7 minutes*
- Sing "Of the Father's Love," "Glory Be to the Father," or other appropriate songs.

## 4. Learning Activity—*15 minutes*
- Look at Learning Activity 3. Place A–J in the correct order. If possible, write the events in the correct order on a chalkboard or whiteboard. **ANSWERS: A**–6; **B**–3; **C**–4; **D**–9; **E**–8; **F**–1; **G**–7; **H**–10; **I**–2; **J**–5; 1–(1) Answers might include: The phrase could imply that the Trinity is not made up of three distinct persons. (2) and (3): Answers will vary; **2** – Answers might include: Many Christians didn't embrace the church's new–found political acceptance; **3**–Answers might include: Cappadocians rejected extreme self–denial and involved themselves in social ministries; **4**–Answers might include: Christians still treat the Trinity as an essential doctrine.

- [If you want to lecture or show a video, do so here.]

## 5. Small Group Discussion and Review—*12–20 or 30–40 minutes*
- Hand a copy of the song lyrics to every student.
- Organize the class into four groups. Give each group one of the 3x5 cards. Say: "*Study the song or verse indicated on your group's card.*" As students read, remind them of these facts: "Glory Be to the Father" was written during or shortly before the controversy about Arius; "Of the Father's Love Begotten" was written soon after the Council of Nicaea, affirming the Creed of Nicaea. Instruct the groups: "*Find one phrase in your verse or song that denies Arius' teachings. Explain how that phrase challenged Arius.*"
- After nine minutes, ask each group, "*Which phrase in your assigned song challenged Arius? How?*" Here are some suggested answers:
"Of the Father's Love Begotten," verse 1: Jesus is the "source"; so, he can't be created.
"Of the Father's Love Begotten," verse 2: This verse calls Jesus "God."
"Of the Father's Love Begotten," verse 3: Christ, Father, Spirit are worshiped as one.
"Glory Be to the Father": Song ascribes equal glory to Father, Son, and Holy Spirit.

## 6. Large Group Discussion—*12–14 minutes*
- Ask: "*When someone says, 'God is blessing our church,' what is usually happening?* [**Allow persons to respond until numeric growth is mentioned.**] *It's easy to assume that growing churches are always "being blessed." Often, that's true.* [Read **Acts 2:41–42**] *But, sometimes, God's people may proclaim the truth with numerically negative results.* [Read **1 John 2:19**] *What was happening in John's church?* [**The church was losing members who weren't true Christians.**] *In God's kingdom, faithfulness matters more than numeric growth. During Constantine's reign, churches grew, but the message became diluted. How might some churches today trade purity for numeric or financial growth? How might our church be*

tempted to dilute God's message for the sake of growth?" [**For each answer, discuss one specific way that your church can avoid that pitfall. Seek points of common ground rather than points of contention.**]

### 7. Upcoming Assignment—*1 minute*
Remind the students: *"Before the next session, each of us will read Chapter Four. Please complete the Chapter Four Learning Activity before coming to the group meeting."*

### 8. Prayer—*3 minutes*
Close the session with a prayer something like this one: *"Lord, we have seen how past Christians misunderstood and misused your message. We admit that we also are guilty. We too are tempted to dilute your message to gain human approval. You know our foolishness. Our wrongs are not hidden from you. Forgive us. Purify us. Love us. Amen."*

### Digging Deeper
*The Trinity* pamphlet (410X) (Rose Publishing)
*Vita Constantini* by Eusebius, 1:28.
*The Rise of Christianity* by W. Frend (Philadelphia: Fortress, 1984) 484–717.
*Constantine the Great* by M. Grant (New York: Scribner, 1993) 135.
*Contra Helvidius* 5 by Jerome

### Words From The Ones Who Were There

**"Glory Be to the Father" ("Gloria Patri")**
*Author unknown (early 4th century, perhaps based on an earlier hymn)*
"Glory be to the Father, and to the Son, and to the Holy Ghost;
As it was in the beginning,/Is now, and ever shall be,/world without end.
Amen, Amen."

**"Of the Father's Love Begotten"**
*by Aurelius Clemens Prudentius (4th century)*
*Translated by John Mason Neale and Henry W. Baker*
*Verse 1*
"Of the Father's love begotten,/Ere the worlds began to be,
He is Alpha and Omega,/He the source, the ending He,

Of the things that are, that have been,/And that future years shall see,
Evermore and evermore!"

*Verse 2*
"O ye heights of heav'n adore Him:/Angel hosts, His praises sing;
Pow'rs, dominions, bow before Him,/And extol our God and King;/
Let no tongue on earth be silent,/Ev'ry voice in concert ring,
Evermore and evermore!"

*Verse 3*
"Christ, to Thee with God the Father,/And, O Holy Ghost, to Thee,
Hymn and chant and high thanksgiving/And unwearied praises be:
Honor, glory, and dominion,/And eternal victory,
Evermore and evermore!"

## CHAPTER FOUR (376–664)
## DISCUSSION AND REVIEW SESSION

### Session Goals
This session will help students:
• Reinforce the knowledge they have gained by reading Chapter Four.
• Consider how Christians today can serve one another instead of seeking power over one another.

### Supplies
• One large piece of poster-board or shelf paper
• A chalkboard or whiteboard or another large piece of paper
• A 3x5 card and a pencil for each student
OPTIONAL: PowerPoint® slideshow for this session, available from Rose Publishing

### 1. Preparation
• Ask God to guide you throughout the session.
• Study Chapter Four and the Chapter Four Learning Activity.
• Use one piece of poster-board to post a sign that reads: *HOW'S YOUR SERVE?*
• At the top of the other piece of paper or on the chalkboard or whiteboard, write: *SERVANT LEADERS OR LEADERS OF*

SERVANTS? Beneath the heading, write: AMBROSE, CYRIL, GREGORY, JOHN CHRYSOSTOM, HILDA, JUSTINIAN, OLYMPIAS, and THEODOSIUS. Post the sign in a prominent place.
• Prepare a brief ten-minute lecture, based on the contents of Chapter Four. Study an encyclopedia article or Internet site about Augustine of Hippo, Benedict of Nursia, or Pope Gregory.
• Select some of the ancient songs that appear in the Leader Guides. Other appropriate songs, found in many hymnals, would include, "Let All Mortal Flesh Keep Silent" (a hymn from around AD 400) or "Be Thou My Vision" (an Irish hymn from the 5th century or earlier).

## 2. Worship—*10 minutes*
• Sing the theme song and three or four other appropriate songs.

## 3. Learning Activity—*4 minutes*
• Review the answers to the Chapter Four Learning Activity: **ANSWERS: 1**–Jovinian; **2**–Ambrose; **3**–Olympias; **4**–Augustine; **5**–Nestorius; **6**–Leo; **7**–Chalcedon; **8**–Justinian; **9**–Scholastica; **10**–Hilda; **11**–pope; **12**–Answers will vary.

## 4. Large Group Discussion and Review—*20 or 35–45 minutes*
• After finishing the learning activity, ask the following questions: "*In AD 381, the First Council of Constantinople confirmed a creed. What do contemporary Christians call that creed?*" (Christians call it "the Nicene Creed," because it echoes the decisions of the Council of Nicaea.); "*What did One-Nature Christians believe?*" (One-Nature Christians thought Jesus' deity absorbed his humanity.)
• [If you want to show a video, do so here.]
• In your lecture: (1) Summarize the chapter in your words. Include any interesting facts that your research uncovered. (2) Talk about one major struggle that Christians faced between AD 370 and 664. (3) Discuss these questions: "How did the cleft between clergy and laypeople enter the churches? Does your church encourage every Christian to be a servant-leader?"

## 5. Individual Life Application—*9 minutes*
• Distribute the cards and pencils. Point to the list of names on the chalkboard. Say: "*On your card, write one name from this list. Beside the name, note whether that person was a 'servant–leader' or a 'leader of servants.' Then, write one reason why you believe your assessment is correct.*" After 5 minutes, allow one person to respond to each name. State clearly that many persons in the chapter may have exhibited both traits at different times in their lives.
• Say: "*At times, Jesus' first disciples fought for power instead of living as servants:* [Read **Mark 10:43–45**] *These words call us to ask ourselves, 'How's my serve? Do I expect church leaders to serve me and my church's needs? Or, have I accepted my God-given responsibility to be a servant–leader in my church?'*"

## 6. Benediction—*2 minutes*
To end the session, read Philippians 2:5–8 and lead a brief prayer.

## Digging Deeper
*Confessions* by Augustine of Hippo
*To Cledonius* by Gregory of Nazianzus, Epistle 101;
*Byzantium: The Early Centuries* by J. Norwich (New York: Knopf, 1989)

## Words From The Ones Who Were There

Translations by Timothy Paul Jones

### "Savior of All Peoples, Come!"
*by Ambrose, Bishop of Milan (late 4th century)*
*Sing to the tune of "Holy Bible, Book Divine" or "Holy Spirit, Truth Divine."*
"Savior of all peoples, come,/Virgin's Son, make here your home.
Be amazed, O sky and earth,/That our Lord chose such a birth."
"Christ, the Father's only Son,/Through his cross our life has won.
Endless will his kingdom be;/When will we its splendor see?"
### "Splendor of God's Glory Bright"
*by Ambrose, Bishop of Milan (late 4th century )*
*Sing to the tune of "Doxology" (Old 100th, Altered)*
"O splendor of God's glory bright,/From light

eternal bringing light;
O Light of lights, life's living spring,/True
Day, all days illumining. Amen."

### *"I Sing As I Arise Today"*
*by Patrick of Ireland (5th century )*
*Sing to the tune of "I Heard the Bells on
Christmas Day" (Waltham)*
"I sing as I arise today; I call upon my Father's
might;
The will of God to be my guide, the eye of God
to be my sight."
"The Word of God to be my speech, the hand
of God to be my stay,
The shield of God to be my strength, the path
of God to light my way."

### *"O God, You Are the Father"*
*by Columba of Iona (6th century )*
*Sing to the tune of "The Church's One
Foundation" (Aurelia)*
"O God, you are the Father of all who trust
in you.
To mankind you have granted faith, life, and
power, too.
O God, you have created earth full of living
things.
You are the righteous Judge and the holy King
of kings."

### *"Father, We Praise You"*
*by Gregory, Bishop of Rome (6th century )*
*Sing to the tune of "Great Is Thy Faithfulness"*
*Verse:*
"All holy Father, Son, and equal Spirit,
Trinity bless-ed, your salvation send.
Yours is the glory, shining and resounding,
Throughout creation, your world without end."

*Chorus:*
"Father, we praise you! Father, we praise you!
Active and watchful, we stand before you.
Singing, we offer our prayers and devotion.
Thus we adore you, our Savior and King!"

### *"King of the Earth"*
*by Gregory, Bishop of Rome (6th century )*
*Sing to the tune of "When I Survey the
Wondrous Cross" (Hamburg)*
"King of the earth and ev'ry life,
Banish our weakness, hate, and sin.

Bring us to heav'n, to praise your name,
With joy and peace that ne'er shall end."
*Sung slowly a capella in unison, this arrangement
sounds similar to a Gregorian chant.*

## Words From The Ones Who Were There

Translations by Timothy Paul Jones

Popular worship band Sending 68 has
partnered with Timothy Paul Jones to produce
contemporary tunes for these two hymns. You
may download recordings and chord charts
for these songs from www.timothypauljones.
com or www.sending68.com. If you wish
to sing these songs in your church or small
group, please obtain a CCLI license for your
organization from www.ccli.com and use the
appropriate CCLI information for the songs.

### *"I Sing As I Arise Today"*
*by Patrick of Ireland (5th century )*
*Verse 1*
"I sing as I arise today; I call upon my Father's
might;
The will of God to be my guide, the eye of God
to be my sight."
*Chorus*
"This is my song; this is my heart's desire.
I in you, you in me, swept up in holy Trinity,
Glory divine, this is my heart's desire."
*Verse 2*
"The Word of God to be my speech, the hand
of God to be my stay,
The shield of God to be my strength, the path
of God to light my way."

### *"You Are King of the Earth"*
*Based on poetry by Gregory, Bishop of Rome
(6th century )*
*Verse 1:*
"King of the earth and ev'ry life,
Shatter our weakness, hate, and sin.
Let your kingdom come and break our pride
Fill us with peace that never will end."
*Chorus:*
"You are King of the earth!
You are King of the earth!
Yet you came to die
and rose to life
forevermore."

"You are King of the earth!
You are King of the earth!
Now reign over us
that we may love
as you love us."
*Verse 2:*
"Praise to Father, Son, and Spirit—
Three–personed God, your salvation send!
Glory divine now shines and resounds,
Throughout creation, world without end!"

# CHAPTER FIVE (496–1291)
# DISCUSSION AND REVIEW SESSION

## Session Goals
This session will help students:
• Reinforce the knowledge they have gained by reading Chapter Five.
• Be encouraged to speak with the compassion of Jesus Christ.

## Supplies
• A half-sheet of paper and a pencil for each student
• A timer
• One large piece of poster-board or shelf paper
• A chalkboard or whiteboard
OPTIONAL: PowerPoint® slideshow for this session, available from Rose Publishing

## 1. Preparation
• Ask God to guide you throughout the session.
• Select two or three songs, including "All Glory, Laud, and Honor," (by Theodolf, one of Charlemagne's aides) which may be found in many hymnals.
• Study Chapter Five and the Chapter Five Learning Activity.
• Use the poster-board to post a sign that reads: *CHRIST-LIKE CRITICISM = COMPASSION + COMPREHENSION + DESIRE TO HELP OTHERS KNOW CHRIST.*

## 2. Before the Session
• As students enter, give each one a piece of paper and a pencil.
## 3. Worship—*5 minutes*
Sing two or three songs that fit this week's theme.

## 4. Learning Activity—*7 minutes*
Discuss the Chapter Five Learning Activity.
**ANSWERS:** 1–B; 2–C; 3–A; 4–C; 5–A; 6–C; 7–C; 8–D; 9–C; 10–A; 11–B; 12–E

## 5. Large Group Discussion and Review—*20 or 40–50 minutes*
• [If you want to lecture or show a video, do so here. 15–30 minutes.]
• Say: *"Glance at Chapter Five. Choose one person mentioned by name in the chapter. Write a series of 'Who Am I?' statements about that person. Include at least three facts about the person."* Here's a sample set of "Who Am I?" statements: *"I seized the Eastern throne;" "Pope Leo III refused to appeal to me because I was a woman;" "I convened the Second Council of Nicaea to end the icon disputes."*
**ANSWER:** *Empress Irene*
• Allow the students 9 minutes to write their "Who Am I?" riddles.
• Have students wad up their "Who Am I?" papers. Set the timer at 1 minute. Tell the students to toss around the paper wads until the timer goes off. At the end, each student should have one paper wad.
• Ask each student to share the statements on his or her paper wad. Urge the group to guess the answer to each riddle.

## 6. Individual Life Application—*12 minutes*
• **Read Acts 18:24–27**. Say: *"Christians should desire to be kind, but being kind does not necessarily mean being silent. Sometimes, Christians must point out errors. Three attitudes should rule Christians when they point out others' errors: (1) Compassion; (2) Understanding; and (3) A desire to guide the offenders toward an accurate knowledge of God's nature. In the early Middle Ages, many Christians condemned Muslims, Jews, and other Christians. Did these three attitudes rule their criticisms?"* [**Allow several responses. Most persons will answer no.**] *"Unfortunately, Christians today sometimes criticize others without first trying to understand them. Name some religious groups with whom we disagree."* [**Write the responses on a chalkboard or whiteboard. Here are some suggestions to guide your discussion: {a Christian denomination similar to your own};**

{a Christian denomination very unlike your own}; Mormons; Jehovah's Witnesses; Muslims.]

• Say: *"The members of some of these groups may be Christians. Others are not. Do you have compassion for the people in each of these groups? Do you understand their basic beliefs? Especially if they aren't Christians, could you lovingly guide them toward an accurate understanding of Christ? Peter said:* [Read 1 Peter 3:15]."

• Say: *"On the back of your paper, list several groups or individuals that you either don't understand or don't feel compassion for. Your list may include family members, fellow–Christians, other races, or other religious groups. Choose to work to understand the people on your list. Then, ask God to help you love them with the love that Jesus demonstrated on the cross."* Allow the students 4 minutes to finish their lists.

### 7. Upcoming Assignment—*1 minute*
• Remind students to complete the Chapter Six Learning Activity before the next session.

### 8. Closure—*5 minutes*
• Close the session with silent prayer. Urge students to pray for people that they listed.

### Digging Deeper
*Byzantium: The Early Centuries* by J. Norwich (New York: Knopf, 1989) 377–380.
*The Story of Christianity* vol. 1, by J. Gonzalez (Harper One; 1984) 262–276.
*Turning Points* by M. Noll (Grand Rapids: Baker, 1997) 134–141.
*The Fourth Crusade* rev. ed. D. Queller (Philadelphia: Penn, 1997) 89–192.

## CHAPTER SIX (673–1295)
## DISCUSSION AND REVIEW SESSION

### Session Goals
This session will help students:
• Reinforce the knowledge they have gained by reading Chapter Six.
• Consider how they can join in God's workings in their areas of influence.

### Supplies
• Four pieces of paper and four pencils

• One large piece of poster-board or shelf paper
• One white robe, one brown robe, and one black robe
• A length of rope to tie around someone's waist
OPTIONAL: PowerPoint® slideshow for this session, available from Rose Publishing

### 1. Preparation
• Ask God to guide you as you prepare for the session.
• Post a sign that reads: *WARNING! GOD IS WORKING HERE!*
• Write one heading on each paper:
(1) MISSIONARY MONKS; (2) MYSTICS; (3) MENDICANTS; (4) SCHOLASTICS.
• Plan to sing some of the following songs; you should be able to find them in most hymnals: "All Creatures of Our God and King" (by Francis of Assisi); "The Day of Resurrection" (by John Damascus); "Jerusalem the Golden" (by a monk from Cluny).
• Study Chapter Six and the Chapter Six Learning Activity.
• Ask three students to arrive at the discussion session early. Dress each one in one of the robes. Tie the rope as a belt around the student with the brown robe.

### 2. Worship—*8 minutes*
Sing the theme song and some of the suggested hymns.

### 3. Large Group Review—*7 minutes*
• Ask the person wearing the white robe to stand. Ask: *"If (name) were a monk, to what order might (name) belong?"* [Cistercian] Ask: *"Why did Cistercians wear white?"* [To avoid any appearance of wealth, they didn't dye their clothes.]
• Ask the person wearing the brown robe to stand. Ask: *"If (name) were a monk, to what order might (name) belong?"* [Franciscan] Ask: *"Why did Franciscans wear brown robes tied with a rope?"* [When Francis first committed himself to Christ, that's what he put on, with a rope from a farmer's scarecrow.]
• Ask the person wearing the black robe to stand. Ask: *"If (name) were a monk, to what order might (name) belong?"* [Dominican

monks wore black robes on top of white robes.] Ask: *"What Scholastic thinker was a Dominican monk?"* [**Thomas Aquinas**].

### 4. Learning Activity—*7 minutes*
• As a class, review the Chapter Six Learning Activity. **ANSWERS:** 1–Bernard; 2–Waldo; 3–Assisi; 4–Anselm; 5–Mendicant; 6–Mystics; 7–Damascus; 8–nuns; 9–Aquinas; 10–Lioba; 11–Bingen; 12–Francis; 13–Cluny; 14–Scholastic; 15–crops; 16–III; 17–God; 18–Cyril.

### 5. Small Group Life Application—*18 or 40–50 minutes*
• [If you want to lecture or to show a video, do so here, 15–30 minutes]
• Organize the class into four groups. Give each group a pencil and a piece of paper. Say: *"On each paper, you'll find the title of a type of Christian mentioned in Chapter Six. In your books, locate the section mentioned on your paper. Find two truths that Christians today can learn from that type of Christian. Write the truths on your group's paper."* Allow students 9 minutes to complete the assignment.
• Ask each group to share its list. Here are some suggestions: Missionary monks reminded Christians to reach out to unreached peoples. Mystics urged Christians to seek deeper relationships with God. Mendicants turned Christians' focus away from their possessions. Scholastics taught Christians to think deeply about their faith.
• Say: *"In this chapter, you learned that even when the established church seemed to fail, God never stopped working. That shouldn't surprise us.* [Read John 5:17] *God is always working! In one place, God may be preparing non–Christians to become followers of Christ. Somewhere else, God may be giving God's people a deeper desire to encounter God anew. Never ask, 'God, are you working here?' God is always working! Ask, 'God, how are you working here? Please prepare me to join you in your work.'"*

### 6. Closure—*5 minutes*
Discuss how God might be working today in unexpected ways. Ask: *"How can you actively join in God's work where you are?"* Discuss three specific answers. Close the session with a brief prayer. Ask God to show the students where God is working in their lives.

### Digging Deeper
*Becket* (10539D) (Vision Video, 150 minutes)
"Bernard of Clairvaux" in *Christian History*, Issue 24.
*Hildegard of Bingen* by S. Flanagan (London: Routledge, 1990)
"Francis of Assisi" in *Christian History*, Issue 42.
*Byzantium: The Apogee* by J. Norwich (New York: Knopf, 1993) 71–79
*History of Christianity in the Middle Ages* by W. Cannon (Nashville: Abingdon, 1960) 106–114.
*The Story of Christianity* vol. 1 by J. Gonzalez (Harper One; 1984) 282–299.
*The Life and Conversation of St. Anselm*, Eadmer 1:22.

## CHAPTER SEVEN (1294–1517) DISCUSSION AND REVIEW SESSION

### Session Goals
This session will help students:
• Reinforce the knowledge they have gained by reading Chapter Seven.
• Look for opportunities to call people to Christ-centered repentance and reform.

### Supplies
• Twelve balloons (*six different colors, two balloons of each color!*)
• One small paper bag
• Six slips of paper
• One large piece of poster-board or shelf paper
• A chalkboard or whiteboard or overheard projector
OPTIONAL: PowerPoint® slideshow for this session, available from Rose Publishing

### 1. Preparation
• Ask God to guide you throughout the session. Is there someone in the study group who annoys you? Pray specifically for him/her. Send an encouraging note to that student, thanking him/her for attending the study.
• Study Chapter Seven and the Chapter Seven Learning Activity.
• On the poster-board, write in large letters:

ARE YOU THE ONE? Post the sign wherever your group meets.
• Put six balloons (one of each color, *not inflated*) in the paper bag.
• On each slip of paper, write one of the following names: CELESTINE V; CATHERINE OF SIENNA; JOHN WYCLIFFE; JAN HUS; THOMAS A'KEMPIS; ERASMUS.
• Place each slip of paper in one of the remaining balloons. Inflate and tie the balloons with the papers inside.
• Place a chair near the front of the room.
• Select several songs that focus on renewal and revival.

## 2. Before the Session
• As students enter, be certain they have completed the Chapter Seven Learning Activity.

## 3. Worship—*4 minutes*
• Sing your theme song and another appropriate song.

## 4. Learning Activity—*8 minutes*
• Ask students to locate Learning Activity 7. Talk about their answers.
**ANSWERS: 1**–Answers will vary, elderly, humble; **2**–Avignon; **3**–Answers will vary, unbridled parties, penance parades; **4**–The Council of Constance deposed all three popes and elected a new pope; **5**–All Christians are equal members of God's church; **6**–They believed Scholasticism was too concerned with unimportant questions that were irrelevant to common people; **7**–Answers will vary, brave, innocent; **8**–They focused on practical, human ideas instead of abstract logic; **9**–Answers will vary, intelligent, humanist; **10**–Answers will vary.

## 5. Large Group Discussion and Review— *20 or 30–45 minutes*
• [If you want to lecture or show a video, do so here, 15–30 minutes.]
• Set a timer for one minute. Have students bat the balloons among themselves until the timer beeps. Whoever is holding a balloon when the timer beeps must keep the balloon.
• Say: "*If you're holding a balloon, pop it. Inside each balloon is a slip of paper. Find in your*

textbook information about the person whose name is written on your paper. Do not show anyone else your paper!*"
• Allow students two minutes to refresh their memories. Say: "*If you got a balloon, you're so special that the class will now interview you! The class can ask you any question about the person whose name is written on your paper except the person's name. Everyone, even the person being interviewed, can use the textbook!*"
• Randomly pull a balloon out of the paper bag. Ask: "*Who popped the (**color**) balloon?*" Ask the respondent to sit in the chair at the front of the room.
• Let students ask questions until someone guesses whose name was written on the paper. Give the person the uninflated balloon that you pulled from the bag as a prize. Allow the person to return to his or her seat. Repeat the process until all six colors have been used.
• Say: "*We have talked about six ordinary Christians. Each one saw a problem and called God's people to repent. The problems they saw affected vital parts of Christian faith, such as the authority of Scripture and personal holiness. Name some similar problems that confront contemporary churches.*"
• Write the students' responses on the chalkboard or overhead transparency. After the list includes 12 items, ask: "*Which problems actually threaten vital parts of the Christian faith? Circle those problems.*"
• Lead the class to select three circled items that specifically could affect their churches. Underline those problems.
• [Read 1 Corinthians 16:14 and Ephesians 4:14–16] Point to the poster. Ask: "*How can we work together to call Christians to deal in a Christ-centered way with the problems we have underlined?* Allow students to respond until they think of three responses. Write the responses on the board.

## 6. Small Group Life Application—*7 minutes*
Organize the class into three groups. Assign one response to each group. Ask each group to pray about its assigned problem. After they've finished praying, students may leave.

## 7. Upcoming Assignment—*1 minute*
As students begin to leave, remind them to

study Chapter Eight and to complete the Chapter Eight Learning Activity before the next session.

## Digging Deeper

*The Agony and the Ecstasy* (24833D) (Vision Video, 139 minutes)

*Henry V* (Fox, 1989, 138 minutes)

*Henry V* (Paramount, 1944, 127 minutes)

*Joan of Arc* (6212) (Vision Video, 100 minutes)

*Joan of Arc* (CBS, 1999, 150 minutes)

*John Hus* (4133) (Vision Video, 30 minutes)

*John Wycliffe* (4053) (Vision Video, 30 minutes)

*A Distant Mirror* by B. Tuchman (New York: Ballantine, 1978) 92–123

*History of Christianity in the Middle Ages* by W. Cannon, 250–292

*Europe* by N. Davies (Oxford, 1996) 409–412

*God's Peoples* by P. Spickard, et. al. (Baker: 1995) 146–148.

## CHAPTER EIGHT (1500–1609) DISCUSSION AND REVIEW SESSION

### Session Goals

This session will help students:

• Reinforce the knowledge they have gained by reading Chapter Eight.

• Consider when professed Christians should and should not separate from one another.

### Supplies

• One sheet of paper and a pencil for each student

• Two large pieces of poster-board or shelf paper

• One large board or an old door or a bulletin board

• Two hammers

• One tack for each student

OPTIONAL: PowerPoint® slideshow for this session, available from Rose Publishing

### 1. Preparation

• Ask God to guide you throughout the session.

• Study Chapter Eight and the Chapter Eight Learning Activity.

• Post a sign that reads: *DIVISION IS NEVER DESIRABLE. WHEN IS IT NECESSARY?*

• On the other poster-board, write the following sentences:

THEY DENY CHRIST'S DEITY; I DON'T KNOW THE SONGS THEY SING; THEY BAPTIZE BY IMMERSION; THEY DENY THE AUTHORITY OF SCRIPTURE; SOMEONE GOSSIPED ABOUT ME; THEIR SERVICES BORE ME; I DISAGREE WITH THEIR VIEW OF THE END-TIMES. Write the phrases in vivid colors. Hang the poster near the front of the classroom.

• At the top of each student's paper, write MY THESES. (If you have access to a photocopier, make a master and reproduce it.)

• Place the hammers, tacks, and board near the front of your classroom.

• Select songs to sing during the session, such as "A Mighty Fortress Is Our God" (Martin Luther).

### 2. Before the Session

As students enter, give each one a pencil and *My Theses* paper.

### 3. Worship—*6 minutes*

Sing the theme song and some other appropriate song.

### 4. Learning Activity—*12 minutes*

Ask students to locate the Learning Activity. Read the suggested answers for each blank in the Chapter Eight Learning Activity. Have students share the words they added in the blanks. **SUGGESTED ANSWERS:** Other answers may also be suitable. **1**–Spanish, Soldier, Jesuit, Catholic; **2**–Studious, French, Fled, Institutes, Geneva; **3**–English, Catherine; **4**–Barrel, Nun, Wife; **5**–German, Translator, Monk, Wittenberg, Theses; **6**–Swiss, Anabaptist, Fled, Zurich, Drowned; **7**–Dutch, Anabaptist, Priest, Fled; **8**–Catholic, Council; **9**–Studious, English, Translator, Priest, Fled, Cambridge, Strangled; **10**–Swiss, Priest, Zurich

### 5. Small Group Life Application—*10 or 25–45 minutes*

• [ If you want to lecture or show a video, do so here, 15–30 minutes.]

• Say: "*Many people left the established church during the Reformation because they believed their church's teachings were no longer biblical.*

Others left because of the church's corruption. A few left because they were disappointed with their church's moral standards. In this session, we'll discuss when Christians should divide from others who profess Christ."
• Organize the class into three groups. Assign each group *one* of the following texts: 1 Corinthians 5:9–13; Galatians 1:6–9; 1 John 2:18–23. Say to each group: *"Ask yourselves, 'According to this Scripture, when should Christians divide?'"* After 8 minutes, allow each group to respond. Here are the suggested responses:
• *If someone who professes Christ defies God's moral precepts …* (1 Corinthians 5:9–13).
• *If someone attempts to alter the plan of salvation …* (Galatians 1:6–9).
• *If someone denies Jesus' identity as Messiah, God, and man …* (1 John 2:18–23).

## 6. Individual Life Application—*14 minutes*
• Say: *"In each situation, someone was endangering a vital part of the Christian faith. I've listed several reasons why people who profess Christ divide. Some endanger vital parts of the Christian faith. Others don't."* **[Read each sentence from the poster.]**
• Say: *"On your My Theses papers, list several situations when Christians should divide from others who profess Christ. Your reasons don't necessarily need to come from my list."* [Allow 5 minutes.] *"Look at each item on your list."* Ask, *"Is this difference essential to the Christian faith? If it isn't essential, cross out the difference. If you're uncertain, circle the difference."* [Allow 4 minutes.]
• Say: *"Let's spend some time praying. Reread your lists. As you read each crossed-out item, ask God to help you accept that difference in other Christians. As you read each circled item, ask God to give you wisdom to know if that is a vital part of the Christian faith. When you finish praying, nail your theses to the board at the front of the class. Let that be your commitment to follow God's leadership when you are faced with a division in the body of Christ."* Nail your own paper on the board to show students what you want them to do. If possible, play meditative background music while students pray and nail their theses to the board.

## 7. Upcoming Assignment and Closure—*3 minutes*
Remind students to complete the Chapter Nine Learning Activity before the next session. Sing a song that reflects the theme for this session.

## Digging Deeper
*A Man For All Seasons* (9967) (Vision Video, 120 minutes)
*Martin Luther: Heretic* (Family Films/ Concordia Publishing, 75 minutes)
*Love God? Sometimes I Hate Him!* by R.C. Sproul (Ligonier Ministries, 50 minutes)
*Renaissance and Reformation* by W. Estep (Grand Rapids: Eerdmans, 1986)
*Here I Stand: A Life of Martin Luther* by R. Bainton (Plume: 1995)
*A Cloud of Witnesses* by C. Weaver and C.D. Weaver (Georgia: Smyth and Helwys, 1993)

## CHAPTER NINE (1510–1767) DISCUSSION AND REVIEW SESSION

### Session Goals
This session will help students:
• Reinforce the knowledge they have gained by reading Chapter Nine.
• Recognize that lasting transformations among God's people must include not only institutional changes, but also individual changes.

### Supplies
• Four sheets of colored paper
• A slip of paper for each student
• One large piece of poster-board or shelf paper
• A copy of the following article, downloadable at www.christianitytoday.com, for each student: W. Russell. "What It Means to Me" in *Christianity Today* (10/26/92): 30–32.
OPTIONAL: Two reliable commentaries on *each* of the following biblical books: Joshua, Isaiah, Genesis and Luke.
OPTIONAL: PowerPoint® slideshow for this session, available from Rose Publishing

### 1. Preparation
• Ask God to guide you throughout the session.
• Study Chapter Nine and the Chapter Nine Learning Activity.

• Use the poster-board to post a sign that reads: *CHANGE! IT'S PERSONAL, TOO.*
• On each colored sheet of paper, write one of these headings: (1) *Does the sun move or does the earth? Joshua 10:12–13.* (2) *Did God ordain Europe's quest of distant coastlands? Isaiah 11:11–12.* (3) *Does God command Canaan's descendants to be slaves? Genesis 9:25.* (4) *Can we use violence to compel people to believe? Luke 14:23.*
• Organize the slips of paper into four equal groups. Write one of the following four texts on each slip of paper, so that there is an equal number of paper slips with each text: Joshua 10:12–13; Isaiah 11:11–12; Genesis 9:25; Luke 14:23.
• Hang a colored sheet of paper in each corner of the room. Prepare a circle of chairs beneath each of the four sheets of colored paper. Be certain that approximately the same number of chairs may be found in each circle and that the total number of the chairs is adequate to seat your entire study group.
OPTIONAL: Place two commentaries, corresponding to the text on the sign, within each circle of chairs.
• Prepare to sing the theme song and another appropriate song, such as the Bohemian Protestant hymn "Sing Praise to God Who Reigns Above."

## 2. Before the Session
• As students enter, randomly hand out the slips of paper.

## 3. Worship—*5 minutes*
Sing the theme song and another appropriate song.

## 4. Learning Activity—*5 minutes*
Review the Chapter Nine Learning Activity as a group. **ANSWERS:** 1–B; 2–G; 3–L; 4–H; 5–J; 6–K; 7–F; 8–I; 9–C; 10–D; 11–A; 12–Answers will vary.

## 5. Small Group Life Application—
*15 minutes*
• Say: *"Each of you should have a slip of paper. The Scripture on your paper matches one of the posters at the corners of the room. Someone in church history misused each of those Scriptures. Go sit beneath your assigned Scripture reference.*

*Carefully study your assigned text as a group. Ask yourselves, 'How did past Christians misuse this text? What is its actual meaning?' Write your answers on the sheet of paper above your circle of chairs."* OPTIONAL: *"Use the commentaries beneath your signs to study the text."*
• Allow 12 minutes for discussion.
• Reassemble the class. Allow each group to talk about its assigned text. Do not allow students to argue or to stray from the subject. Here are some suggested responses:
(1) Galileo realized that the earth rotates around the sun. Church leaders tried to use Joshua 10:12–13 to prove that the sun rotates around the earth. Yet the Bible portrays historical events from a human perspective. From Joshua's perspective, the sun did seem to stand still.
(2) Columbus claimed that Isaiah 11:11–12 proved that God had ordained his quest. Yet, in its context, the passage refers to Israel's return from exile, not to Columbus' journey.
(3) Slave owners used Genesis 9:25 to say that God wanted Africans to be slaves. Yet the Bible never clearly affirms that this text refers to Africans. Furthermore, Noah—not God—is speaking here. The Bible never affirms that God approved Noah's curse.
(4) Settlers used Luke 14:23 to justify their violence against non-Christian natives. Jesus did compel people with convincing words. Yet he never approved violence as an evangelistic methodology.
• **[Read Deuteronomy 18:20.]** Say: *"Today, God doesn't call Christ's people to kill false prophets. But it's still a serious matter to misapply God's words. How can Christians today avoid misusing biblical texts?"* Use the article "What It Means to Me" to guide a discussion about misusing biblical texts.

## 6. Large Group Life Application—
*10 or 25–40 minutes*
• [If you want to lecture or show a video, do so here, 15–30 minutes.]
• Say: *"Christianity changed radically in the Reformation. Many of the changes were needed, and the changes did solve some problems. Yet the changes failed to solve all the problems. Perhaps people failed to see that change can't be confined to institutions. Real change must begin with the individual. How do Christians today try to*

transform institutions and fail to see changes that are needed in individual lives?"
• Here are some suggested responses: *When a church doesn't grow, members criticize the staff instead of making certain that they're right with God; When God's presence seems absent, churches try new programs instead of seeking authentic spiritual awakening.*

### 7. Individual Life Application—*5 minutes*
Urge students to ask themselves, How do I fail to see areas in my life that need to change? Spend a few moments in silent prayer. If possible, play a meditative song as people pray. End the time of meditation with an appropriate prayer, such as: *Lord, we also have misused your words. We have expected institutions to change when, in truth, it is we ourselves who need to change. Show us our sins. Cleanse our sins. Give us strength to turn from them. Amen.*

### 8. Closure—*2 minutes*
Remind students that, before the next group meeting, they should complete the Chapter Ten Learning Activity.

### Digging Deeper
*God's Peoples* by Spickard, P. and K. Cragg, eds. (Grand Rapids: Baker, 1994) 216–227.
"Columbus and Christianity" in *Christian History* Issue 35
*A History of Christianity in the United States and Canada* by M. Noll (Grand Rapids: Eerdmans, 1992) 12.
*The Story of Christianity* vol. 1, by J. Gonzalez (Harper One; 1984) 382–411.
*This Rebellious House* by S. Keillor (Downer's Grove InterVarsity, 1996) 26–37.
*Cromwell* (0003) (Vision Video, 139 minutes)
*The Mission* (0303) (Vision Video, 125 minutes)
"Baptists" in *Christian History* Issue 6.
"John Bunyan" in *Christian History* Issue 11.

### CHAPTER TEN (1620–1814) DISCUSSION AND REVIEW SESSION

### Session Goals
This session will help students:
• Reinforce the knowledge they have gained by reading Chapter Ten.

• Consider how the unchanging Word of God can intersect the ever-changing cultures of mankind.

### Supplies
• Eight overhead transparencies and an overhead projector or a hymnal for each student that includes the songs listed below or a digital projector and computer to project lyrics on a screen
• Eight 3x5 cards
• One large piece of poster-board or shelf paper OPTIONAL: PowerPoint® slideshow for this session, available from Rose Publishing

### 1. Preparation
• Ask God to guide you throughout the session.
• Use the poster-board to post a sign: *HOW CAN CHRISTIANS ADAPT TO THEIR CULTURE WITHOUT COMPROMISING THEIR FAITH?*
• On each card, write one of these statements. *Include the numbers on each card!*
1. Before the 1700s most Christians sang only psalms, like "Lift Up Your Heads," a paraphrase of Psalm 24:7–10.
2. In the 1700s Pietists, like the Moravians, wrote songs that focused on their relationship with Jesus. Nikolaus Zinzendorf, a Pietist, wrote "Christian Hearts, in Love United" and "Jesus, Lead the Way."
3. Through the Moravians, God drew John and Charles Wesley to Christ. "And Can It Be" captures the heart of the Wesleys' faith.
4. For a few years, George Whitefield and the Wesleys split over predestination. Had they not reunited, you might never have sung, "Hark! The Herald Angels Sing." Charles Wesley wrote the song—but we usually sing Whitefield's altered version.
5. Isaac Watts was another Pietist hymn–writer. Isaac Watts wrote "I'll Praise My Maker." Around 1737 John Wesley modified Watts' original words.
6. Deism focused people on God's creation. In "I Sing the Mighty Power of God," Watts praised God as the Creator without reducing God to a distant creator and nothing more.
7. Unlike Deists, Watts and other Pietists went beyond praising God as the Creator. In

"When I Survey the Wondrous Cross," Watts worshiped Christ as his Redeemer and God.
8. John Wesley and other Great Awakening preachers spoke against slavery. In 1764 a slave trader named John Newton became a Christian. He rejected his old ways and wrote "Amazing Grace."
• Locate these hymns: "Amazing Grace" (Newton); "And Can It Be" (Wesley); "Christian Hearts, in Love United" or, "Jesus, Lead the Way" (Zinzendorf); "Hark! The Herald Angels Sing" (Wesley/ [Whitefield]); "I Sing the Mighty Power of God" (Watts); "I'll Praise My Maker" (Watts/Wesley); "Lift Up Your Heads" (Weissel); "When I Survey the Wondrous Cross" (Watts). If your church's hymnal does not include these songs, you can write the lyrics of public domain hymns on transparencies.
• Enlist musicians and a song leader to direct the hymns.
• Study Chapter Ten and the Chapter Ten Learning Activity.

## 2. Before the Session
• As students arrive, distribute the cards to students who can read well publicly and who are willing to read aloud. Comment that the cards are numbered. The first card will be read after the opening song. The second card will be read after "Lift Up Your Heads," and so on.

## 3. Worship—*30 minutes*
• Sing the theme song or another appropriate song, such as, "O For a Thousand Tongues to Sing" (Wesley).
• [Read Psalm 78:12–23] Say: "*The ancient Hebrews reviewed their history through this psalm. Let's follow their example. Let's review our Christian heritage through God's gift of music! So ...*" [Read Psalm 78:1–8]
• Ask the student who received the first card to read his/her card aloud. After each reading, the song leader should immediately lead everyone in singing the first verse of the suggested hymn. Continue until all eight cards have been read and the group has sung all eight hymns.

## 4. Large Group Review—
*7 or 20–35 minutes*
• [If you want to lecture or show a video, do so here, 15–30 minutes.]
• Quickly review the Chapter Ten Learning Activity.
**ANSWERS:** 1–Roger Williams; 2–Anne Hutchinson; 3–Jonathan Edwards; 4–Nikolaus Zinzendorf; 5–Susanna Wesley; 6–George Whitefield; 7–John Wesley; 8–Sarah Crosby; 9–Answers will vary 10–Answers will vary. Use the definitions of Deism and the Enlightenment listed at the beginning of Chapter Ten to help students answer these questions.

## 5. Life Application—*12 minutes*
• Say: "*In the 1700s, Deism threatened Christianity. According to Deists, God was the Creator—but little more. Many people who called themselves Christians embraced Deism. By the late 1700s and early 1800s, many churches had abandoned the Bible's depiction of God. They had adapted their beliefs to their culture until they had nothing left to believe in. What false ideas about God are popular in our culture?*" [**Allow students to respond until they come up with 3–5 ideas. The ideas may be perversions of Christian truth (like the denial that Jesus is the only way of salvation) or of Christian practice (like changing the Christian faith to appeal to non-believers). List the ideas on a chalkboard, whiteboard, or transparency.**]
• Say: "*Like many false ideas, some forms of Deism arose from a desire that seemed good—a longing for tolerance and peace. Why did the false ideas that we've listed arise?*" [**As students respond, try to help them see that false ideas usually arise from desires that seem good. The problem is that people fail to locate the right response to their desires.**]
• Say: "*Christians must never adapt their faith to false beliefs. But Christians can let non-believers' longings help them understand how to respond to false ideas in their culture. Name some right responses to the desires that led to the false beliefs that we've listed.*" [**Allow students to respond until at least several specific responses surface.**]

## 6. Upcoming Assignment and Closure—
*3 minutes*
• Lead a brief prayer. Ask God to help your students respond appropriately to false beliefs.
• Remind the students to complete the Chapter Eleven Learning Activity before the next session.

### Digging Deeper
"George Whitefield" in *Christian History* Issue 38.

"The American Revolution" in *Christian History* Issue 50.

*This Rebellious House* by S. Keillor (Downer's Grove InterVarsity, 1996) 70–102.

*The Baptist Heritage* by L. McBeth (Nashville: Broadman, 1987) 124–136.

*A History of Christianity in the United States and Canada* by M. Noll (Grand Rapids: Eerdmans, 1992) 132–136.

## CHAPTER ELEVEN (1780–1914) DISCUSSION AND REVIEW SESSION

### Session Goals
This session will help students:
• Reinforce the knowledge they have gained by reading Chapter Eleven.
• Become more aware of how God may be working in their lives.

### Supplies
• Christmas decorations (e.g., a small tree, tinsel, lights, etc.)
• A piece of paper and pencil for each student
• A photocopy of the essay "Christmas Wasn't Born Here" for each student. Your local library should be able to locate the essay. The article may be found on the Internet or in printed form—K.L. Woodward, "Christmas Wasn't Born Here." *Newsweek* (12/16/96): 71.
• A chalkboard
• One large piece of poster-board or shelf paper
• Biographical articles about five of these people: William Carey, Amy Carmichael, Fanny Crosby, Sarah Grimke, Ann H. Judson, Lottie Moon, C. H. Spurgeon, Hudson Taylor, Sojourner Truth, William Wilberforce. You can find articles through:
—The Internet (*www.christianhistory.net www. gty.org/~phil gospelcom.net/chi/glimpses/ indexpage.htm*)

—Your local library (*Oxford Dictionary of the Christian Church* and encyclopedias)
OPTIONAL: PowerPoint® slideshow for this session, available from Rose Publishing

### 1. Preparation
• Ask God to guide you throughout the session.
• Study Chapter Eleven and the Chapter Eleven Learning Activity.
• Post a sign that reads: GOD'S ONLY BOUNDARY IS HIS OWN NATURE!
• Trim the classroom with the Christmas decorations.
• Arrange the biographical articles, papers, and pencils on tables.
• On the board, write the names of people about whom you located articles.
• Select two or three songs to sing during the session, such as "It Came Upon a Midnight Clear" (a 19th-century Christmas song), "Faith is the Victory" (one of Ira Sankey's hymns), "Mine Eyes Have Seen the Glory" (a song from the Civil War), or some of Fanny Crosby's hymns.

### 2. Before the Session
• As students enter, be certain they have completed the Chapter Eleven Learning Activity.
• Give each student a copy of the essay "Christmas Wasn't Born Here" to read as other students arrive.

### 3. Worship—*10 minutes*
Sing the theme song and two or three 19th-century hymns.

### 4. Learning Activity—*12 minutes*
Review Chapter Eleven Learning Activity. These answers are suggestions: **ANSWERS:** 1–modern, optimism, progress; 2–Carey challenged his church's refusal to obey this text; 3–To reach the Chinese, the Taylors adopted Chinese culture; 4–The Restorationists wanted Christians to forsake denominations so that they could obey this text; 5–God used Lydia's prayers to bring Charles to salvation; 6–feelings; 7–Both White and Miller believed persons could predict Christ's return; 8–(a) Jesus is God, John 1:1; (b) Jesus was virgin–born, Matthew 1:18; (c)

Jesus died as a sacrifice for sinners, 1 John 2:2; (d) Jesus arose from the dead and will come again, Acts 1:3–11; (e) The Bible contains no errors, 2 Timothy 3:16–17.

## 5. Large Group Reflection and Review—
*5 minutes*
• Say: *"In the 1600s and 1700s, few Christians in England or the Americas observed Christmas. When Christmas was celebrated, it was—in a nineteenth century bishop's words—'a day of worldly festivity, shooting, and swearing.' In the 1800s, Clement Moore published a poem titled 'Twas the Night Before Christmas.' According to a Dutch legend, St. Nicholas dropped dowries down chimneys for poor girls. Moore's poem popularized the legend of St. Nicholas in America and England. By 1843, Christmas had become a time to stay home with one's family. Yet the new Christmas focused on human reason and human goodness. In Charles Dickens'* A Christmas Carol, *the spirit of Christmas, not Jesus Christ, is what transforms Scrooge. Many nineteenth–century people had placed human boundaries—boundaries like faith in human reason, human goodness, and human progress— around God's boundless work until they no longer felt a need for a personal relationship with Christ. Today, Christians still try to limit God's work at times. We may try to restrict the Spirit's movements to our denomination, a certain race, or certain traditions. We sometimes forget that God's only limit is God's own nature, as expressed in Scripture."*

## 6. Research and Sharing—*20 minutes*
• Say: *"On the board, I've listed five names. Each of these people allowed God to break human boundaries—to go 'out of bounds'—in his or her life. Use the resources on the tables to research one of these Christians. On your paper, list (1) an intriguing fact about the person, (2) one way that the person moved beyond human boundaries, and, (3) how Christians today can break similar boundaries."*
• Allow students 12–15 minutes for research.
• Organize the class into three roughly equal groups. Have students share their lists with one another within their groups. Each group should select the most interesting list from among its members.

• Ask each group to share its chosen list with the entire class. On the chalkboard or whiteboard, list the ways that God can work through Christians today to break human boundaries.

## 7. Closure and Upcoming Assignment—
*8 minutes*
• Lead the class in prayer. Ask God to guide each student to recognize God's limitless capacities. Urge students to study Chapter Twelve and to complete the Chapter Twelve Learning Activity before the next meeting.

## Digging Deeper
"Charles G. Finney" in *Christian History* Issue 20.
*A History of Christianity in the United States and Canada* by M. Noll (Grand Rapids: Eerdmans, 1992) 176, 317–323, 370–372.
*How the Churches Got to Be the Way They Are* by                  G. White (SCM Press, 1991) 13–16, 69–71.
*The Scandal of the Evangelical Mind* by M. Noll (Grand Rapids: Eerdmans, 1993)
*Amazing Grace* (20th Century Fox, 2007; 118 minutes)
*Children's Heroes: Damien, Robert Raikes, William Carey* (4208) (Vision Video, 9 minutes each)

## CHAPTER TWELVE (1906–2010) REVIEW AND CLOSURE SESSION

### Session Goals
This session will help students:
• Reinforce the knowledge they have gained by reading Chapter Twelve.
• Consider how to use the knowledge they have gained from their study of church history.

### Supplies
• Black bread (such as pumpernickel), Swiss cheese, sauerkraut, ice cream and sundae toppings, bananas, sunflower seeds, tortilla chips, Italian-flavored snacks or pizza, Polish sausages, trail mix, Graham crackers
• One of the videos suggested in Digging Deeper
• One large piece of poster-board
OPTIONAL: PowerPoint® slideshow for this session, available from Rose Publishing

## 1. Preparation
• Ask God to guide you throughout the session.
• Post a sign that reads: *HOW DID YOU GET TO BE THE WAY YOU ARE?*
• Ready the DVD player and projector or television.
• Prepare food, flatware, plates, and drinks.
• Enlist an accompanist and song leader.
• Study Chapter Twelve and the Chapter Twelve Learning Activity.

## 2. Before the Session
• As members enter, make certain they have finished the Chapter Twelve Learning Activity.
• Ask some members, *"Is there a song or Scripture that has become more meaningful to you because of this study?"* Compile a few songs and Scriptures.

## 3. Worship—*12 minutes*
• Sing the theme song as well as, if possible, the songs that have become more meaningful to members as a result of this study.
• Read some of the Scriptures that have become more meaningful through this study. Ask the class: *"How have these songs and Scriptures become more meaningful to you through this study?"* Allow several students respond.

## 4. Large Group Review—*Time will vary*
• Ask members to locate the Chapter Twelve Learning Activity. Say: *Each of the first ten answers relates to one of the foods on the table. Randomly point at foods and ask: What question and answer might [food] suggest?* Please recognize throughout this activity that the connections between the foods and the facts may not be immediately clear. Have fun!
**ANSWERS: 1**–Russian Orthodox Church (Black bread is often considered to be a Russian staple); **2**–Karl Barth (He was Swiss.); **3**–Dietrich Bonhoeffer (He was German and sauerkraut is a German food.); **4**–Sunday (ice cream sundae); **5**–William Bryan (He participated in the famous "Monkey Trial," and monkeys are known to eat bananas.); **6**–Pentecostals (Sunflowers are often associated with Kansas, where some aspects of the Pentecostal movement began.); **7**–John XXIII (He was an Italian pope; pizza is an Italian food.); **8**–John Paul II (He was Polish.); **9**–World Council of Churches (Trail mix—The WCC is a mixture of various groups.); **10**–Billy Graham (Graham crackers).
• Share your answers for question 11. Use the definition at the beginning of Chapter Twelve to answer question 12.
• Begin the video. Members can eat as they watch the video together. After the video, read aloud a segment of Chapter 12 that relates to the video. Briefly discuss the video, asking, "What parts of this video made more sense because of what you learned in *Christian History Made Easy?*"

## 5. Life Application—*12 minutes*
• Ask: *To what areas of your Christian life can you apply what you have learned through these studies?* Let students respond until three specific responses surface. Write the responses on a chalkboard.
• Read aloud the quote from Gavin White in "Final Reflections." Lead the class in prayer. Ask God to help members to use their new knowledge of their Christian heritage in their daily lives.

## Digging Deeper
*Dietrich Bonhoeffer* (4137) (Vision Video, 60 minutes)
*The Hiding Place* (8024) (Vision Video, 145 minutes)
*Inherit the Wind* (United Artists, 128 minutes)
*Shadowlands* (4054) (Vision Video, 73 minutes)
*A Primer on Postmodernism* by S. Grenz (Grand Rapids: Eerdmans, 1996)
"The Monkey Trial and the Rise of Fundamentalism" in *Christian History* Issue 55.
*After Modernity. What?* by T. Oden (Grand Rapids: Zondervan, 1991)
*No Place for Truth* by D. Wells (Grand Rapids: Eerdmans, 1993)

# INTRODUCTORY LEARNING ACTIVITY

How much do you know about church history?  Fifteen key names from church history are hidden in the word-search.  Each name completes one of the sentences below.  Feel free to use a hymnal or Bible. If you don't know an answer, guess!

| R | E | F | F | E | O | H | N | O | B |
|---|---|---|---|---|---|---|---|---|---|
| E | L | A | S | C | A | S | A | S | Q |
| N | S | G | R | A | H | A | M | L | D |
| I | P | A | U | L | T | B | C | E | R |
| T | U | T | N | S | R | R | A | F | A |
| N | R | A | N | I | A | E | L | F | G |
| A | P | Y | O | M | B | H | V | I | E |
| T | E | E | E | O | H | T | I | L | D |
| S | T | L | G | N | O | U | N | C | L |
| N | E | S | R | S | U | L | L | Y | I |
| O | R | E | U | U | S | H | A | W | H |
| C | R | W | P | H | E | G | R | A | H |
| M | O | T | S | O | S | Y | R | H | C |

1. According to tradition, _____ was crucified upside down.
2. Early Christians met in _____ (Romans 16:5).
3. Emperor _____ claimed that he saw a cross in the sky.
4. John _____ 's nickname meant "Golden-Mouth."
5. One bishop accused _____ of Bingen, a mystic, of heresy.
6. Many Protestants call John _____ "the Morning Star of the Reformation."
7. Martin _____ wrote "A Mighty Fortress Is Our God."
8. John _____ wrote the *Institutes of the Christian Religion*.
9. Menno _____ was an early Anabaptist leader.
10. Bartolome de _____ fought his country's exploitation of Native Americans.
11. Charles _____, who wrote the hymn "And Can It Be", was part of a "Holy Club" at Oxford University.
12. Charles _____ was an English pastor in the mid-1800s.
13. Karl _____ 's commentary on Romans criticized the liberal theology of the 1800s.
14. Hitler had Dietrich _____ executed in 1945.
15. Billy _____ has been called the "best loved American Christian."

# CHAPTER ONE LEARNING ACTIVITY

This quiz will help you review what you read in Chapter One.
Try to answer the questions without looking back in the book.

## TRUE OR FALSE

1. ___ Roman citizens rarely served only one god.
2. ___ Nero started the fire in Rome.
3. ___ Peter was probably crucified upside down.
4. ___ Romans loved anything new.
5. ___ Non-Christians often attended Christian worship services.
6. ___ During the first century, the Jewish faith was legal in the Roman empire.
7. ___ Domitian refused to let anyone call him "God."
8. ___ The temple was destroyed in AD 64.
9. ___ After the temple burned, Jewish leaders urged synagogues to accept Christians.
10. ___ Emperor Domitian ignored the Christians.

## FILL IN THE BLANKS

*(Answers to these two questions will vary.)*

11. Name two reasons Christianity was unpopular in the first and second centuries.

    a. _____

       _____

       _____

    b. _____

       _____

       _____

12. God uses social and political factors to produce spiritual results. List two social or political factors that God used to expand the church's mission.

    a. _____

       _____

       _____

    b. _____

       _____

       _____

# CHAPTER TWO LEARNING ACTIVITY

This quiz will help you review what you read in Chapter 2.
Place the correct letters in the blanks.

1.  In the late first century, overseers and elders were _____.
    A. the same position
    B. slightly different positions
    C. nonexistent

2. According to the Gnostics, _____ was evil.
    A. everything spiritual   B. everything physical   C. Christ

3. Marcion created the first _____.
    A. creed     B. church     C. list of authoritative writings

4. The church's responses to Gnosticism included _____,
    and overseers.
    A. a canon, a creed
    B. a canon, a Bible
    C. a cannon, a sword

5. The Rule of Faith is still used, in a slightly altered form.
    Christians call it _____.
    A. the church newsletter
    B. the Baptist Hymnal
    C. the Apostles' Creed

6. Rome's overseer became powerful because _____ and because two apostles died
    in Rome.
    A. Rome was an important city
    B. he was intelligent
    C. of his wife

7. When eastern Christians refused to celebrate Easter on the same day as
    Romans, _____ excluded eastern Christians from fellowship with
    Roman Christians.
    A. Elmo              B. Anicetus              C. Victor

8. The New Prophets made _____ .
    A. fun of the Trinity   B. some false predictions   C. love not war

9. Eastern Christians celebrated Easter during the _____.
    A. Jewish Passover     B. winter   C. Super Bowl

10. The church's holiness depends on the _____.
    A. holiness of its members   B. Holy Spirit   C. holy overseers

# CHAPTER THREE LEARNING ACTIVITY

Number the following events in the correct order. You will probably need to refer back to Chapter Three. To help you get started, two events are already numbered. Write 2 beside the next earliest event, 3 beside the event that occurred next, and so on.

A. ___ The Donatists ask Constantine to settle a church dispute.
B. ___ Diocletian and Galerius persecute Christians for the last time.
C. ___ Constantine supposedly sees a cross in the sky.
D. ___ Julian, an opponent of Christianity, becomes the emperor.
E. _1_ Constantine restores Arius and exiles Athanasius.
F. _7_ All Romans must obtain sacrifice certificates.
G. ___ The Council of Nicaea agrees that Jesus is one essence with the Father.
H. ___ In Alexandria, Eastern and Western Christians agree that God is three persons with one essence.
I. ___ Cyprian allows persons to reenter their churches if they show outward signs of sorrow.
J. ___ Beneath a cross, Constantine marches into Rome.

Answer the following questions.

1. Many Eastern Christians disliked the phrase in the Creed of Nicaea that described Jesus as being "of one essence with the Father." Why?
_____
_____

   Restate the phrase "of one essence with the Father" in your own words. _____
   _____

   How would you explain the phrase to a sixth-grade Sunday school student? _____
   _____

2. Why did many fourth-century Christians flee to the desert?
   1) _____
   2) _____

3. The Cappadocian communities for nuns and monks, founded by Macrina and Basil, weren't like other religious communities. What made their communities different?
   _____
   _____

4. How do the Council of Nicaea's decisions affect your church today?
   _____
   _____

# CHAPTER FOUR LEARNING ACTIVITY

This quiz will help you review what you read in Chapter Four. In the word search, locate ten key words from the chapter. Write the words in the blanks.

| | | | | | | | | | |
|---|---|---|---|---|---|---|---|---|---|
| C | H | A | L | C | E | D | O | N | S |
| Y | I | C | O | O | S | R | L | E | Q |
| R | L | I | L | P | O | P | E | S | J |
| I | E | T | Y | S | R | E | M | T | D |
| S | N | S | M | T | B | Q | O | O | L |
| C | I | A | P | A | M | U | E | R | I |
| H | T | L | I | N | A | D | L | I | H |
| E | S | O | A | T | S | A | N | U | D |
| V | U | H | S | C | H | O | L | S | L |
| O | G | C | Y | R | I | E | V | E | I |
| J | U | S | T | I | N | I | A | N | H |
| S | A | N | A | I | N | I | V | O | J |

1. _____ did not like the division between clergy and laypeople.

2. Before he became Milan's bishop,_____ was a governor.

3. _____ used her inheritance to give slaves their freedom.

4. Ambrose's preaching impressed_____.

5. _____ was misunderstood when he criticized a common title for Mary, "God-Bearer."

6. _____ convinced Attila the Hun not to plunder Rome.

7. In AD 451 the Council of _____ used Leo's *Tome*, Cyril's writings, and the Nicene Creed to explain the relationship of Jesus' two natures.

8. _____ convened the Second Council of Constantinople, AD 553.

9. _____ and her twin brother, Benedict, built religious communities in Italy. Their guideline was Benedict's *Rule*.

10. Even though she was English, _____ defended Celtic-Irish traditions at the Synod of Whitby.

11. Gregory is sometimes called "the first _____ ."

12. What person in this chapter would you most like to meet? Why? What questions would you ask her or him? (*Answers will vary.*) _____

# CHAPTER FIVE LEARNING ACTIVITY

This quiz will help you review what you read in Chapter Five.
Choose the word or phrase that completes each sentence.

1. Muslims worship _____.
   A. Muhammad              B. Allah              C. idols

2. The Second Council of Nicaea allowed Christians to _____.
   A. worship idols.      B. idolize icons      C. revere icons

3. Pope Leo III crowned King Charles of the Franks as the _____.
   A. Roman emperor    B. Roman bishop   C. Saxon emperor

4. The forged *Donation of Constantine* granted lands to the _____.
   A. Eastern church  B. English church  C. Roman church

5. Pope Leo IX ("Bruno") _____.
   A. promoted priestly celibacy        B. pardoned Henry IV

6. The purpose of the First Crusade was to _____.
   A. sack Constantinople  B. kill Jews  C. conquer Jerusalem

7. Pope Innocent III _____ the attack on Constantinople.
   A. ignored         B. encouraged         C. forbade

## Match each statement below with its source.

8. _____ Third Council of Constantinople

9. _____ The Roman Nicene Creed

10. _____ Pope Urban II's sermon

11. _____ Humbert's bull

12. _____ Fourth Lateran Council

A. "If anyone out of devotion sets out for Jerusalem, the journey shall be seen as penance."

B. "Michael Cerularius and his followers be damned."

C. "[The Holy Spirit] proceeds from the Father and the Son."

D. "We glorify two natures and two wills agreeing within [Jesus] for the salvation of humanity."

E. "His body and blood are . . . in the sacraments."

# CHAPTER SIX LEARNING ACTIVITY

This crossword puzzle will help you review what you learned as you read Chapter Six. Try to complete the puzzle without looking at the chapter.

1. In 1112, _____ of Clairvaux became a Cistercian monk.
2. When _____ died, he remained under his church's condemnation.
3. The founder of the Franciscan order was from _____.
4. _____ was an archbishop of Canterbury.
5. _____ preachers traveled throughout medieval towns.
6. _____ wanted to encounter God directly
7. John _____ lost his right hand and his freedom when someone lied about him.
8. English and Irish monks and _____ spread the gospel through self-sufficient religious communities.
9. Thomas _____ combined Aristotle's logic with devout Christian faith.
10. _____ and Boniface were English missionaries to Germany.
11. Hildegard, a mystic, directed a convent near _____, Germany.
12. After his conversion, _____ gave away his possessions and cared for lepers.
13. Duke William gave up his hunting dogs to build a new monastery at _____.
14. _____ scholars, like Anselm and Aquinas, integrated God's revelation with human reason.
15. English and Irish monks used their top-quality _____ to generate interest in the Christian faith.
16. Although he thought Francis' rules were too strict, Pope Innocent _____ approved Francis' movement.
17. In this chapter, you learned that _____ is always working.
18. From a human viewpoint, _____ and Methodius failed as missionaries. Yet God turned their efforts into a success.

# CHAPTER SEVEN LEARNING ACTIVITY

This learning activity will help you review what you learned as you read Chapter Seven.

1. What sort of pope was Celestine V? _____
   _____

2. For 72 years the popes reigned from _____,
   a village on the French border.

3. Name one way people responded to the Black Death.
   _____

4. How did the Roman Catholic Church end the Great Papal
   Schism? _____

5. Wycliffe believed all Christians were responsible to study
   and understand the Bible for themselves. Why? _____
   _____
   _____

6. Why did many members of the Common Life Movement
   dislike Scholasticism? _____
   _____

7. List two words that might have described Joan of Arc.
   (a) _____ (b) _____

8. Why did many fifteenth-century Christian scholars call
   themselves humanists? _____
   _____

9. List two words that might have described Erasmus.
   (a) _____ (b) _____

10. God isn't on the side of any human regime. God is on the
    side of his own character. Christ demonstrated God's
    character through a cross—not through military conquests.
    Rent and watch the videos *Joan of Arc* and *Henry V*.
    Each film portrays a battle from the Hundred Years' War.
    When and how did the English (*Henry V*) and the French
    (*Joan of Arc*) both assume God was on their side?
    _____
    _____

11. When and how do Christians today assume that God takes
    political sides?_____
    _____
    _____

# CHAPTER EIGHT LEARNING ACTIVITY

In each blank, write words from the list that relate to the name beside the blank. Most words in the list will be used more than once. After you finish the learning activity, add one word of your own in each blank.

| | | | |
|---|---|---|---|
| Anabaptist | Dutch | Jesuit | Studious |
| Barrel | English | Monk | Swiss |
| Cambridge | French | Nun | Theses |
| Catherine | Fled | Priest | Translator |
| Catholic | Geneva | Soldier | Wife |
| Council | German | Spanish | Wittenberg |
| Drowned | Institutes | Strangled | Zurich |

1. Ignatius Loyola _____

2. John Calvin _____

3. Henry VIII _____

4. Kaetie Luther _____

5. Martin Luther _____

6. Felix Manz _____

7. Menno Simons _____

8. Trent _____

9. William Tyndale _____

10. Ulrich Zwingli _____

# CHAPTER NINE LEARNING ACTIVITY

This quiz will help you review what you read in Chapter Nine.
Match the statements with the people or events.

1. _____ Jacob Arminius
2. _____ Galileo
3. _____ Huguenots
4. _____ Bohemian Protestants
5. _____ Puritans
6. _____ King James
7. _____ John Smyth
8. _____ John Bunyan
9. _____ Westminster Assembly
10. _____ Bartolome de Las Casas
11. _____ Pedro Claver

A. "Always a slave of Africans."

B. People must choose to cooperate with God.

C. "The chief end of man is to glorify God . . . ."

D. "The Indians are our brothers."

E. "Am I not free to dissent from Vieyra's opinion?"

F. Brothers of the Separation of the Second English
   Church in Amsterdam.

G. Mathematically, a sun- centered universe makes the
   most sense.

H. Threw two Catholic envoys through a window, marking
   the beginning of the Thirty Years' War.

I. Wrote Pilgrims' Progress.

J. Wanted earthly joy to lead them to glorify God.

K. Disliked the Puritans' Geneva Bible.

L. Were slaughtered on St. Bartholomew's Day.

12. The movie *The Mission* portrays the demise of one Jesuit
    mission. Check out the movie from your library or video
    store. After you watch the movie, reread the stories about
    the sugar plantations, Las Casas, and Claver. How did the
    movie help you understand the Jesuit missions?

    _____

    _____

    _____

    _____

    _____

    _____

# CHAPTER TEN LEARNING ACTIVITY

This quiz will help you review what you read in Chapter Ten. Fill in the blanks.

1. Under_____, Rhode Island became a haven for religious refugees.

2. The Massachusetts Bay Colony exiled _____ because of her unpopular views.

3. By contemporary standards, _____ would have been a boring speaker.

4. Count _____ started round-the-clock prayer meetings which the Moravian Brethren continued for more than 100 years.

5. Hundreds of people came to _____'s home, to hear her speak. One of her sons wrote more than 5,000 hymns.

6. _____ disagreed with the Wesleys about predestination.

7. _____ , the founder of the Methodist movement, opposed the Revolutionary War.

8. During the Great Awakening, _____ preached throughout England. Her preaching tours continued for 20 years.

9. Review the section entitled, "You Say You Want a Revolution in Human Reason?" Look up "[the] Enlightenment" in an encyclopedia. Define the Enlightenment in your own words.

   _____

   _____

   _____

10. Review the sections that explain Deism. Name two ways that Deism differs from biblical Christianity. Find a Scripture that gives God's view of each difference. List the differences and the Scriptures below.

    A. _____

    _____

    B. _____

# CHAPTER ELEVEN LEARNING ACTIVITY

This quiz will help you review what you read in Chapter Eleven.
Fill in the blanks.

1. List two words that describe the 1800s:
   (a) _____ (b) _____

2. How does Matthew 28:19-20 relate to William Carey?
   _____
   _____

3. How does 1 Corinthians 9:20-23 relate to Hudson and Maria
   Taylor? _____
   _____

4. How does John 17:20-21 relate to the Stone-Campbell
   Restoration Movement? _____
   _____

5. How does James 5:16 relate to Lydia Andrews and Charles
   Finney? _____
   _____

6. List one word that describes the teachings of Kant and
   Schleiermacher. _____
   _____

7. How does Mark 13:30-32 relate to William Miller and
   Ellen G. H. White? _____
   _____

8. List the five fundamental beliefs that were affirmed at the
   1895 Bible conference. Locate a Bible verse that relates
   to each one. (a)_____
   (b) _____ (c) _____
   (d) _____ (e) _____

# CHAPTER TWELVE LEARNING ACTIVITY

This "Who Am I?" exercise will help you recall what you learned as you read Chapter Twelve.

1. When the Russian Revolution occurred, we lost our special status. Who are we? _____

2. When I saw my professors' names on a statement that supported World War I, I forsook liberal theology. Who am I?
   _____

3. I guided a seminary for the Confessing Church. Hitler himself decreed my death. Who am I? _____

4. I was a popular fundamentalist evangelist. When Congress prohibited alcoholic beverages, I preached a funeral for "John Barleycorn." Who am I?_____

5. I prosecuted John Scopes in the famous "Monkey Trial." Who am I? _____

6. Our movement began in Kansas and spread to Azusa Street in Los Angeles. Who are we? _____

7. I was a 76-year-old Italian cardinal when I became pope. I convened the Second Vatican Council in Rome. This council urged Roman Catholics to study the Bible. Who am I? _____

8. I asked God's Spirit to heal my homeland. Ten years later, Communism collapsed. Who am I? _____

9. Delegates from Orthodox, Anglican, and other Protestant churches joined to form our ecumenical group. Who are we?
   _____

10. I was a founder of *Christianity Today*. I have been called "the best-known and best-loved American Christian." Who am I?
    _____

11. Check out the movie *Inherit the Wind* from your library or video store. The movie depicts the "Monkey Trial" of 1925. The movie changes several key facts and scenes. (Bryan becomes "Brady"; Darrow becomes "Drummond"; Scopes becomes "Cates.") Still, it's a useful resource to help Christians think about their beliefs. How did the movie help you understand American fundamentalism in the 1920s?
    _____

12. Define "postmodernity" in your own words:
    _____

# A

Abelard, Peter 78
Africa 32, 35, 38, 54, 65, 152, 184, 186, 187
African-Americans 145, 148, 155, 159, 160, 174, 185
African Methodist Episcopal Church 145, 148
A'Kempis, Thomas 99, 118
Albigensians 62, 74
Alfred the Great 78
Allen, Richard 145, 148
Ambrose of Milan 49, 51, 54
Anabaptists 104, 112, 113, 114, 119, 128
Anglican Church 117, 120, 122, 127, 134, 146, 147
Anselm 88, 98
Apollinarianism 46
Apostolic Fathers 8
Aquinas, Thomas 78, 88, 89
Arianism 32
Arius 38, 39, 40, 41, 49, 56
Arminianism 123, 145
Arminius, Jacob 123
Asbury, Francis 134
Athanasius 32, 40, 41, 42, 44, 54
Atheism 17, 103
Augustine 8, 46, 53, 54, 55, 59, 60, 80, 120, 150
Azusa Street Revival 164, 183, 184

# B

Baptism 23, 27, 36, 40, 50, 55, 67, 71, 83, 86, 90, 98, 112, 113, 128, 129, 134, 184
Baptists 120, 127, 128, 129, 137, 145, 148, 150, 151, 153, 160, 163, 173, 174, 177
Barleycorn, John 170
Barth, Karl 167, 168, 169, 170, 174, 179
Bartolome de Las Casas 131
Basil of Caesarea 32
Bede the Venerable 78

Benedict, Saint 58
Bernard of Clairvaux 78, 83, 84
Bernard, Saint 84
Beza, Theodore 104
Black Death (Plague) 94, 95, 96
Blandina 8, 19
Bonaventure 78
Bonhoeffer, Dietrich 173, 174, 175, 176
Boniface VIII, Pope 92, 93
Boxer Rebellion 148
Bryan, William Jennings 172, 173
Bucer, Martin 104
Bunyan, John 127, 128, 129

# C

Calvinism 123, 124, 134, 145, 151
Calvin, John 104, 110, 111, 169
Cane Ridge Revival 152
Cappadocia 32, 44, 45, 51
Carey, William 150, 151, 152
Carlstadt 104
Carmichael, Amy 152
Catherine of Sienna 95
Catholicism 74, 75, 76, 78, 85, 90, 117, 180
Celestine V, Pope 93
Celtic-Irish Christians 46, 59, 60
Charlemagne 62, 68, 75, 80
Children's Crusade 78
China (Chinese) 78, 120, 148, 152, 183, 184, 206
Chrysostom, John 52, 53
Cistercians 78, 84
Civil War 160, 163
Claver, Pedro 132, 133
Clement of Rome 8
Columbus, Christopher 130
Conciliarism 90
Constantine, Emperor 32, 36, 37, 38, 39, 40, 41, 52, 62, 67
Consubstantiation 104
Copernicus 124, 125, 140
Coptic Orthodox 57
Council of Chalcedon 46,

57, 62
Council of Constance 90, 98
Council of Constantinople, First 46, 50
Council of Constantinople, Second 46
Council of Constantinople, Third 62
Council of Ephesus 46
Council of Florence 90, 104
Council of Nicaea 32, 39, 40, 50, 62, 66
Council of Pisa 96, 98, 104
Council of Trent 118
Covenantalism 148
Crusades 71, 72
Cyprian 32, 35, 36
Cyril 56, 57
Cyril and Methodius 82, 83

# D

Damascus, John 81, 82
Damien 152
Darby, J. Nelson 148
Darrow, Clarence 172, 173
Dead Sea Scrolls 12, 164
Declaration of Independence 147
Deism 134, 141, 146, 147
Descartes, Rene 120
Diocletian, Emperor 32, 36
Dispensationalism 148
Docetism 20, 24
Dominicans 78, 89, 120
Domitian, Emperor 16
Donatism 32, 36, 38
Duke William III 81

# E

Eastern Orthodoxy 62, 71, 74, 75, 77, 78, 85, 100, 187
Eckhart, Meister 90
Eck, Johann Maier 104
Edict of Milan 32, 38
Edwards, Jonathan 142, 145
Emerson, Ralph Waldo 148
Enlightenment 134, 140, 141, 150
Erasmus, Desiderius 90, 102, 103, 107, 110, 113

Eusebius of Caesarea 32
Evangelicalism 164, 167, 176, 177, 178, 180, 181, 182

**F**

Fell, Margaret 134
Feudal System 64, 65, 95
Finney, Charles 148, 154
Fosdick, Harry Emerson 164, 171
Fox, George 134
Franciscans 78
Francis of Assisi 78, 87
Fundamentalism 163, 164, 171, 173, 176, 178, 179, 180

**G**

Galileo Galilei 125
General Council 46
Gnosticism 20, 23, 24, 25, 26, 28, 54, 62, 74, 159
Graham, Billy 127, 145, 151, 177, 178, 179
Great Awakening, First 134, 142, 143
Great Awakening, Second 153, 154
Great Awakening, Third 160
Great Cappadocians 32, 44, 50
Great Depression 173
Gutenberg, Johann 101
G.W.F. Hegel 148

**H**

Halfway Covenant 139
Heidelberg Catechism 104
Heinrich Bullinger 104
Helena 32
Henry, Carl F.H. 177, 178, 179
Henry VIII, King 115, 116
Henry V, King 99
Hilda of Whitby 60
Hildegard of Bingen 83, 85
Hippolytus 20
Holiness Movement 148
Hubmaier, Balthasar 104
Huguenots 111, 122

Hus, Jan 90, 97, 108, 134
Hutchinson, Anne 137, 138

**I**

Icons 66, 81, 82
Ignatius 8
India 78, 118, 130, 151, 152, 180, 184
Innocent III, Pope 62, 73, 74, 86, 87
Investiture Dispute 62
Ireland 60
Irenaeus 20

**J**

James I, King 126
Jansenism 120
Japanese Christians 120
Jerome 32, 42, 43, 55
Jerusalem 8, 10, 14, 15, 20, 22, 29, 31, 65, 71, 72, 78
Jerusalem Council 8
Jerusalem Temple 8
Jesuits 118, 120, 133
Joan of Arc 99, 100
John I of the Cross 120
John Paul II, Pope 181, 182
John XXIII, Pope 90, 180, 181
Josephus 8, 14
Julian, Emperor 41
Julian of Norwich 90
Justin Martyr 8, 16, 17

**K**

Kant, Immanuel 148, 155
Kierkegaard, Soren 148
Kimbangu, Simon 184
King James Bible (Version) 104, 127
King, Martin Luther, Jr. 127, 185
Kung, Hans 164

**L**

Lateran Council, Fifth 104
Lateran Council, First 62

Lateran Council, Fourth 62, 74, 78, 86
Latin America 184, 187
Leo III, Pope 68
Leo IX, Pope 70, 81
Leo X, Pope 103, 107, 108, 115
Lewis, C.S. 177
Loyola, Ignatius 118
Luther, Martin 104, 106, 107, 108, 109, 115, 117, 144

**M**

Marcella 43
Marcion 20, 24, 25, 26, 27, 28, 29
Marsilius 90
Masada 14, 15
Massachusetts Bay Colony 136, 138, 139
Maximilla 20, 30
Melanchthon, Philip 117
Mendicants 85, 86, 88
Mennonites 114, 146
Methodists 120, 134, 144, 145, 148, 153, 160, 183
Miller, William 159
Milton, John 120
Milvian Bridge 37
Modern Age 150, 152, 160, 162, 163, 164, 169, 170, 185
Monophysitism 46
Monotheletism 62
Montanism 20, 30
Moody, Dwight L. 161, 162
Moravian Brethren 134, 143
Mother Teresa 180
Mueller, George 148
Muhammad 65, 100
Munster massacre 113, 114
Muslims 62, 65, 66, 71, 72, 73, 74, 81, 82, 85, 90, 100, 101, 130
Mysticism 83, 99

**N**

Nero, Emperor 8, 10, 11, 14, 15

Nestorianism 46, 78
Newton, Isaac 140
Nicene Creed 32, 39, 41, 44, 46, 49, 50, 57, 67, 69, 70, 71, 76
Niebuhr, Reinhold 169, 170, 175
Northampton Awakening 142

**O**

Oecolampadius 104
Olympias 51, 52, 53
Origen 20, 25, 35
Ottoman Empire 90, 100

**P**

Papias 8
Parham, Charles Fox 164, 183
Pascal, Blaise 120
Patrick, Saint 60
Paul III, Pope 118
Pelagius 46, 55
Pentecostalism 164, 183, 184
Photius 70, 77, 82
Pierce, Bob 164
Pietism 134, 142, 143, 144
Pius IX, Pope 160, 161
Polycarp 8, 17, 19, 25, 28, 29
Postmodernism 164, 166, 185, 186
Presbyterians 104, 117, 120, 129, 152, 153, 160
Prohibition 170
Protestantism 117, 123
Puritans 120, 126, 127, 128, 129, 136, 137, 138, 139

**Q**

Quakers 120, 134, 146

**R**

Rauschenbusch, Walter 148
Reformation 104, 111, 117, 169
Reformed Churches 104
Renaissance 90, 93, 101, 103, 110, 114
Restorationists 153, 154
Revolutionary War, American 146
Ricci, Matteo 120
Rule of Faith 20, 26, 27, 28, 30

**S**

Salem Witch Trials 139
Schleiermacher, Friedrich 155, 156, 157, 167, 176
Schweitzer, Albert 164
Scofield, Cyrus I. 148
Scopes, John 172, 173
Scopes Trial 172
Separatists 120, 126, 127, 129, 134, 136, 137
Seventh-Day Adventists 159
Seymour, William 164, 183
Simons, Menno 113, 114
Singh, Sundar 184
Slavery 78, 131, 132, 133, 145, 146, 152, 158, 159, 160
Smyth, John 128
Social Gospel 148, 158, 160
Sor Juana Ines de la Cruz 120
Spanish Inquisition 90, 101, 131
Spurgeon, Charles H. 158
Stone, Barton W. 153
Syrian Orthodox 57

**T**

Tertullian 20, 30
Theodore of Mopsuestia 46
Theodosius 46, 50, 51, 52
Theological Liberalism 156, 164, 167, 168, 169, 170, 171, 173, 176, 186
Theotokos 46, 56
Tillich, Paul 164
Trajan, Emperor 8, 14, 15, 16
Transubstantiation 62
Truth, Sojourner 159
Tyndale, William 104, 114, 115, 116

**U**

Uniats 104
Unitarianism 141

Urban II, Pope 71, 72

**V**

Vatican Council, First 161, 180
Vatican Council, Second 181
Vespasian 8, 15, 16
Vieyra, Antonio 120
Vulgate 32, 43, 104

**W**

Waldensians 78, 86
Waldo 78, 86
Wesley, Charles 143, 144
Wesley, John 134, 143, 144, 145, 146
Whitefield, George 144, 145
Wilberforce, William 158
Willar, Frances 163
Williams, Roger 134, 137, 138, 147
Women's Christian Temperance Union 163
World War I 167, 168, 169, 170, 173
World War II 175, 176
Wycliffe, John 97, 98, 103

**Z**

Zinzendorf, Nikolaus 134, 143
Zwingli, Ulrich 104, 109, 110, 112